History
of an
Argentine Passion

by
Eduardo Mallea

Translated, with
an Introduction and Annotations, by
Myron I. Lichtblau
Syracuse University

LATIN AMERICAN LITERARY REVIEW PRESS
SERIES: EXPLORATIONS
PITTSBURGH, PENNSYLVANIA, 1983

The Latin American Literary Review Press publishes Latin American creative writing under the series title *Discoveries,* and critical works under the series title *Explorations.*

Library of Congress Cataloging in Publication Data:

Mallea, Eduardo, 1903–
     History of an Argentine passion.

     (Explorations)
     Translation of: Historia de una passión argentina.
     Bibliography: p.
     1. Mallea, Eduardo, 1903–   —Biography.
2. National characteristics, Argentine. 3. Authors,
Argentine—20th century—Biography. I. Title.
II. Series: Explorations (Pittsburgh, Pa.)
PQ7797.M225Z46513 1982   863 [B]   82-20816
ISBN 0-935480-10-2

History of an Argentine Passion can be ordered directly
from the publisher:
Latin American Literary Review Press
P.O. Box 8385, Pittsburgh, Pennsylvania 15218

In loving memory of my father,
Samuel Lichtblau (1888–1981),
who will be missed by all who knew him.

Contents

Preface   i
Introduction   v
Bibliography   xiv
Author's Preface   xiii
    I. The Atlantic   1
   II. The Metropolis   15
  III. The Visible Argentina   48
   IV. The Invisible Country   65
    V. Scorn   81
   VI. Kinds of Consciousness   86
  VII. America   97
 VIII. Meditations   112
   IX. The North, The South   122
    X. The Spirit of Giving and the Spirit of Freedom   134
   XI. The Country Like Lazarus   143
  XII. The Invasion of Humanity   153
 XIII. The Severe Exaltation of Life   166

Preface

At a time when Hispanic American fiction is at the forefront of world letters, it seems appropriate to bring out a translation of a seminal essay by one of Argentina's most important contemporary novelists. Several of the novels and short stories of Eduardo Mallea (1903-1982) have already reached the English-speaking reader in translation—*The Bay of Silence, All Green Shall Perish, Fiesta in November, Chaves,* "Conversation," and "Human Reason." But none of his essays has thus far been translated to English, although they form an integral part of his literary production. Thus, this translation of *Historia de una pasión argentina*, by far Mallea's most important essay, will help provide the English-speaking reader with greater understanding of the author and his world of fiction.

My interest in Mallea dates back some thirty years, when I read several contemporary Latin American novelists for a course I was taking at Columbia University. My introduction to Mallea was *The Bay of Silence,* a long but very rewarding novel about young idealistic Argentines seeking to find themselves in a society inimicable to their needs and aspirations. The work left such a deep imprint on me that I set out to read other works of Mallea and to examine them critically. The fruit of this interest has been several articles and a book on Mallea's style; the present translation of *History of an Argentine Passion* is the culmination of that interest.

A word about the translation. In a sense, all translation borders on the creative because an exact, one-to-one correspondence between words in any two languages rarely exists. I have tried to be as faithful to the Spanish text as possible without doing violence to the English translation. At times this faithfulness was sacrificed for clarity of meaning or smoothness of expression. Readability with textual reliability is what I have sought to attain at all times. To this end I have taken some liberties with syntax, word order, sentence construction, and even punctuation. On many occasions, the course of Mallea's thought process, of which his prose style is the written manifestation, can not be followed directly or exactly in English. To do so would not only deform the English but would also prevent capturing the true meaning of the original Spanish in all its vigor, expressiveness, and subtle connotations.

I wish to express my appreciation to Dr. John James Prucha, vice chancellor for academic affairs at Syracuse University, for necessary funds to do research in Buenos Aires in July, 1978, for his financial support of this book, and for his frequent words of encouragement for my scholarly work. I am grateful to Dr. Volker Weiss, vice president for research and graduate affairs, for a generous subvention. I would also like to thank Dr. Gershon Vincow, dean of the College of Arts and Sciences, for granting me a research leave of absence in the fall of 1980 to complete the manuscript. I also acknowledge the assistance of Dr. Louis W. Roberts, executive chairman, Faculty of Foreign Languages and Literatures, in clarifying certain Latin references and in seeing this project through to completion. My thanks, too, go to Dr. Daniel Testa, former associate chairman, Spanish and Portuguese, for his constant support of the project.

I am very much indebted to Eduardo Mallea and to Editorial Sudamericana of Buenos Aires for granting me permission to translate *Historia de una pasión argentina* to English.

Many other friends and colleagues have helped me in the preparation of this book, and to all of them I am deeply indebted: to Reinaldo Ayerbe, Alberto Blasi, Jaime Ferrán, Ignacio Izuzquiza, Susana Leiva, Jorge Luis Romeu, and Raquel Romeu for patiently aiding me with troublesome expressions in the text; to Joann Cannon, A. Leland Jamison, John H. Matthews, James Soffietti, and Gerd K. Schneider for assisting me with several of the annotations. In addition, I am thankful to the professional staff of Bird Library of Syracuse University, *La Nación* and *La Prensa* of Buenos Aires, the Instituto de Literatura Argentina, the Academia Argentina de la Lengua, and the Asociación de Escritores Argentinos.

I should also like to acknowledge the kindness and unselfish interest of Yvette Miller, without whose very able editorial advice and assistance this book could not have been brought to publication.

Finally a word of thanks to Julie Riggall for her typing services.

—*M. I. L.*

DeWitt, New York

Note: As this book was being printed, I learned of the death of Eduardo Mallea in Buenos Aires on November 12, 1982. I deeply mourn his passing. His life as a man and as a writer has meant much to me personally and intellectually.

Introduction

Referring to the "novel of the land" that characterized Spanish American fiction from about 1920 to 1940, the Chilean critic Fernando Alegría stated that ". . . on humanizing the pampa, the jungle, the mountains and the rivers, in reality it dehumanized man."[1] The statement aptly describes this *criollista* novel that put an end to the dominating influence of European models in the nineteenth century. The novel of the land was essentially a homage to the American scene, an awakening to her mighty physical presence. In casting off its European bonds and asserting itself as an original and independent art form, the *criollista* novel distorted the total picture of America, presenting only the most distinctive but not necessarily the most representative features of her culture and civilization—the jungles of Colombia, the limitless and solitary pampa of Argentina, the vast plains of Venezuela, the high plateau of Bolivia. Nature, as the implacable enemy of man caught helplessly in her grip, became the real protagonist and an almost deterministic force in shaping man's destiny. The novel subordinated man to his environment and made him a victim of nature's evil power.

Criollista novelists like the Venezuelan Rómulo Gallegos (1884–1968), the Colombian José E. Rivera (1889–1929), and the Argentine Ricardo Güiraldes (1886–1927)[2] captured well the consciousness and spirit of the land. But it was left to a succeeding generation of writers, of which Eduardo Mallea is a leading figure, to capture the consciousness and spirit of man in his fundamental essence, of man not necessarily in conflict with nature, but in a deeper conflict with himself and with his emotions, feelings, and ideologies. The novel that emerged in the 1940s and matured in the 1950s became more universal in the themes it presented and the values it treated. Now man was the protagonist, and his struggles and aspirations and anguish became the source from which writers drew their narrative material.

In Eduardo Mallea, Argentina found the spokesman for its deepest and most genuine values and beliefs. Other writers before him—Carlos María Ocantos (1860–1949) and Manuel Gálvez (1882–1962)[3]—had portrayed the external realities of the country but seldom succeeded in penetrating its inner core. The frustration and pain Mallea feels on observing the erosion of Argentina's character and traditions pervade both his personal life and his literary works. Mallea cuts deeply into Argentina's spirit and analyzes with a rare degree of perceptiveness the emotional and mental states of twentieth-century Argentines caught up in an illogical world of changing mores and philosophies. He is an intellectual and psychological novelist who understands that man's anguish results more from a struggle of forces within his own psyche than from external, environmental forces.

Mallea's position in Spanish American literature is firmly fixed, although he is no longer in the forefront of fiction writing. In novels such as *Fiesta in November* (1938), *The Bay of Silence* (1940), *Everything Green Shall Perish* (1941), and *Chaves* (1953), Mallea portrays unhappy Argentines who find no solution to the solitude, agony and alienation that accompany them at every moment. Mallea's novels are frequently static, introspective, with little external movement, but they are profound studies of the interaction between the human mind and human emotions. Mallea's world is the inner world of man seeking to reconcile opposing or incompatible forces in his life: logic and reason versus emotion; conscience versus will; idealism versus pragmatism; conformity versus resistance.

Man's inability to communicate with his fellow man lies at the base of Mallea's thinking and is used almost as a leitmotif in many of his best works. Man's suffering stems in part from his unwillingness to give of himself to others. John Donne's words that "No man is an island entire of itself, every man is a piece of the continent, a part of the main,"[4] may serve Mallea well as an appropriate maxim whose truth he demonstrates in all his essays and works of fiction.

Mallea's whole life has been his literature, although, like many other Hispanic American writers, he attended law school until he realized his true vocation lay in the world of letters. His literary inclinations soon led him to work with a group of young writers in founding a magazine called *Revista de America* (1923), which he fictionalizes in *The Bay of Silence* under the name of *Basta*. Mallea wrote little for the *Revista de America,* but immersed himself completely in the artistic and literary scene of Buenos Aires and became well respected for his aesthetic sensitivity and discernment. As his reputation grew, Mallea contributed to other journals and newspapers, and in 1934 he began a longtime association with *Sur,* which under the vigorous editorship of Victoria Ocampo[5] became one of the best and most influential literary magazines in Hispanic America. Equally significant in Mallea's career was his association with the prestigious *La Nación* of Buenos Aires and in particular his editorship of that newspaper's Literary Supplement from 1934 to 1955.

Mallea's trips to Europe in 1928 and 1934 broadened his literary base and fed his intellectual longing for new cultural experiences. In 1955, he became Argentine's delegate to UNESCO in Paris and in 1956 traveled to New Delhi to represent Argentina at the UNESCO meeting. Honors quickly came to Mallea. In 1940, he became the president of the Argentine Association of Writers. In 1945 he won the coveted First National Prize of Letters and a year later the Grand Prize of Honor of the Argentine Association of Writers. The Forti Glori prize and the Grand National Prize of the Arts followed in 1968 and 1970 respectively.

*   *   *

Mallea's literary formation took place in the post–World War I period under the influence of the vanguard movements then in vogue— ultraism, dadaism, creationism, cubism.[6] Novelty and artistic refinement in literary creation were the goals; evasion of observed reality was in many cases the means. Mallea wrote no poetry, but his first published work, *Stories for a Despairing Englishwoman* (1926), reveals the aesthetic and verbal sensibility so characteristic of the vanguard writers of the time. Mallea was silent for nine years following the appearance of these short narratives. Then, in 1935 he published two volumes of essays, *Knowledge and Expression of Argentina* and *European*

Nocturn, and a year later *The City on the Motionless River,* a work containing some of his most incisive short stories. *History of an Argentine Passion* was published in 1937[7] and thus predates all his novels. It would seem that at this point in his career Mallea was uncertain whether to devote his greater energies to the essay or to fiction. What is clear is that several of Mallea's novels, notably *The Bay of Silence* and *Simbad* (1957), reveal an essayistic tone that makes the narrative frequently heavy and somewhat tedious. The great Colombian writer Germán Arciniegas[8] once said that "the best of Mallea is in his *History of an Argentine Passion*" and other critics have likewise seen in this work one of Mallea's greatest achievements. The 170-page essay can very well stand on its own as a powerful expression of Mallea's ideology, but it takes on added importance because the author treated many of its themes in subsequent works of fiction. Mallea's existential view of life, his vision of a perverted Argentina, his search for Argentina's true identity, his concept of man's isolation and torment—all these ideas were first formed and developed in *History of an Argentine Passion* and later fictionalized and made the conceptual basis of his entire literary production. Indeed, any critical appreciation of the profound meaning of such novels as *The Bay of Silence, Chaves,* or *The Eagles* (1943) can come only through an understanding of the philosophical and social ideas presented in this seminal essay. The close artistic and thematic relationship between Mallea essayist and Mallea novelist is always present; the convergence is nowhere more evident than in *History of an Argentine Passion.*

The essay is at once an impassioned statement of Mallea's intellectual and philosophical credo and a bitter denunciation of what he perceives as his country's reprehensible utilitarianism, superficiality, and pretension. The work reveals Mallea's painful anguish over the destruction of Argentina's values and the bankruptcy of its ideals. It is both Mallea's spiritual autobiography and Argentina's national biography, for as the author examines his own feelings and beliefs, he lays bare the quintessential characteristics of his troubled country as he envisages them. Mallea's stance is that of a liberal intellectual who sees the Argentina of the 1930s dominated by a conservative, even repressive oligarchy that has betrayed the fundamental truth and moral order on which the country was built.

* * *

What makes *History of an Argentine Passion* such a fascinating document is that it serves as the point of departure for all of Mallea's thought. Few modern writers have a greater thematic and stylistic unity in their works. It would be well to point out here those themes common to *History of an Argentine Passion* and to Mallea's fiction. The renowned Spanish critic Amado Alonso wrote in a review of Mallea's novel *Fiesta in November* that "It is in part a novelized version of *History of an Argentine Passion.*"[9] The concept of emotional mutism implicit in Mallea's description of the provincial Argentine in chapter four, is projected fictionally in many characters such as Agata Cruz in *Everything Green Shall Perish,* Riguroso Barboza in *In the Growing Darkness* (1973), and above all in Chaves in the novel that bears his name. The concept of the two Argentinas, the visible and the invisible Argentina, is patently brought out in the inner turmoil of Martín Tregua, the disillusioned and frustrated young writer in *The Bay of Silence,* and in Fernando Fe's struggle to achieve artistic perfection in *Simbad.* Among the themes treated in the essay and later developed in fiction are the lack of real communication among men, seen throughout *The Bay of Silence, All Green Shall Perish* and "Conversation"; the anguish and alienation of such characters as Jacobo Uber, Gloria Bambil and Tomás Botón in the stories comprising *The City on the Motionless River* and *The Waiting Room* (1953); the crisis of national identity and values as portrayed in *The Eagles* and *The Tower* (1951); the relationship between Argentina's ethnic roots and the assimilation of European culture, as is revealed explicitly in *The Bay of Silence* and implicitly in *Fiesta in November;* the concept of a spiritual and ethical renovation on the part of Argentine youth; the plea that authentic Argentines, thwarted temporarily but not defeated, have courage and await better days, in the same way that Martín Tregua takes refuge in his bay of silence. In addition, the figure of the retired American actress in chapter nine, toward whom Mallea feels a strong spiritual attraction because she resembles the true, invisible Argentines, is transformed into the Señora de Cardenas, the "you" to whom Martín Tregua addresses his words as narrator of *The Bay of Silence.* The points of contact between *History of an Argentine Passion* and Mallea's fiction appear in several other forms as well. Ernest Lewald points out that in some chapters of the essay Mallea "visualizes an Argentina filled with men and women who are very nearly replicas of those found in *The City on the Motionless River.*"[10] Lewald points out too that Bahía Blanca, where Mallea lived as a boy and which he nostalgically describes in *History of an Argentine Passion,* appears as the native city of Fernando Fe, the protagonist of *Simbad.*

*   *   *

The concept of the visible and the invisible Argentina is central to Mallea's philosophy; the juxtaposition of the two terms creates a focal point for the reader and holds his interest through the maze of rational explanations and illustrative examples that abound in the essay. The visible Argentina is the materialistic, ostentatious, false veneer that the country, especially Buenos Aires, lives with from day to day. It represents all that is pernicious in Argentina: artificiality, sham, shallowness, venality, lack of human warmth, dissembling, and above all the betrayal of the country's true spirit. The visible Argentina is the "show," what Mallea calls the "representing" of life instead of the genuine "living and doing." Mallea explains:

> Of all those who touch Argentina's surface, the worst, the most harmful and the most condemnable is the person who has substituted "representing" for living. We are not dealing with a universally common type, but with our own particular type of social virtuoso of fraud. Behind a learned and cultured appearance, his so-called ideas are numerous and his belief nil. His whole performance is gestures, acting out a role; even when he thinks, he gestures.[11]

The invisible Argentina is what Mallea would like the country to become, what it once was. The invisible Argentina is the heart, the genuine soul and spirit of the country, its authentic but hidden values, its potential greatness. Invisible Argentina is prevented from manifesting itself and shaping the destiny of Argentina by the destructive forces within the visible Argentina, by the spurious voice of an Argentina that would subvert its true essence and sell out to opportunists, profiteers, demagogues and mercenary political leaders. On one occasion Mallea states:

> What I call the invisible Argentina is not, in a simplistic way, the rural man as opposed to the city man. The difference lies in the fact that there exists one kind of man whose moral physiognomy is that of our cities and another kind whose moral physiognomy is that of our unspoiled nature, of our natural nature. It does not matter that one who exemplifies the qualities of this latter group may live in the city, nor does it matter that a person who has the moral physiognomy of our cities may live in our hinterland. This may be a fortuitous circumstance. What is important is not where these people are, but what they are like.[12]

*   *   *

Around the figures of two well-known authors—the American Waldo Frank (1889–1967) and the Estonian Count Hermann Alexander Keyserling (1880–1946)—Mallea further develops his concepts of Argentina's inherent character and ultimate destiny. He saw in the writings of these two men antithetical perceptions of Hispanic America. Frank, author of such works as *Virgin Spain* (1926), *The Rediscovery of America* (1928), and *America Hispana* (1931), knows the Hispanic mind, understands the Hispanic character, sympathizes with the yearning of all Latin Americans for self-determination, and reaches out to find the underlying causes of their social ills and national unrest. Keyserling, social theoretician and mystic, who wrote, among other works, *The Travel Diary of a Philosopher* (1925), *America Set Free* (1929), and *South American Meditations on Hell and Heaven in the Soul of Man* (1932), has the stereotypic negative view of Hispanic America as a wild, primitive, untamed continent in which instinct prevails over reason and logic. Mallea contrasts Frank's deep insights into Hispanic culture with Keyserling's utter ignorance of America, which leads to his biases and antipathy against the essence of the American spirit. Responding to Keyserling's odious phrase, "the reptilian world of South America," Mallea writes with obvious anger:

Count Keyserling does not seem to know the deeds that shaped the American people, indeed is unaware of the "sense" of its original thought, of its literature and imagination, of its inspiration, and in order to enunciate his general postulates, he has taken the reality of our nation at its point of new pregnancy, in its state of second pregnancy. The frequently somnolent and sluggish sight of pregnancy—pregnancy of destiny and therefore of consequence—has been interpreted by him as telluric blindness. He has extracted from Argentina's soul only the image of a life sunk in emotional apathy, in the swamp of sweet and heavy blood, submerged in its lack of inspiration.[13]

Mallea's "passion," as he uses the term in the title of his essay, is his deep feeling for Argentina, his almost obsessive preoccupation with his country's true identity, with its welfare and moral character. The author's passion becomes unbearable pain, intense suffering, as he meditates on the wretched social conditions he finds all around him. Argentina agonizes and Mallea agonizes along with her. The many biblical references throughout the text suggest that Mallea may be relating his own passion to Christ's passion. But Mallea's message goes beyond this: the country itself must struggle to overcome powerful negative forces, and then emerge victorious. Argentina has allowed itself to be duped; it must now recognize its moral weakness, identify its detractors and betrayers, and take stock of its real worth as a nation and as a people.

For Mallea a life without spiritual values is a barren life; a life without the guiding presence of God is void. The writer's abiding religious faith is felt throughout *History of an Argentine Passion* and expressed in various ways, from the use of metaphors, symbols, and Bible quotations to the constant repetition of the words "soul," "spirit," "essence," and "root." Mallea's philosophy becomes almost a theocentric system in which divine intervention is seen pervading life and giving strength, meaning, and purpose to man's existence. Mallea's sense of religion is that of an active, vital, vibrant force that inspires and orients, that provides order and direction to the lives of Argentines who face the chaos and impersonality of the modern world.

*   *   *

On April 30, 1937, in *El Hogar,* Benigno Herrero Almada[14] published an interview he had with Mallea regarding his forthcoming book, *History of an Argentine Passion.* Herrero transcribes the answers Mallea gave to several questions concerning the genesis and content of the work. Mallea envisaged the essay as a call to Argentine youth to rise up against the false and distorted values dominating Argentine life and commit itself to working for a better Argentina. In this regard it is interesting to note that some thirty-five years before, in 1902, the Uruguayan José Enrique Rodó similarly addressed the youth of America in his famous essay *Ariel,* in which a distinguished professor speaks to his students on the occasion of his retirement from the university.

History of an Argentine Passion achieved immediate critical success and brought Mallea to a position of importance in Argentine literature. The essay received highly favorable reviews in newspapers and magazines both in Argentina and throughout Hispanic America, and Mallea was quickly recognized as a serious, discerning interpreter of Argentine culture. Critics saw the author's broad vision of his country as emerging initially from his boyhood residence in the vast, windswept, arid central plain south of Buenos Aires, in the region of Bahía Blanca. In the popular newspaper *El Mundo,* Horacio Rega Molina wrote when the essay first appeared that "I have read nothing truer and deeper about what we Argentines are and what we should be than *History of an Argentine Passion.*"[15]

In the journal *Mediodía Literario,* the Argentine Lizardo Zía comments that ". . . never before has an act of faith been expressed so purely so that we Argentines may see ourselves wholly, like a tree that looks into its very roots."[16] In the Literary Supplement of *La Nación,* an anonymous reviewer, using the words of the French novelist Maurice Barrès, calls the work an "ideological novel" and considers its greatest virtue to be "the vehemence for love."[17]

The important literary journal *Nosotros* published two book reviews of *History of an Argentine Passion* in the November, 1937, issue. Aníbal Sánchez Reulet states categorically in one review that with his book

Mallea is the first author in Argentina and perhaps in the Spanish-speaking world to create the genre which he calls the novel-essay: "*History of an Argentine Passion* is a novel which tries to show the development of a thought; an essay in which a thought lives fictionally . . . Thus, in Mallea's work we witness the dramatic growth of a passion and its painful conversion to an idea."[18] In the second review, Herminia Brumana states frankly that before reading *History of an Argentine Passion* she was not enthusiastic about Mallea's writings. But after seeing her own suffering reflected in the essay, she counted herself as one of those whom Mallea identifies as "sleepless Argentines, taciturn Argentines, who suffer Argentina like a pain in the flesh."[19]

In the March, 1938, issue of *Sol y Luna*, the renowned Argentine poet Leopoldo Marechal[20] published his impressions of the essay in the form of a public letter to Mallea. For Marechal the essential theme of the work is the awakening of Argentina's inner resources and strength to build a more unified and enlightened country.

Reviews of *History of an Argentine Passion* appeared in three successive issues of *Sur,* from November, 1937, to January, 1938. In the first review, Bernardo Canal Feijoo sees a "cyclical relationship"[21] between Mallea's essay *European Nocturn* and *History of an Argentine Passion.* In the latter work, Canal Feijoo states, the prodigal son returns to his "center, . . . wounded by the lessons life taught him in his wanderings."[22] Canal Feijoo points out that it was necessary for Mallea to have gone through the anguish of those experiences in Europe to awaken to the deep passion he now feels for Argentina. The second review in *Sur,* written by Ana Margarita Berry,[23] praises Mallea's skill in characterization and description and adds that *History of an Argentine Passion* should have a place in universal literature. For Berry, the essay has perfect structural unity, despite the diversity of themes and narrative modes. In the third review, Emile Gouiran, a French critic residing in Argentina, writes that *History of an Argentine Passion* is "the most beautiful book I have read in Argentina in the past five years."[24] He emphasizes particularly Mallea's humanness, his feeling for the most basic human values and aspirations. Gouiran shares Mallea's disdain for Keyserling and says that the Baltic count's shamefully prejudiced view of America should not even be accorded space in the essay.

In 1938 *Sur* also published Luis Emilio Soto's *Crítica y estimación,*[25] a volume of literary essays which includes a chapter on *History of an Argentine Passion* and Mallea's concept of the invisible Argentina. Soto presents one of the fullest early analyses of the essay, judging it the work of a sensitive humanist and patriot whose anguish leads him to ask the same question about Argentina that the great statesman Domingo F. Sarmiento[26] posed some seventy-five years before: "Who are we?" Soto also states that the first two chapters of *History of an Argentine Passion* can be considered Mallea's "provincial recollections," a reference to the title of one of Sarmiento's most important books.

Professional critics in other Spanish American countries frequently mixed their encomiastic comments on Mallea's profound feeling for his native land with statements about the essential oneness of all the American nations. Mallea's anguish, Argentina's anguish, are seen as America's anguish. Emilio Champion, writing in *El Comercio de Lima* on June 12, 1938, referred to the book as "profoundly American" and placed Mallea, along with Jorge Luis Borges[27] and Victoria Ocampo, in the first rank of American prose writers and among the "goldsmiths of the word in prose."[28]

*　　*　　*

Whether in his essays or in his fiction, Mallea's style[29] has always manifested two distinct modes: the heavy, dense, psychologically or philosophically oriented style, overloaded with an academic lexicon and frequently characterized by an abstraction that derives from his thought process; and the lyrical, rhythmical, cadenced, almost poetical style, exalted and impassioned, spontaneously moving and emotive. Nowhere are these two antithetical prose styles more manifest than in *History of an Argentine Passion.* Mallea is capable of reaching sublime heights of poetic inspiration in his prose writing, or descending into a morass of tangled abstruseness and wordiness. He can write the most beautifully expressive prose worthy of any anthology or he can write long paragraphs of flat, dry prose that can try the patience of even the most avid Mallean enthusiast. At his worst, Mallea is unable to extricate himself verbally from his own complex intellectual web of thoughts and ideas; at his best Mallea's prose can be sheer beauty of form and word. Mallea can move us with his descriptive power or tire us with an excess verbalization of philosophical concepts.

Mallea's style is expansive rather than succinct; he protracts the expression of his thoughts and ideas and seems to go in endless circles to express emotions and feelings. Basically, he mistrusts the single word to convey meaning or nuance of meaning. Instead, he uses a multitude of synonymous words, groups of similar words, and all sorts of associative and repetitive devices that cumulatively approach the desired meaning. One of the hallmarks of Mallea's style is his ingenious linguistic play to capture the intensity and subtlety of his intellectual and emotional world. His prose gropes for new and at times daring ways of verbal expression; yet the prime function of his language is never linguistic cleverness, but the transmission of thought and feeling in the most effective way possible. Few writers have achieved such harmony of theme and style.

The frequent abstractness of Mallea's thought is counterbalanced by his genuine concern for people, both as individuals and as collective Argentines. As a social critic, Mallea thinks first in broad, general concepts, then sees these same concepts in more specific, personal terms, whether in reference to himself, to the people around him, or to those he casually observes or reads about. His concern for man is at the heart of his anguish over Argentina's way of life and its ultimate destiny. His concern for man takes him on long walks through the busy, anonymous capital to try to understand and touch Argentina's genuine spirit. It is this concern for individual man that makes him feel provincial life so intimately, that makes him empathize with the rural Argentine at work in the fields, that makes him see beauty and value in honest simplicity.

Mallea's fiction and Mallea's essays are two distinct but interrelated facets of the same creative mind. Mallea reaches his greatest heights in fiction—*The Bay of Silence, All Green Shall Perish, Fiesta in November*—when he uses themes that issue from the same intellectual and emotional wellspring that inspires his essays, particularly *History of an Argentine Passion*. Few writers in Hispanic America have fused the essay and fiction with such oneness of literary purpose, artistic sensitivity and, perhaps what is most important, consciousness of mission as expositor of their country's social and moral condition. As long as Mallea's novels and short stories continue to interest readers because of their affirmation of man's relationship to himself and to society, so too will *History of an Argentine Passion*, for they are complementary aspects of his deep preoccupation with what Argentina is and will become.

Notes

1. Fernando Alegría, *Novelistas contemporáneos hispanoamericanos* (Boston: D.C. Heath, 1964), p. 1.

2. Gallegos is the author of *Doña Bárbara* (1929), a novel of the Venezuelan plains in which the civilizing force of one man, Santos Luzardo, is pitted against the lawlessness of a willful and destructive woman. An educator and statesman besides a great novelist, Gallegos was president of his country from 1947 to 1948. Rivera is the author of *The Vortex* (1924), in which the protagonist, Arturo Cova, finally succumbs to the relentless evil of the Colombian jungle. Güiraldes wrote the classic *Don Segundo Sombra* (1926), an almost mythologized idealization of a gaucho whom an orphaned youth tries to emulate.

3. Called by some the Balzac of Argentina, Ocantos is the author of a twenty-volume series of novels called *Novelas Argentinas,* published between 1888 and 1929. Gálvez is the author of many commercially successful novels, such as *The Normal School Teacher* (1914), *The Metaphysical Ill* (1916) and *Nacha Regules* (1919), as well as a series of novels on the Paraguayan War of 1867–1870 (1928–1929).

4. "No man is an island . . ." From Donne's *Devotions upon Emergent Occasions, XVII.*

5. Victoria Ocampo (1893–1980). Essayist, editor and woman of letters. As editor of *Sur,* she exerted a tremendous influence on Argentine cultural tastes and expression. For a very fine literary biography of Ocampo see Doris Meyer's *Victoria Ocampo: Against the Wind and the Tide* (New York: G. Braziller, 1979).

6. Excellent commentaries on Mallea's literary career are found in John H. R. Polt's *The Writings of Eduardo Mallea* (Berkeley: University of California Press, 1959) and in H. Ernest Lewald's *Eduardo Mallea* (Boston: Twayne Publishers, 1977).

7. *History of an Argentine Passion* was first published by Editorial Sur, Buenos Aires, in 1937. The editorial house Espasa Calpe, Madrid/Argentina, in its Austral collection, published an edition in 1940 and again in 1942, 1944, 1945, 1951 and 1969. Emecé Editores, Buenos Aires, published the essay in 1961 in its *Complete Works of Eduardo Mallea*. Editorial Sudamericana, Buenos Aires, came out with an edition of the essay in 1961, 1968 and 1975. The edition I have used for this translation is that of Espasa Calpe, 1969, and all references in the text refer to this edition.

In all editions of *History of an Argentine Passion* except the first, there appears a five-page prologue by Francisco Romero entitled "New Discourse on Method," in which the Argentine poet and critic discusses interesting parallelisms between René Descartes's famous essay *Discourse on Method* (1637) and Mallea's work. Romero argues that both writers attempt to show how they reach the criterion for truth; to do this they record the experience step by step under the scrutiny of the watchful reader. For Romero, Descartes communicates the "essential nature of things," Mallea the substance of "being Argentine."

8. Germán Arciniegas (b. 1900). Colombian essayist, diplomat and professor. Works: *These People of America* (1945), *The Continent of Seven Colors* (1965).

9. Amado Alonso, "Fiesta en noviembre," *Sur,* Vol. 44 (May 1938), p. 66.

10. Ernest Lewald, *op. cit.,* p. 51.

11. *History of an Argentine Passion,* p. 53.

12. *Ibid.,* p. 70.

13. *Ibid.,* p. 119.

14. Benigno Herrero Almada , "¿Un libro admonitorio publicará Mallea?", *El Hogar,* Buenos Aires (April 30, 1937), p. 10.

15. Horacio Rega Molina, "Notas sobre *Historia de una pasión argentina,*" *El Mundo,* Buenos Aires (December 13, 1937), p. 8.

16. Lisardo Zía, "Conversación ideal con Eduardo Mallea," *Mediodía Literario,* Buenos Aires (April 11, 1938), p. 4.

17. Anon., "Historia de una pasión argentina," *La Nación,* Buenos Aires (September 16, 1937), p. 4.

18. Aníbal Sánchez Reulet, "Pasión e idea de la Argentina," *Nosotros,* Año II, Núm. 20 (November 1937), pp. 307–308.

19. Herminia C. Brumana, "El último libro de Mallea," *Nosotros,* Año II, Núm., 20 (November 1937), p. 310.

20. Leopoldo Marechal, "Carta a Eduardo Mallea." *Sol y Luna,* Buenos Aires, Vol. I (March 1938), pp. 181–182.

21. Bernardo Canal Feijoo, "Historia de una pasión argentina," *Sur,* Vol. 38 (November 1937), p. 82.

22. *Ibid.,* p. 74.

23. Ana Margarita Berry, "Historia de una pasión argentina," *Sur,* Vol., 39 (December 1937), p. 83.

24. Emile Gouiran, "Una interpretación argentina: *Historia de una pasión argentina,*" *Sur,* Vol. 40 (January 1938) p. 78.

25. Luis Emilio Soto, "Eduardo Mallea y su visión de la Argentina invisible," in *Crítica y estimación* (Buenos Aires: Editorial Sur, 1938), p. 87.

26. Domingo Faustino Sarmiento (1811–1888). Argentine essayist, educator, statesman, and president of his country from 1868 to 1874. In 1835, Sarmiento was exiled to Chile for attacking the dictatorial regime of Juan Manuel Rosas. His famous essay *Civilization and Barbarism: The Life of Juan Facundo Quiroga,* published in Santiago in serial form in 1845, is both a biography of one of Rosas' henchmen and a perceptive study of Argentina's social, cultural and political systems, with particular reference to the gaucho's nomadic and independent way of life. Sarmiento wrote *Provincial Recollections* in 1850, a book dealing with his early formative years in the northern city of San Juan.

27. Jorge Luis Borges (b. 1899). Universally recognized Argentine poet, short story writer, and essayist. Works: *The Moon Opposite* (1925), *The Garden of Forking Paths* (1942), *The Aleph* (1949), *Death and the Compass* (1951), *Other Inquisitions.* (1952).

28. Emilio Champion, "En torno a un libro de Eduardo Mallea," *El Comercio de Lima* (June 12, 1938), p. 4.

29. See Myron I. Lichtblau's *El arte estilístico de Eduardo Mallea* (Buenos Aires: Editorial Goyanarte, 1967).

Bibliography

I. On *History of an Argentine Passion.*

Anon. "Historia de una pasión argentina." *La Nación,* (Sept. 26, 1937), p. 4.
Anon. *"Historia de una pasión argentina." Noticias Gráficas,* Buenos Aires (Oct. 3, 1937), p. 13.

Anon. "Notas sobre *Historia de una pasión argentina.*" *El Mundo,* Buenos Aires (Dec. 13, 1937), p. 8.

Anon. (C.Z.). "Vigencia de una pasión argentina." *La Nación,* Buenos Aires (Dec. 2, 1962), p. 1.

Berry, Ana Margarita. "*Historia de una pasión argentina.*" *Sur,* 39 (Dec. 1937), pp. 76–85.

Brumana, Herminia C. "El último libro de Mallea." *Nosotros,* II, No. 20 (Nov. 1937), pp. 309–10.

Canal Feijoo, Bernardo. "Historia de una pasión argentina." *Sur,* 38 (Nov. 1937), pp. 74–82.

Champion, Emilio. "En torno a un libro de Eduardo Mallea." *El Comercio de Lima* (June 12, 1938), p. 2.

Gouiran, Emile. "Una interpretación argentina: *Historia de una pasión argentina.*" *Sur,* 40 (Jan. 1938), pp. 75–78.

Grieben, Carlos F. "Una pasión argentina." *El Mundo,* Buenos Aires, (July 22, 1956), p. 24.

Herrero Almada, Benigno. "¿Un libro admonitorio publicará Mallea?" *El Hogar,* Buenos Aires (April 30, 1937), p. 10.

Lewald, H. Ernest. *Eduardo Mallea.* (Boston: Twayne Publishers, 1977), pp. 19–20, 50–57.

Marechal, Leopoldo. "Carta a Eduardo Mallea." *Sol y Luna,* Buenos Aires, Vol. I (March 1938), pp. 180–82.

Polt, John H.R. *The Writings of Eduardo Mallea.* (Berkeley: University of California Press, 1959), pp. 10, 12, 14, 15, 26, and *passim.*

Rega Molina, Horacio. "Notas sobre *Historia de una pasión argentina,*" *El Mundo,* Buenos Aires (Dec. 13, 1937), p. 8.

Sánchez Reulet, Aníbal. "Pasión e idea de la Argentina." *Nosotros,* II, No. 20 (Nov. 1937), pp. 307–09.

Soto, Luis Emilio. "Eduardo Mallea y su visión de la Argentina invisible," in *Crítica y estimación* (Buenos Aires: Editorial Sur, 1938), pp. 81–93.

Stabb, Martin S. *In Quest of Identity: Patterns in the Spanish American Essay of Ideas, 1890–1960.* (Chapel Hill: The University of North Carolina Press, 1967), pp. 161–69.

Topete, José Manuel. "Eduardo Mallea y el laberinto de la agonía: *Historia de una pasión argentina.*" *Revista Iberoamericana,* XX, No. 39 (March 1955), pp. 117–51.

Wolkonsky, Olga. "Una crítica atrasada de un libro que no lo será jamás: Reflexiones sobre la *Historia de una pasión argentina* de Eduardo Mallea." *Correo Literario,* Buenos Aires, Vol. III, No. 28 (Jan. 1945), pp. 1 & 7.

Zía, Lisardo. "Conversación ideal con Eduardo Mallea." *Mediodía Literario,* Buenos Aires (April 11, 1938), p. 4.

II. On Eduardo Mallea

Alegría, Fernando. *Breve historia de la novela hispanoamericana.* México: Ediciones de Andrea, 1959, pp. 231–36.

Chapman, Arnold. "Sherwood Anderson and Eduardo Mallea." *Publications of the Modern Language Association of America,* LXIX, No. I, (1954), pp. 34–45.

Chapman, Arnold. "The Spanish American Reception of United States Fiction, 1920–1940." (Berkeley: University of California Press, 1966), pp. 65–71.

Chapman, Arnold. "Terms of Spiritual Isolation in Eduardo Mallea." *Modern Language Forum,* XXXVII, No. 1–2 (1952), pp. 21–27.

Dudgeon, Patrick. *Eduardo Mallea. A Personal Study of His Work.* (Buenos Aires: Agonia, 1949).

Earle, Peter G. and Mead, Robert G. *Historia del ensayo hispanoamericano.* (Mexico: Ediciones de Andrea: 1973), pp. 127–30.

Ghiano, Juan Carlos. *Constantes en la literatura argentina* (Buenos Aires: Editorial Raigal, 1953), pp. 109–28.

Lichtblau, Myron I. "El arte de la imagen en *Todo verdor perecerá. Revista Hispánica Moderna,* XXIX, No. 2 (1963), pp. 121–33.

Lichtblau, Myron I. *El arte estilístico de Eduardo Mallea.* (Buenos Aires: Editorial Goyanarte, 1967).

Lynch, William. "The Universal Values of Eduardo Mallea." *Saturday Review of Literature,* XXVII, No. 11 (March 11, 1944), p. 9.

Mallan, Lloyd. "Tom Wolfe or Argentina." *Kenyon Review,* VI, No. 3 (1944), pp. 476–81.

Montserrat, Santiago. "Eduardo Mallea y la Argentina profunda." *Sur,* 123 (Jan. 1945), pp. 72–83.

Morsella, Astur. *Eduardo Mallea.* (Buenos Aires: Editorial Mac-Co, 1957).

Petersen, Fred. "Notes on Mallea's Definition of Argentina." *Hispania,* XLV (Sept. 1962), pp. 621–24.

Rivelli, Carmen. *Eduardo Mallea. La continuidad temática de su obra.* (New York: Las Americas Publishing Company, 1969).

Rodríguez Monegal, Emir. *Narradores de esta América.* (Montevideo: Alfa, 1969), Vol I, pp. 249–69.

Zum Felde, Alberto. *Indice crítico de la literatura hispanoamericana. La narrativa.* (Mexico: Editorial Guarama, 1959), pp. 435–46.

III. Other Works Consulted

Alegría, Fernando. *Novelistas contemporáneos hispanoamericanos.* (Boston: D.C. Heath, 1964), p. 4.

Alonso, Amado. "Fiesta en noviembre," *Sur,* 44 (May 1938), p. 66.

Chesterton, Gilbert Keith. *Chaucer.* (New York: Greenwood Press, 1956), p. 28.

The Complete Works of Saint John of the Cross. Translated and edited by E. Allison Peers from the critical edition of P. Silverio de Santa Teresa (Wheathamstead/Hertfordshire: Anthony Clarke Books, 1974), p. 420.

Crawford, William Rex. *A Century of Latin American Thought.* (Cambridge: Harvard University Press, 1961).

Eleven Plays by Henrik Ibsen. (New York: Random House, n.d.), p. 377.

Keyserling, Count Hermann. *Meditaciones suramericanas.* Trans. Luis López-Ballesteros. (Santiago de Chile: Editorial Zig-Zag, 1933).

Keyserling, Count Hermann. *South American Meditations on Hell and Heaven in the Soul of Man.* Translated from German, in collaboration with the author by Theresa Duerr. (New York and London: Harper & Brothers, 1932).

Kierkegaard, Soren. *Either/Or: A Fragment of Life.* Vol. I. Translated by David F. Swenson and Lillian Marvin Swenson. (Princeton: Princeton University Press, and London: Humphrey Milford, Oxford University Press, 1944), p. 28.

Meyer, Doris. *Victoria Ocampo: Against the Wind and the Tide.* (New York: G. Braziller, 1979).

Pascal, Blaise. *Pensées. The Provincial Letters.* (New York: The Modern Library, 1941), p. 231.

Author's Preface

*"Millions of spiritual creatures
  walk the earth."*
*"Unseen, both when we wake and
  when we sleep."*

Milton, *Paradise Lost*

After many years of futilely trying to attenuate the affliction my country has caused me, I feel the need to shout out my anguish to the world. From that anguish is born this reflection, this almost unutterable fever that irremediably consumes me. This despair, this love—hungry, impatient, vexing, intolerant—, this cruel vigil.[1]

And suddenly this country exasperates me, depresses me. I rise up against that depression; I touch my country's flesh, her temperature; I watch for the slightest movements of her conscience; I examine her gestures, her reflexes, her inclinations. And I stand up against her, I reproach her, and I violently summon her to show her true self, her deep self, just when she is about to accept myriad invitations to go astray.

I feel the presence of this land[2] like something corporeal—like a woman of incredible secret beauty whose eyes have the color, the majesty, the solemn loftiness of the country's northern skies and jungle waterfalls. Her body is long, narrow at the waist, broad at the shoulders, smooth. Her softness is the provinces.[3] Her live offspring still embryo-like: the active inner soul of the territories, the political divisions, the cities. her head lies close to the tropics but has none of their frenzy, near and distant at the same time time—something distinctive. Her matrix is in the estuary,[4] an exceedingly strong matrix of humanity, which penetrates deep into the land by means of two powerful river beds. Her trim figure, her whole nervous system, seem to rest, erect and eternal, on the vertebral column of the Andes. Woman's smooth bust around beautiful pectoral turgescences: the deserts, the plains, the mountains of the untamed north. Her stomach, large and flat like those in normative sculpture: the pampa.[5] Her long and well-proportioned legs are like the long, stony hills of Patagonia,[6] not without the common down-like grasses of the valleys. Her feet become slender toward the south, rest on the glacial straits, touch the barren and deserted slopes of Cape Horn and let the British—at one time despised—amuse themselves with the unconnected slipper-shaped Falkland Islands.[7]

I want to see my country in this way, like a woman, *mater*,[8] because woman is what attracts love. What can the country born of this women, *mater*, be? Virility, serenity, fortitude, intelligence and virile beauty, in terms of human qualities; we can not imagine any one betraying a beautiful womb before birth.

The truth: the country born from that womb has been all of that. And with something more. With something still more. In our nation intelligence was always a form of goodness. To love in spirit is to have compassion, Unamuno[9] said, and the one who has the greater compassion loves more.

I wanted to know which of those virtues exist and which are in danger of dying out.

I do not want a soliloquy, but a dialogue with you, with the Argentines I prefer. What fruitful results would this confession have other than the responses? What effectiveness other than the restlessness it awakens, the care, the scruples it rouses—the state of consciousness capable of creating with its own condition. I can not teach, I can not—nor do I wish to—exact any thought, I can not instruct. I only want to stir your feelings, to have you react emotionally along with me.

Sleepless Argentines, on toward our Argentina, toward a difficult Argentina, not toward an easy Argentina! Toward a state of intelligence, not toward a state of shouting. By intelligence I mean activating a feeling of distrust in ourselves together with trust. Only this is fruitful. As long as we just vegetate in certain vague states of well-being, we shall continue to forget a destiny; and what is more, the responsibility for a destiny. By intelligence I mean the total understanding of our obligation as men, the insertion of this vibrant understanding in our nation's course, the insertion of a moral code, of a defined spirituality in all our natural activities.

Argentines, taciturn Argentines,[10] Argentines who endure Argentina like a physical pain, it is necessary to go toward that goal, not to stop.

It is you I am addressing. Not others. Not the Argentine who gets up, views the dawn in terms of business, vegetates, speculates and procreates. Not the so-called political bigwig, generally sold to ignominious moneyed interests (and involved in these interests is the bribe, which imposes on certain types of men the dark blindness of not knowing, the cloudy destiny of not understanding and the sad ring of the fraudulent sell).[11] Nor am I addressing those who "control" and "exploit" Argentina. No. But you, who perhaps form part of that submerged, genuine Argentina, to whose richly deserved and solemn glory this book is dedicated. You, who are the age of dawn.

Those other men are irrational, the irrational (to be candid, the animal) part of our country. And only to the extent that a man's rational side is strong does intrinsic nationality, inherent nationality, grow toward its basic foundation. There is nothing sadder nor more frightening than the nationalism of unreasoning men. It is not by accident that animals recognize as their territory only that area used for defense and food gathering. The higher a being's rationality, the larger is the tree its nation plants and spreads out in that being. Only one thing I fear and it is love without intelligence of the heart, because this is the kind of love that kills as it protects.

We are exposed to so many social ills in this country of so much sun and so much land and so much sky that the only way I see to combat them is through a categorical, radical and full mobilization of our collective consciences. Mobilization is maturation. It is when all the particles of a living organism are set in violent motion, in excitation, that the organism begins to bear ripe fruit, when that whole organism moves in the direction of its secret prescience and all its cells have acquired a kind of organic lucidity. And if we are still green as a nation, still unripe, it is not because we are "a young nation"—a candid, innocent lie since we can speak of neither the young nor the old in this world, and in any case one is in effect even older because of certain frustrations in youth. If we are still green, it is because our consciousness is retarded, because it has not developed from its primal sources, from its wellspring, but has remained within itself, as if closed off. We are without real fruit and only the branches of our native tree have begun to spread out because of the false space of an illusory supercivilization. The sons of the sons of Argentines, what will they be like? That is a question that should deeply concern us. I know what they will be like in their outward form, but I do not know what they will be like in their moral form. I know they will be rich, I know they will be physically strong, technically able. What I do not know is whether they will be Argentines. And I do not know this because I see that their parents today have already lost the sense of being Argentine.

The sense of being Argentine.[12] This phrase sounds strange just pronouncing it, because it scarcely means anything to us and does not find in the individual the necessary credulous and responsible area of concern. It is a vacuous phrase like those vacuous voices speaking in America of things of the spirit and culture, that is, in purely verbal and not consubstantiated terms. And if this basic phrase is a vacuous one, we should not complain loudly to the heavens, but to our souls, to our own souls. We should complain to our souls because we stand before the verification of a certainty, namely that our consciousness remains immature and that we run the risk not of continuing to be but of becoming more and more immature men.

Our founding fathers were not immature men. But we are becoming increasingly so through an involution, through a process of involution in the face of which we must stop and say "No." Instead of lingering over our affliction, absorbed in arid, cloistered reflection, we should feverishly rush out of our room and announce to all our neighbors our critical decision and our hunger for betterment, our answer "no" to that inert advance whose stride is like a heavy drowsiness settling over men, multitudes, and cities.

No. The Argentina we want is something else. Different. With a consciousness in movement, a consciousness that is what it should be, namely, natural wisdom. If, according to the Socratic theory expressed by Plato in his *Phaedo*,[13] knowledge is recollection, then what we need at all times is recollection, that is, prior knowledge of the origin of our destiny; and in the origin of our destiny lies the origin of our feelings, behavior and very nature. Our future is potentially contained in our natural origin. If we lose the memory, that is, the knowledge of our inner origin—what can we be but a kind of errant optimism? To have originated is constantly to originate, to be born is to continue to be born. If we do not know how and for what reason we carry such constant rebirth within us, this ignorance will be tantamount to a repeating death under the guise of self-perpetuating life.

The ultimate result of these reflections is that they allow me no peace. Each day I see contemporary Argentina lose her true character in one act or another. One moment, she is here, present; another moment she is lost. It is useless to try to summon her to a self-examination. Her voice today is battered down by a detailed accumulation of ignorance, producing in her an attitude similar to that of certain youthful ages, which makes us laugh and discourages us at the same time. What are we to do face to face with this country in which the parable of the Prodigal Son[14] is reproduced? The country has set out in search of pleasure and wealth; we can not help but notice that she has also drawn too far away from something which she should never draw away from: the sense of her inner progress.

Furthermore, countries, like men—I repeat once more, oh Lord, like men—are not masters of their destinies but of the roads their lives take. The existence of each living species on this planet knows no ultimate end. It is all road. Men are living roads; the winged insect that dies in oil is a road. Life is a road, death a road. Everything is a road. The body is a road and the soul a road toward a remote consummation. Love is a road, charity a road, hatred which divides is a road, and hope that arises in the east with each new dawn. The apparent motionlessness of the moving constellations is a road. Doubt, joy and agony. The man who lurks in the shadows to strike his treacherous blow is a road, as is the woman who—blood of her blood—kills the one she loves. A road is the dream of the taciturn, the courage of the daring, the activity of the active, the laziness of the lazy, woman's periodic indisposition and her twilight delirium at the height of her poetic anguish. A road too, is a child's walking, the atheist's cruel reserve, the evil Christian's lie, the prosperous man's pride and the poor man's bitterness. Those are all roads.

We are poor masters of our roads when we begin to neglect them, because then, as the parable from the Scriptures says, he who goes out in search of opulent days and nights sadly returns as a swine keeper. Machiavelli,[15] with his provident discretion and his dark, captious, imbecile-like face (just as he is stll seen in a corner of the duke's Florentine chamber), knew this only too well when he advised Lorenzo the Magnificent:[16] "Some have believed and others still believe that God and Fortune so govern events in this world that the wisdom of men can neither effect any changes in these events nor remedy them. But I dare venture the opinion that if half of our actions depends on Fortune, we men govern at least the other half."

In truth, nothing is controlled, for we live on the level pampa, on even ground, from which point no commands are given. But we are or cease to be according to whether or not we have the courage of our conscience. This, which may appear to be a small thing, is so transcendent that because of it alone a man was arrested in the olive orchard and put to death on Friday in late afternoon. And in the same way the good and the bad thief were executed and an evil judge was disgraced and some centurions saddened without apparent reason, and many people buried alive in the catacombs of the Roman countryside. And down through the ages men have fought against each other as the only way of giving of themselves, and at the end of their lives, in the cruelest moments of their wars, there is a faint moan and a belated longing for peace and survival.

Only in recent decades has our nation gone astray, only since the turn of the century, a little more than thirty-odd years. I have seen the early immigrants and the later ones; one can study in them, as in the deep lines of worry on a face, the story of our decadence as a country even more than as a nation or as a state. (And may those annoyed by this kind of truth not be too scandalized. The greater their feeling of scandal, the worse their guilt will be when enough people are determined to be better). I have seen foreigners who came to our country when the voices of our greatest minds were still alive. And for those men the essence of Argentina was a state of religiousness. Those men from countries where human effort has lost its effectiveness acquired a wholly new devotion to earth and tree, house or man, to everything around here. They witnessed the almost heroic rise of a nationality in which everything was still to be created, from the city parks, the line of demarcation for urban dwellings, the martial songs, the foresight of politics, the organic reality of the country as regards extrinsic and intrinsic elements, to the visible articulation of its intelligence. These were the moral and material deeds of a territory marvellously offered to the future. But this was not an illusory and empty future, but an active and inhabited future, a present future, like the future of everything created by a volative act, in which the concept of future is merely the progress or subsequent form of a present act. And before the spectacle of that authentic potential greatness, the men who came from other lands withdrew into themselves, totally consubstantiated, and grew silent.

In the aged figure of such men I have seen the imprint of this feeling of fervor, so simple, so emotional, and so pure. And their presence touched me with an emotion that sprung from my land, because in those faces full of black wrinkles like those of ancient tillers, faces already friends with the eternal and without earthly greed, that expression endured. It was none other than the expression of a new world, the spectacle of a dawn that ceaselessly advances toward midnight and then begins again. All around these men, these foreigners, they had heard the sounds of wisdom, the sound of ideas, of feelings, hopes, gestures, wills in action, the sound of a world of newcomers procreating itself, not unconsciously, but rather like the newborn who opens the way alone in the darkness of the maternal womb. They spoke of things Argentine, of the old guardians of our nationality, of unforgettable mental lapses in public addresses (like Avellaneda's[17] speech when San Martín's remains[18] were repatriated). They spoke of such and such a sensitive virtue in such and such a newcomer to the new land, with the same tender and slightly solemn voice with which they had learned to read in the Ecclesiastes in the land of their birth beyond the ocean.

And I have seen the latest immigrants.[19] In vain I have sought to discover in those younger faces of ambitious men the mental radiance to understand something besides the letters of the huge, bright signs in the city, to hear something besides the café songs, to see something besides the physical image of a comfortable country, in short to perceive something more defined and profound than the mere feeling of a pretentious national orchestration. I have seen them, happy on the outside, dead on the inside. Tied to our destiny without knowing us, even without feeling us, without feeling beyond our skin.

Are they to blame? No, my countrymen, we are. Because their deafness is a way we have of alluding to our own mutism. We prefer not to think of our emotional mutism. We think it is enough just to shout out to ourselves: Forward, and God will provide.

What deception! What deception, for God will not provide. It is so written: "He who wants to save his soul shall lose it."[20] He who *wants* to save his soul; thus our free will destroys us when it is not directed toward a transcendental principle, when we let it slip through the guiding hands of our virtue, our heart and our knowledge. And these hands are not only the fertile hands of man, but the branches of the primal tree, the beginning of all principles, because there is no principle that does not flourish from those three branches.

At this point it is inevitable for me to begin by speaking about myself. So inevitable, so necessary! I have already said that these pages are prompted by an anxiety, an aspiration, a need for dialogue. I want to have some Argentine faces turned for a moment toward my grief, toward my own struggle, my own hopes, my agonies and my rebirths as I live with a country that keeps me on the bitter edge of constant vigil. My word is scarcely more than fervor now. I just wish to share that fervor with others, that is, to confess, to let others know my faith. There is no sound friendship that is not based on an uninterrupted confession, on understanding, seeing and feeling everything by confessing it. Confession means unity, without which there can be nothing between you and me, my reader, who is to judge me, love me, hate me or tolerate me.

Accordingly, the aim of this book is quite ambitious and the objective too large. Because its aim and objective are to find some people along the way, stop with them and have them tell each other the reasons for their contrition and their faith, and then say: "For this we live, for this we suffer, for this we struggle, for this we love, for this we shed our blood and for this we die."

I do not know that there is on this earth any other possibility for consolation, except faith itself.

Notes

1. These last two sentences serve as a good example of one of the notable characteristics of Mallea's style: the concatenation of several words or phrases of related or even synonymous meaning which cumulatively express the author's thought or emotion.

2. Argentina, covering about 2200 miles from north to south and about 900 miles at its greatest width, comprises four major geographic regions: the humid, tropical and semi-tropical northern parts, which include forest lands; the arid and semi-arid western parts, which include the Andean mountain system; the dry lands of Patagonia; and the Pampa.

3. Argentina has twenty-two provinces, among them Buenos Aires, Cordoba, Jujuy, La Pampa, La Rioja, San Juan, and Tucumán. The struggle between the provinces and Buenos Aires has been at the center of Argentine political life for over two centuries and to this day represents a source of national divisiveness.

4. Reference to the Río de la Plata (River Plate), which is really an estuary formed by the confluence of the Paraná and the Uruguay Rivers. Buenos Aires lies on the western bank of the estuary and Montevideo on the eastern, some one hundred miles away.

5. Pampa. The vast grass-covered plain in central Argentina, extending some 700 miles north-south and 400 miles east-west. The fertile pampa, comprising about 25% of the area of Argentina, is prodigiously suited for cattle and sheep raising and for the cultivation of wheat, cereal, and other grains. But the pampa is more than just a geographic area where the gaucho once roamed, is more than the heartland of Argentina. For many Argentines it is the symbol of the nation's spirit, its roots and traditions.

6. Patagonia. Region near the southern tip of South America, partly in Argentine territory, partly in Chilean. Sheep raising is a major industry in this windswept area.

7. The Falkland Islands. Located in the South Atlantic Ocean some 300 miles east of the Straight of Magellan. The islands have been a British colony since 1833, although Argentina has always claimed the territory.

8. Mater. The Latin word for "mother," used here symbolically as source, origin, life, or essence.

9. Miguel de Unamuno (1864–1936). Renowned Spanish novelist, poet, and thinker. He greatly influenced Mallea in the formulation of his existential philosophy involving man's irreconcilable anguish and alienation in a chaotic society. Unamuno's most famous work, *The Tragic Sense of Life* (1921) undoubtedly was read and admired by the young and impressionable Mallea.

10. Taciturn, silent, reticent, uncommunicative, withdrawn are all terms that recur so often in Mallea's fiction that they constitute a leitmotif. This psychic state in which so many of Mallea's characters find themselves can be termed emotional mutism. Either the quality of mutism itself or a symbolic representation of it is used so frequently in character delineation that it is more than a convenient means of indicating a mood or condition. The idea of mutism is rarely treated as something ephemeral within the psychological makeup of the character. Rather, it is a deeply ingrained state of mind that forms an integral part of the whole personality. As used by Mallea, mutism implies the lack of communication among men, an inability to enter into emotional liaisons with others. When Mallea writes of mutism, he is setting up a hostile mood, establishing an atmosphere of incompatibility. In varied narrative forms, the concept of mutism is encountered in almost all of Mallea's novels and brought out most vigorously and creatively in *Chaves* (1953).

11. Mallea sees Argentina dominated politically by the powerful, entrenched forces of the oligarchy. He fears that the conservative, even repressive policies of this group have stripped Argentina of its once progressive spirit and authentic values, morally debilitating the nation and leaving it a victim of pernicious opportunists and grafters. In September 1930, an Army revolution toppled the regime of President Hipolito Irigoyen, who had been elected by the Radical party (Unión Cívica Radical) for a second term in 1928. In this coup, the military had the support of the Conservative, or National Democratic party, to which the wealthy landowners and the Church alligned themselves. General José F. Uriburu served as president of the revolutionary government from 1930–1932, and General Agustín P. Justo from 1930–1938, during which periods the country was dominated by the conservative oligarchy.

12. Mallea writes here of a concept of nationhood (*Argentinidad*) that can be applied to other Hispanic American countries as well, i.e., *Mexicanidad* or "being Mexican." *Argentinidad* encompasses more than patriotism, loyalty, national pride or even ethnic identity. It lies at the root of one's innermost sense of belonging, of feeling Argentine, of living Argentina's traditions and values.

13. *Phaedo*. One of Plato's (427–347 B.C.) great dialogues, written around 365 B.C. The work describes the last day in the life of Socrates, Phaedo's teacher. The dialogue also contains a discussion on the immortality of the soul.

14. The Prodigal Son. The parable set forth by Jesus (Luke 15:11–32) to the scribes and Pharisees. The younger of two sons squanders his inheritance in a life of dissipation, but his subsequent ill fortune makes him see the error of his ways. He repents and returns home, where he is well received by his father. When the older son becomes indignant at this action, the father says that he is now happy that he has his son once again, resuscitated from the dead.

15. Niccolo Machiavelli (1469–1527). Italian statesman and author of *The Prince* (1532), which sets forth principles that a ruler should follow, among them that he should avail himself of any means to gain his goals.

16. Lorenzo de Medici (1449–1492). Called Lorenzo the Magnificent, he was the most celebrated of the Medici family. It was largely through his efforts that Florence became the most powerful State in Italy.

17. Nicolás Avellaneda (1836–1885). Argentine president from 1874–1880. His administration was marked by relative domestic tranquility and great financial and material advancement. He also did much to encourage immigration and further education at all levels.

18. José de San Martín (1778–1850). Argentine general in Hispanic America's struggle for independence against the Spanish yoke. He is Argentina's national hero and its symbol of strength, traditional virtues and fierce patriotism and loyalty.

19. Immigrants. Argentina, with a land area of 1,079,000 square miles and only 26,000,000 inhabitants, has always been sparsely populated except for the city of Buenos Aires. The great Argentine statesman, Juan Bautista Alberdi, said that "To govern is to populate." The Argentine government has always encouraged immigration. First the Spanish, then the French, English, German, Italian and Jew have all come to Argentine shores and contributed greatly to the forging of a modern nation. The ageless conflict between the immigrant and the native is nowhere more pronounced than in Argentina. The problems of assimilation, adaptation, loyalty, prejudice and opportunity have been colorfully treated by many Argentine novelists and dramatists, among them Manuel Gálvez and Florencio Sánchez (1875–1910).

20. From Mark 8:35.

I.
The Atlantic

The bay. Awakening to the feeling for
the land. First reflections looking out
on the plains. Mrs. Hilton's school.
The children of immigrant settlers.
The world begins.

I had almost no infancy in the city.

I first saw the light of day in an Argentine bay city[1] on the Atlantic. A few days later, the constant muffled noise of the continuously shifting dunes, the country's variable climate and the fierce wind would be rocking me, as if this motion were some strange deity's grim act of playing. My father[2] was a hospital surgeon; my mother a gentle woman, the salt of the earth in her serene goodness. Both were so hardworking and decent by nature that I always saw in them something good salvaged from man's shipwreck. My first friend was the ocean-blown wind, which in my imagination was a wolf to arouse my fears or a dog to frolic with. In the middle of winter nights, the roaring wind accompanied my mother in her vigil, while my father performed operations by himself in cottages and remote areas, cutting into wounded flesh. His vigorous hand collected no fee. If he had to charge those who could afford it, he did; if he had to give free medicine to the poor, he did that too, and generously. When I was twelve, I began to understand what that stream of poor people coming to his clinic meant. They came to look at him silently and trustingly. Sometimes they would bring fowl, other times they would bring nothing but painful trust, that surrender full of sad hope. In that house, where we disdained the almighty peso, the doors were kept open during the day, for those who came not seeking a cure for some ailment came to ask advice.

The dry weather of the south held the bay in its grip. For days on end, the only thing heard in the city was the roaring of the furious wind and the sound of the dunes shifting the sand. Only laborious work could distract the men from the persistent bad weather in the cold Atlantic city. It was terribly difficult to live in that severe, merciless climate. Not even a meadow around the whole city; no colors, no sun for days and days, but instead the gray stone, the gray wind, the gray sand. And the gloomy atmosphere, the endless afternoons, the sudden and deep nights. At times a fine rain, then the wind again, the fog, the dust from the sand dunes that furiously punished our eyes. My father would return in the night carriage after seeing his patients. The heat from the stoves and the light from the lamps kept the whole family warm as the storm raged outside. While my parents and my brother were reading, I would suddenly lift the curtain up, stick my nose to the glass and look out into the night. Everything appeared full of imaginary monsters. And when someone laughed in that house a cynical echo seemed to answer from outside. No, there was no easy life for this smalltown doctor. We were in the middle of the desert. No one could live there without some sacrifice; in that region every living thing belonged to the desert, the wind, the sand.

Many ships stopped at that ocean port along Magellan's route to Cape Horn.[3] Looking toward the south, I wondered what that vast desert was like, to which these latter-day navigators came from time to time with the echo of the opposite hemisphere in their mouths lacerated by bad weather and bad liquor. Lost along the streets crowded with sawmills,[4] and then along the wharves crowded with elevators, bridges and cranes, I approached those ships with great curiosity.

Hasty readings of Reclus[5] had taught me little about what each region of our planet offered those professionals of the sea, who resembled certain Asiatic monks because of their contempt for death and a kind of sacred and inhuman hermeticism.

My mother, my eight-year-old brother and I—the three of us—lived almost in silence around the central figure of my father. He was a man of enormous energy and great tenderness, of strong character and high intelligence, of abundant moral and verbal wisdom. He had such a refined and elegant demeanor that it was difficult to tell which aspect of his character was the more genteel, that abiding generosity of heart, or that concise, fervent, delicate speech with which he openly expressed all his thoughts and gave them dignity. My father was related to Sarmiento and his family's history is recorded in several chapters of *Provincial Reminiscences*. My father belonged to that group of men of tough moral fiber who appear during the difficult years of a nation's social formation. He had to travel long distances in his horse-drawn carriage to perform surgery or deliver babies in the hinterland of southern Buenos Aires province, where many times his life was threatened if the patient made little progress. He knew Dante,[6] *The Prince*,[7] and Molière[8] to perfection. He was also active in politics and was wounded in a leg after writing critical articles in a militant newspaper. Even as a young boy I would admire certain concrete things in my father: his mental vigor, his zealous and even violent honesty, his profound generosity, his culture, the extraordinary courage of his convictions. And all these things were defended by his great physical courage. At eighty, this man would have the spirit of a man of thirty, the intelligence of an intellectual in his prime, the consistency of character of a fighter without a army.

To temper his surgeon's arm and test his valor with men, my father fenced every morning with his instructor. What I remember of my first years is a boy curiously watching those bouts in the vast, wide-doored vestibule of our city home. Then that door would open and patients would begin to come in; later, Mr. Saint-Hilaire would arrive to teach my brother violin, Madame Thérèse Frigé to practice French with my father, and Mrs. MacGregor to teach me the rudiments of piano. With this woman my mother would play Handel's *Largo*.[9]

I was eleven when the war broke out in Europe. The information I received about it was only indirect, through my parents' conversations and through those French publications that reached my house containing horrible photographs of the wounded—ah, Miss Cavell in her long uniform, the words *Nach Paris*[10] on the doors in sinister charcoal, the military edicts, the insolent inscriptions! My recollection of the war is linked to the works of Croce,[11] Barrès,[12] Ferrero,[13] Bernstein,[14] Lavedan,[15] all of whom my father read; in short, to the awakening of my adolesence—the instincts, curiosities, dreams, ambitions.

It is natural for every organism to have its healthy parts and its sick parts, its unintelligent parts and its intelligent parts. Of all social organisms the one most characterized by its negative parts is the bourgeoisie, of which there are two kinds, the dull, sleepy, lizard-like bourgeoisie and the idealistic bourgeoisie. This is a form of disconformity, however relative it may be. And artists generally spring from a paternal human climate into which the disquieting seed of disconformity has penetrated. As for me, I come from the latter kind of bourgeoisie, from an idealistic bourgeoisie. I hope that some day this idealistic bourgeois residue disappears, leaving only a man whose spirit knows no material interest.

One day my father stood up at a municipal board meeting and shouted out: "I'm not voting for this because I'm an honest man." And with no bitterness he gave up his career as a public servant; he would no longer fight politically except in the last campaign of the only party he ever joined, the old illustrious Unión Cívica[16] (Radical party), for whose leader Udaondo—a good friend, too—he would gladly have shed his blood. But Beazley's candidacy[17] was unsuccessful and the party withdrew from the political arena. My father would have preferred anything to joining another party, but many members of the Radical party thought differently and later became extremists and other things. (In spite of these isolated and fortuitous defections, rarely has Argentine civic-mindedness reached a higher degree of collective honesty than during those years of orderly government and repudiation of the oligarchy. The years immediately preceding 1916 witnessed the arrival on the political scene of a vigorous group of worthy men wno felt that public office demanded the highest integrity). "We shall not get rich as long as I live," I heard him tell my mother one night, and she supported him in his convictions, in his self-imposed poverty, in that Spartan simplicity and iron-tough character that meant he never accepted a situation of dependency. At this time, he left politics almost completely—he had been and still was one of the most important men in his party, one of the men loyal to Udaondo. Around this time, too, 1914–1915, my father began to give up medicine, which he had practiced for almost thirty years, to devote himself *corpus et anima* to his children's education. We were then three, and the oldest studied law in Buenos Aires.

My first conscious contact with my land occurred at that time. One awakens to that feeling or not; perhaps one can live a thousand lives without even touching it. I had that feeling for the first time in the long, solitary afternoons in that southern city, when I stood on the rear balcony of my house and saw the never-ending hills which separated the city from the sand dunes and the open country. That was the pampa, the remote horizon, the plains, the desert. As I went up the distant slope, from time to time I passed a swarming throng at a funeral; the procession ascended, then suddenly disappeared. Some hundred meters beyond, the impoverished countryside began under an incomparable sky. Human destinies, with their conversations and sudden turns, scarcely disturb the earthly dialogue with the clouds or the fate of the invisible wheat that grows from the dead grain and then starts again. As Lucan affirms in the *Pharsalia*,[18] there is a certain point of the mountain from which armies in combat seem motionless. And at the end of that flat vastness, all action seems futile in the eyes of this mother, the indomitable land; only thought reaches it and subjugates it. Engrossed in thought, I saw nothing but the naked land, our land, the clean and austere immenseness, the Argentine plain.

As an adolescent without reasoning power to classify and discriminate, everything seemed to me more categorical than man in a land devoid of limits. This is so, perhaps, because every idea is of a material nature in its infancy, and matter does not hold sway over matter. My spirit dozed, dreamed; my whole being was absorbed in the landscape; my spirit rested for a while in the small hills and then continued on toward the plain rapidly and yet quietly.

I would often stay alone in our house with the servants, and while they played their card games with dirty, kitchen-stained cards, I went up to the balcony to recite the Angelus.[19] Thanks to that rite, I awakened to the primordial essence of my land and was transfixed before the silence and the solitude of the melancholy plains. Empty land and cities—the whole country was like that—empty land and cities, dizzy noise and solitude. And as the days went by—August followed July, September followed August—my soul accommodated itself more and more, with greater breadth and profundity, to the form of that nature that surrounded me, a flat surface on which nothing resounded without a tenderly savage and taciturn touch.

Tenderly savage and taciturn land where each day I became aware of the name of a new town, an increase of a few million people, the diverse directions of unleashed progress. To the north, to the south, to the east and west, towns grew—furtive mushrooms beside the rock of a multitudinous center. To the north the sugar mills were grinding; to the northeast the juice of abundant vines ran through the presses; toward the Andes, the pampa, towards the center the cattle and the grain multiplied biblically. In the capital, precious stones and gold grew abundantly; speculation was active. Opulent fruit came from municipal governments. The morning sower's joy proliferated everywhere. And toward the south, the promised land, the hierarchical paradise after so much amazing work, the so-called pharaonic railroads were spreading out. Ah, man's frivolous condition! All of that was the Prodigal Son's first steps.

Behind the external splendor was naked man, standing before naked earth, natural man face to face, alone, with his inner destiny. Alone with his destiny, not as one individual of a class, not as just a part of a collective social destiny, not as a being controlled by chance, not as a subject of the two choices—work and crass, opportunistic profit—but as a person with evident dreadful freedom and perilous fate, as a person facing the Last Judgment[20] and not the transitory and happy Judgment. And the Last Judgment will not come with the end of the world; each day secretly indicts us. The person confronting other men, the land, religion, the naked person—that person had remained behind. He was coming along behind, a somber shadow that follows one who squanders.

The child in me tirelessly looked out onto the plains. From that perspective, I saw everything clearly, like that furthest point in the background in which primitive man seemed to place his whole sentient vision: the color of the horizon that gives spirit, light, tone and accent to the unformed mass. That whole wild expanse—I began to think as the adolescent in me disappeared—was going to be conquered by only one thing, by a moral system as strong and as well-defined as itself: idea, passion or feeling.

Where was I to look for that idea, that passion, that feeling? I looked for that sign in my classmates all around me, first in elementary school, then in high school. In the former, an English school run by the iron hand of Mrs. Hilton—a corpulent, bronze-skinned Australian who ruled us with the whip, although she was always fair, as befits the best of the strong—there were grouped together the blond children of the many immigrant settlers, children of Danes, of Norwegians, of Welshmen, of Germans, of Frenchmen, of Celts. There I played with the Jorgensen boys, there I knew the Rasmussen brothers, and the Denholm and the Le Tesson children. There I openly admired the most skillful and brave among them, Hector and Stanley Geddes, both older than I, whom I accompanied more than once as their squire in their bloodless bouts. Ah, Hector and Stanley Geddes—one dead, the other, who knows where he is?—who did not deign to look at their younger fellow student, who always took the other side in arguments, who were so haughty, bold and aggressive in that Atlantic city. How much silent devotion I gave them!

I especially remember the winters at Mrs. Hilton's school. The large deserted rectangular courtyard, the two enormous rooms, separated by a glass partition. The two classes, the upper and the lower, contained all the grades. We all sat down there in the morning—the bully Valpoli, whose fingers would cruelly choke his victims, as well as the girls with auburn braids and bright eyes. While those fifty pupils boisterously played during recreation, I preferred to watch, to admire them, to hate them or love them depending on their character, and to uncover for good or evil the secret of all those incipient vocations. Like the comet's tail in the cosmic dust, in those brief recess periods my spirit followed this or that rapture of another soul, that precocious delinquent's rebelliousness or the meek, docile boy's early unction, and I was astonished at what my imagination had projected for the future destinies of these two opposite types of boys.

When they called on me to run, my performance was mediocre. While my legs urged me on, a different kind of urging was still greater—my astonishment, my reflection, my meditating shyness. They were days of discovery in both human and physical relationships and I had new reasons for surprise and fascination, from the symmetrical nervation of the leaf to the composition of sand, from the omnipotence of the classics to the village girl's simple tale, from the rites of the Sunday liturgy and the image of the crucified Lord to the sweet secret mystery of grace on the faces of the girls crossing the cathedral square with their hair blowing in the late afternoon wind.

But astonishment means losing a period of time; to be astonished is to stop. And among all those turbulent young lives, only mine was slow, awkward, inefficient. They considered me hopeless for games—but I rebounded from that deficiency with my fantasy sated, my small eyes ardent with lucidity and discovery, my soul in suspense. Once the children played Execution, or Firing Squad. A ball served as a projectile; the terribly skillful executioner threw it lightning fast from a considerable distance just when the condemned man started running to try to save his life. When it was my turn, I waited, and when the other boy raised his hand from afar, I opened my eyes and ran sideways. But he threw the ball and let out a savage guffaw. He had figured out exactly how far a timid boy would spring. And I felt the projectile explode like a whiplash square on my cheek. Ah, anticipation! Everything would always reach me in life like that, wounding me as I was getting out of the way, as a result of someone else's treacherous calculation that my calculation would be wrong, at the very instant of rising up from the ground with open, startled, ardent eyes!

Le Tesson, Bigliardi, Denholm, Valpoli, Battistoni, how I captured in you the wayward birds! For while you may have forgotten me as you scattered over the four corners of the earth and relegated me to a dark attic of your soul, without ever remembering me, I still think of all of you, I visit you at this belated convocation.

The proximity of these immigrant children, of those near-foreigners, exalted me in a somber and secret way. I felt their tenacity quietly influencing my country's destiny. I loved them. For them I would have given all of my childhood ambitions, my health and my blood. For them I began to love their countries' books, the heroic legends and the first adventure books written in the language of Sir Walter Scott.[21] During their hectic games, they mixed their old, ingrained words with their newly acquired Spanish. They brought to us their natural knowledge of adversity.

I love them. Many afternoons, when the wind dragged the dunal sand from the ocean, I returned from school with one of them and we crossed the municipal square. No matter what topic they touched on, these boys, who were really hardly more than children, were very definite about their inclinations, tastes and plans. Years later, at the Colegio Nacional, I could not find in my Argentine classmates the same determination shown by those immigrants. The design to build a country could be seen in the beauty of the girls—with bright eyes and fine skin, a Flossie Rae, and Elsa Bogges, proud and with a northern appearance—as well as in the apparent aridness and harshness of the boys. They well knew the role they were to play in that construction, the role that belonged to each person, whether his vocation was a cattle dealer or an industrialist.

Although Mrs. Hilton's whip never touched me, it did teach me many things. It taught me what the presence of an order, a system, does to each man, how it enriches and strengthens him; it taught me what kind of aristocracy imposes the acceptance of a logical order on the soul. She imposed an order, with her bronzed, Maenad[22] trimness and her stern gray eyes, but when necessary her heart replaced hardness with tenderness in those stony features. I knew nothing about Australia, but Mrs. Hilton herself loomed large enough so that I did not have to learn more about that nation. Her whip, applied on the hands of pupils who lied—so many times mercilessly on Le Tesson, whom she then threatened to send to a warship as further punishment—or on the hands of pupils who "snitched" or who enjoyed being lazy, taught me that man has no alternative but to have society impose justice on him, inasmuch as one does not punish oneself.

In the long afternoons, under the Tiepolo sky,[23] I would read in the garden until night closed in. My world of fantasy, both in human and divine form, was like waves which the sea stretched out before me from the depths of the pages I voraciously read as I bit my nails. On cold days my mother told me to change clothes, fearful that the biting air would cut into me. I went upstairs to the third floor where the bedrooms were, as if in a dream: the fictional characters lived in me more than did familiar reality. Little Dorrit[24] played with the strange inhabitant of the abbey, with Stephen Gray; and Sexton Blake[25] filled me with burning envy and ambition to be a detective.

Then I went from the British school to the National School and for the first time had contact with Argentine teachers. They were indolent doctors or lawyers who indolently taught grammar or arithmetic.

Interest in their students began and ended with the class hour. If I had once learned in English who San Martin was, I tenaciously began to forget it here. My classmates' attitude was different and was created out of that indolence, out of the teacher's perpetual negligence. No one was concerned about anything except living comfortably, with little reading and less review. At the time, the change from the serious Nordic character to the Argentine's leisurely manner was not an unpleasant one for me. Rather than listening in class to all those yawning men of learning, I wanted to feel and touch the city, the teeming streets, the plains, the port, my inseparable books, the classics— Dumas,[26] Dickens,[27] Stevenson[28] and Gaboriau.[29] What attracted me too was the behavior of men and the glances of women. Since I had no sisters, or female cousins or friends, the world of women was as strange to me as a remote continent. I had almost always kept a silent distance from the girls at the British school. But now, with the awakening not only of my natural instincts, but also of an active imagination, my whole being wanted to know about that secret and modest feminine world, about the reasons for the power that women had over me, about the frequent evasive glances, flirtations, cruelties, reticences, coddling and other feminine ways.[30]. My habits as a shy, solitary person, a wanderer, created in me a strange attraction to women, an attitude of strange respect. They alone would later teach me to feel and understand lucidly and profoundly certain things of the human heart. They alone would later give me, in the most difficult stages of my life, in the most turbulent of certain nights, the warm bread of joy.

Some mornings I would go with my father to the hospital, the carriage first jolting on the stone roadway, then riding more smoothly as it passed the country houses, between the myrtles and the tamarisks. The patients hurried to fuss over the director's son and invited me to taste delicious broths. I still remember a wonderful dish made of thistle and spices. To repay them, I brought them European magazines with photographs taken at the Marne[31] or Charleroi:[32] executions, trenches, the wounded and the dead lying face down in the dry earth. At times, while my father worked in the white rooms, I would be busy listening to the coachmen's prattle close to the veranda, near Corso, our shiny-coated horse. I felt close to the soil in which these houses were rooted, close to the huge cedars, the diosma bush and the thyme.

I opened my sensitive nose to the earth's pure smell, my eyes to the sky so blue and smooth that neither cloud nor fog interrupted the pale indigo arch. And the Atlantic wind surrounded me, bathed me. My father finally came out and sat down with a sigh, worried about one case and happy about another, his face at once smiling and austere. I felt his hand rest on my arm, that thumb on which a scalpel had left its mark. Contact with this kind of inner nobleness and love filled my silence with sudden joy. No hunger has ever been so strong in me as my hunger for those kinds of men in whom life's terrible law of living is redeemed by a plethoric effusion of nature and the heart. Hunger for those altruistic men who keep nothing for themselves except the will to give. Moved by sadness, inhibitions and deep anguish, I drew no self-satisfaction then from things—nor have I subsequently—for they are the apotheosis of motionlessness and in me never did anything but increase tragic speculations. What is in motion, on the other hand, what is alive and vital, is what responds to love's only impulse. And it was from those people rich in emotive action that I always extracted life, in its exalted forms, in its wellspring. God knows that neither water nor food has made me seek these things if they were not pure—and in humanness I know no other purity but piety.

Piety, charity; the three theological virtues are summed up in that one alone. Charity engenders faith and also hope. And I can not conceive of any true act of love which is not an act of piety of the flesh, through which the flesh itself, rather than being condemned forever, is saved by self-denial.

Notes

1. Bahía Blanca. Important city on the Atlantic Ocean, in the southernmost part of the province of Buenos Aires. Population: 93,122. The harsh, arid climate, with fierce, biting winds, no doubt left its mark on Mallea's rather reticent and stern character. In 1951 Mallea published the novel *All Green Shall Perish,* in which there is an obvious parallel between the harshness and aridness of Bahía Blanca and the emotional barrenness of the unloving couple,

Agata and Nicanor Cruz. Much of the beautiful imagery in the novel involves analogies between the severity of the land and the sterility of the couple's relationship.

2. As r.e can judge from the tone of the text, Mallea's father left a deep and lasting imprint on Eduardo. His father was stern but never harsh, and always showed loving care. Through his father's words, Mallea learned humility and integrity; through his deeds he learned compassion for the downtrodden and the poor.

3. Reference to Ferdinand Magellan (1480–1521), the Portuguese navigator who first circumnavigated the earth, discovering the strait that connects the Atlantic to the Pacific at the southern end of South America.

4. The protagonist of Mallea's novel *Chaves* is employed in a sawmill, where the constant, irritating noise contrasts sharply with his silence and emotional withdrawal.

5. Jean Jacques Elisée Reclus (1830–1905). French geographer, author of *The Earth* (1868), *The Earth and its Inhabitants,* 20 vols. (1876–94), and *Man and the Earth* (1905).

6. Dante Alighieri (1265–1321). The great Italian poet, author of *The Divine Comedy,* (1308–1320), a journey through hell, purgatory, and heaven.

7. Reference to Machiavelli's *The Prince.*

8. Molière. Jean Baptiste Poquelin (1622–1673). The renowned French satirical dramatist, author of *The Misanthrope* (1666), *The Doctor in Spite of Himself* (1666), *Tartuffe* (1664), and *The Miser* (1668).

9. George Frederick Handel (1685–1759). German-born composer, most famous for his oratorio *Messiah* (1741). Wrote more than forty operas. In *Serse* (1738) there appears the tenor aria "Largo."

10. *Nach Paris.* German slogan used in World War I, meaning "On to Paris."

11. Benedetto Croce (1866–1952). Italian critic and philosopher, author of the four-volume *Philosophy of the Spirit* (1909). In 1903, Croce founded the literary and philosophical journal *La Critica* and became one of its major contributors.

12. Maurice Barrès (1862–1923). French novelist and essayist whose works reveal a strong nationalistic and patriotic fervor. Barrès is the author of *A Free Man* (1889), *The Soul of France* (1915), and *The Underlying Spirit of France* (1917).

13. Guglielmo Ferrero (1871–1942). Italian historian whose many works include *The Greatness and Decline of Rome* (1907–09), *The Ruin of Ancient Civilization* (1921), and *The Life of Caesar* (1933).

14. Aron Bernstein (1812–1884). German Jewish journalist, essayist, and short story writer who played an important role in establishing Reform Judaism in Berlin. He is the author of *History of Revolution and Reaction in Germany*, 3 vols. (1883–1884).

15. Henri Leon-Emile Lavedan (1859–1940). French playwright. Among his most famous comic plays are *Le Prince d'Aurec* (1892), *Le Marquis de Priola* (1902), *Le Goût du Vice* (1911) and *Servir* (1913).

16. The "Unión Cívica" (Civic Union) came into being in 1888 under the leadership of Leandro Alem (1842–1896) and Aristóbulo del Valle (1845–1896). Guillermo Udaondo (1859–1923) was an important member of this party that played a decisive role in forcing the resignation of President Juárez Celman during the Revolution of 1890. In 1891, the most liberal segment of the Unión Cívica formed the Unión Cívica Radical and over the next two or three years became the leaders of the Radical party. Udaondo was unsuccessful as a candidate for Congress and for president of Argentina, but in 1916 became head of the Unión Cívica Radical. Under Presidents Hipólito Irigoyen (1916–22; 1928–30) and Marcelo T. de Alvear (1922–1928), elected by the Radical party, Argentina enjoyed considerable democratic government. From 1916 to 1930, the Radical party was supported by the middle class and a sizeable portion of the working class.

17. Francisco J. Beazley (1864–1924). Argentine civil servant and educator. He was vice rector of the Colegio Nacional from 1890 to 1892 and chief of police in Buenos Aires from 1896 to 1904.

18. Marcus Annaeus Lucanus (A.D. 39–65). Roman poet born in Cordoba, Spain, nephew of the philosopher Seneca. Lucan is the author of the epic *Pharsalia,* an account of the civil war between Caesar and Pompey.

19. Angelus. Roman Catholic prayer in honor of the mystery of the incarnation. It is recited three times a day, at 6 A.M., noon, and 6 P.M. The bell tolled at these times is called the Angelus bell.

20. Last Judgment. The Christian doctrine that states that at the end of this world the dead shall be raised and stand in judgment.

21. Sir Walter Scott (1771–1832). Scottish romantic poet and novelist who influenced the development of historical fiction in Hispanic America. Works: *The Lady of the Lake* (1810), *Rob Roy* (1818), *Ivanhoe* (1820).

22. In Greek mythology, Maenads were Bacchus's female worshipers. The term refers to a dissolute woman, a reveler.

23. Giovanni Battista Tiepolo (1696–1770). Italian painter whose most famous works include *Christ in the Garden of Olives* and *Madonna in Glory.* The striking clarity of the colors he used gave rise to the expression "a Tiepolo sky."

24. Little Dorrit. Heroine of the novel (1855) by Charles Dickens that bears her name. Little Dorrit was brought up in jail, where her father was imprisoned for failure to pay his debts.

25. Sexton Blake. British detective hero, created by Harry Blyth. The character of Sexton Blake first appeared in a story called "The Missing Millionaire," published in a boys' weekly, *The Halfpenny Marvel,* on December 20, 1893. Some 4000 Sexton Blake novels have been subsequently written by over 200 detective writers.

26. Alexander Dumas, father (1802–1870). French dramatist and novelist, author of the widely read works *Napoleon Bonaparte* (1831), *The Three Musketeers* (1844) and *The Count of Monte Cristo* (1844). It is possible that Mallea may be referring to Dumas's illegitimate son of the same name (1824–1895), the author of *Camille* (1852).

27. Charles Dickens (1812–1870). The great English novelist was extremely popular in Latin America, many of his works being serialized in the leading newspapers of the capital cities. Among his most famous works, no doubt read by Mallea, are *Oliver Twist* (1837), *David Copperfield* (1849), *A Tale of Two Cities* (1859), *Little Dorrit* (1857), and *Sketches by Boz* (1836).

28. Robert Louis Stevenson (1850–1894). Scottish novelist and poet, most famous for *Treasure Island* (1883), *The Strange Case of Dr. Jekyll and Mr. Hyde* (1886), *Kidnapped* (1886) and *The Master of Ballantrae* (1889).

29. Emile Gaboriau (1835–1873). French writer of detective stories who created the popular characters Père Tabaret and Monsieur Locoq.

30. Many of Mallea's female characters exhibit very negative qualities: aloofness, superficiality, coldness, emotional retreat. Despite this bias, there are few Hispanic American novelists who have penetrated the female psyche so deeply and with as much acumen as Mallea.

31. Marne. River in northeastern France. On September 9, 1914, the Allies stopped the German Armies in the first battle of the Marne.

32. Charleroi. Small industrial city in south central Belgium. Invaded by the Germans in 1914, the city became the scene of bitter fighting.

II.
The Metropolis

*Another birth. Approaching
intelligence. Friendship with the
angry ones. The passion of sensibility.
The beginning of the fight. First
fundamental questions. The passion of
the anguished creators. Basic inquiry
regarding essence and the land. Man
and his relationship to the real world
and to the ideal world.*

1916. Buenos Aires[1] and awakening to a new consciousness, or rather, the awakening of consciousness. Driven by his most basic concern, the education of his children, that fifty-eight-year-old physician who had denied himself so many things severed all ties with his profession and came to the capital to care for his two sons near the University. The older son studied jurisprudence; I was still in high school. It is a serious task to educate, and my father knew how to do it only one way— austerely.

So I suddenly find myself in Buenos Aires, in the very center that monopolizes the government and thought of the country. Everything seems momentous to me, extraordinary. In the city, I stand for hours in amazement before the sight of Babylon[2] that maintains the shape of the plains in the midst of its pungent strength and almost savage wealth. The men seem strong to me; the women, beautiful. It is adolescence's lustful time, when youth, somewhat frightened, gratifies its desires in houses of prostitution and seeks amorous adventures in sleazy hotels with large-busted women of loose morals. I poke around the bookstores; I wander through the streets. I stop before every store window as I would before the make-believe world of jewels, furniture, steamships, restaurants, bazaars, elegant ways of men and women with expensive labels. I enter the darkness of the movie houses, I stop to see the crowds pass by. I am fulfilled, I am happy. Some day that city will read what I write. But, does it read now what I read? I don't want to ask myself anything; my joy is too great as I contemplate the city of more than two million inhabitants, of more than two million destinies that can be narrated like a story.

But the school environment, the classrooms at the high school, were not different from those I had left behind. I had to walk through many city streets and squares to get to those cold rooms. There I found warmth of other companions my age and another kind of coldness, the coldness of my teachers. During five years in secondary school,[3] I knew more than forty teachers; in gratitude I remember only two. One was M. François, my French instructor; the other was Wilkens, who taught physics.

My literary vocation first showed itself in my need to create myths whose real beauty was similar to the beauty that had produced such a great effect on me. I was not content to exalt myself, to cry and to learn; I needed to exalt others, to make others cry, and also—in a puerile way—to instruct. I began to write stories and secretly send them to some of the children's magazines I read. When I first saw them published, I felt I was walking through the streets in the aura of a happy hallucination. "To write!" I thought. What a poor ingenuous boy I was, reading the biographies of Hugo[4] and Leon Tolstoy[5] and trying to emulate them.

I was then fourteen. Motion pictures, which were almost as old as I was, grew up with me; how my imaginative nature was abetted by that art! Hours and hours in the darkness glued to the adventure reflected by a milky halo on the silver screen. Since my father wanted us to have physical education too, I joined a club where they taught boxing—this word was anathema then in Buenos Aires, at a time when Maeterlinck[6] was praising "the noble art of self defense" in Belgium and Bombardier Wells[7] and Carpentier[8] were the idols of London and Paris. Each day in the ring I was supposed to learn how to be a good loser, how not to flaunt my strength so that I might show improvement with each lesson, how not to expect anything which does not come from the strength I generate within myself. Before dinner, all limbered up, I had Danish in a pastry shop near the club; and as I crossed the streets toward Esmeralda, my eyes filled with the lights, the charm, the excitement, the sense of humanity, the traffic on Carlos Pellegrini and Suipacha Streets, from Cangallo to Paraguay, those arteries[9] beating with the pulse of the city as rich as Croesus.[10] Ah, those evenings as an adolescent in Buenos Aires, a nascent interest in those sallow-skinned girls with a haughty air and bright eyes. Blind desire for strange trips to that closed-off land—women! At that time everything seemed prodigious; to see, touch, smell, hear, taste; to extract from everything living a certain effusion, an ecstasy; to approach everything alive with a shudder, in a deeply intense way, with vibrant vehemence and even joy or tears. Daring and timid at the same time, I ran through the streets behind the demonstration acclaiming this or that hero. I had one purpose in mind: to demonstrate ardently, to provide direction for my enthusiasm, an outlet for my tendency to stand in wonder at things. To stand in wonder! I asked for nothing else, wanted nothing else. To stand in wonder, it did not matter at what, just as long as I stood in wonder and provided that the shadow of a divine likeness is read into the object of wonderment.

A fatal constant then prevailed over my chance meetings: my arriving too late to meet different kinds of people, not only thought of abstractly but actively sought. At that time when deception and discord were rife, however detached I might have felt from my prosaic surroundings, I failed to come across even one deeply worried, genuine, and upright person. I never even suspected that there could live in the city that motley group of tough, wayward, and hot-headed adolescents from which finally emerge two or three authentic creative artists to serve as guides to a whole generation.

The only people I saw around me were those who showed a Boeotian[11] dislike for things of the mind, who were incapable of devouring a book—even of reading one—of having an absurd dream or carrying in their soul that foolish flame to ignite a Utopia or an act of heroism or mysticism. It was unusual to see a student read books outside of the required texts. One morning as I was sitting in the trolley that took me to school, Mr. Wilkens, our physics instructor, a relatively young man, happened to sit down beside me and noticed to his great surprise that I was reading Charles Dickens's *Sketches by Boz*[12] in English. After that, he became my most sympathetic teacher, even though he was the one most feared by the students because he was so strict and severe in his teaching. Of a noble Danish family, whose roots lay deep in Jutland, he was a man of great distinction, remote, understanding, aristocratic in his bearing, a descendent of the Vikings. He soon left Argentina for his native land. He was a man accustomed to paying due respect to the uses of intelligence, and although the most rigid of the physics teachers—an often dry science—he knew, as his colleague Sir James Jeans states, that the great poets have done much more to comprehend the real world than the great physicists.

At this time, I wanted to associate closely with those people who could foster the cultivation of intelligence. Later, that longing was transformed into another, more profound and identifiable longing— that of searching for a dialogue with intelligent women, a dialogue of friendship with intelligent men. I could not conceive of any man who did not have as his basic foundation a constant reflective sensibility. If I ever had strong class prejudice, this was it.

I was not concerned about those men with infallible intelligence. I was interested in those human beings full of doubts who would find their dawn and continue on ahead. Not pure function, but the substance of intelligence. In this sense, each day I felt a greater abomination for dogma, a greater inclination toward the spirit that is active in each and every circumstance of man's existence, whether it be literary, sentimental, sensual, physical or moral. Hatreds and preferences grew in me. Execration of the presumptuously dogmatic, passion for the creators. Execration of the arrogantly learned, passion for those who admit they rise each day to states of ignorance, passion for those who perceive how their own virgin newness, their horror at cold, systematic concepts and mechanized intellectualization are awakened each day. Execration of the one who superciliously sits on his throne of learning.

All this would quickly lead me to the company of the great rebels of literature. To those who have not been content just to write, to those who have shouted out, to those who have not been content merely to live, to those who have endured the universe. To those who have not stopped when confronted with passion and conflict; to those who have shed their clothes and gone to face the terrible sea, who have remained human even in defeat, rich in valor, alive, more than alive—almost dead by dint of so much living. It was the moment in which I looked desparingly for certain somber acts of heroism. I had left behind me the period when I made a pact with pure sentiment, I left behind Dickens, Manzoni,[13] Mistral,[14] Hugo, Chateaubriand,[15] de Vigny.[16] Now literature could give me only the heroic—not the epic as a theme, but the crucial, bloody heroic action of some stormy and anguished poets. I can not imagine how this sudden solicitude came over me after so many years of sentimental vegetation. Perhaps because the almost exclusive reading of novelists had left a germinative well of human experience in the depths of my spirit. Throughout my adolescence, Thackeray,[17] Meredith,[18] Hardy,[19] Maupassant,[20] Turgenev,[21] the northern writers, the Goethe of *Werther,*[22] Balzac,[23] Stendhal,[24] even the pompous and lonely D'Annunzio[25] had all stored up, refined and distilled a strange prescience of man and an unhappy feeling in the face of destiny. Confronted with such philosophic currents, my spirit withdrew. My nascent inclination toward tragic-minded creative writers comes from several sources: Greek tragedy begun by Aeschylus[26] as well as the decadent Latin theater; the lack of influence I felt of English romantic poetry (whose suggestive voices were too rhetorical to move me emotionally) and the very real influence of Sterne's satire and aristocratic humor in *Tristram Shandy,*[27] the influence of Sir Thomas Brown's perceptive "human science" in his *Religio Medici;*[28] the crepuscular philosophy emanating from the apparently gratuitous anecdote of Daniel Defoe;[29] and finally the basic cruelty of Stevenson's life.

Life has only two sources of nourishment, and action was not exactly nourishment for my life. When action does not nourish a man's existence, that existence is nourished by passion in the sense of suffering and sacrifice. And this passion, in turn, can be conscious or blind in the body that endures it. If it is blind, the torment is bearable, the penury becomes almost physical; but when it is conscious, when it is a passion of sensibility, then the person enduring it feels flayed, bloodied, almost dead by virtue of living under such extreme conditions. In my case, the extreme lay in the passion of a soul stirred by a terrible hunger for everlastingness and unity. Could I in some way have my thought endure, have it reach a greater limit than the choices available to a life beseiged by an awareness of its irremediable boundaries, of its physical solitude and of an apparently irredeemable inner emptiness which I had filled with spiritual acts, knowledge, beliefs, experiences? I began to walk through museums, I squeezed into the last seats in lecture halls, I went to listen to public lectures whose titles quickly fanned my desire to take in all that knowledge. Daring and impatient even within my inhibitory timidity, with the ardor which my own appetite inflamed and preserved, I walked around, curious and tense, like one wanting to search for everything, to be affiliated, to clutch something; and I returned to my room full of bitter desire for so many things I failed to find. Taciturnly, I sat down late to eat with my family. This strange, silent, somber boy with a face more sentient than intelligent, with small despairing eyes, with a precocious mutilation of the happiness that should be present in his young eyes, did not surprise that whole family of sentient people, who were also silently human. They saw me eat and listen; no one bothered me; then I went out to think, out into the night, which is always a beloved place to the shy and the lonely, and I walked for long hours.

Only utter weariness brought a sort of order to so much stormy disorder. In that act of slowly retiring for the night and sometimes carrying on like a madman a mumbled inner dialogue with the things I had seen, heard, and felt, I regained a certain hope issuing from as many mouths as my voracious desire had, my desire for no small glories, no small exaltations, no small loves. My part was—and in my interminable sleeplessness my lips also whispered that without saying so—to live in the lake of burning fire, in the lake of the Apocalypse: *pars illorum erit in stagno ardenti igne.*[30] But was that torment going to be eternal in a joyless life; or is it that suddenly, one day or other, through creation, through thinking, writing and feeling again, and then again thinking and again writing, through that dialectic profession of the soul, the torment was going to be redeemed, to be full of light like the streets I liked to find at night in the city on leaving the suburban darkness.

All that was not enough. Alone facing the world and infinite space, this young man who changed everything—ambitions or gluttony—

for an intense moment of human happiness or copious grief, saw a Pascalian[31] fear appear in his reflective horizon. Fear of his own vegetative limitation, of what there was in him tied to the earth, of what there was in him underneath, underlying. Fear of what that impelling force toward the spiritual still left unredeemed in him. When in the war years I would hear the echo of that distant clamor, my agitated spirit also felt that immense pain, that tearing of the flesh in the fields of despoiled earth and ruins. My love was for France and England, but my suffering was universal. One day I enthusiastically joined the great Francophile demonstration that led to the burning of the German Club one late summer afternoon. Count Luxburg had insulted our country and I could no longer hold back my vindictive anger. As an adolescent *sans culotte,*[32] almost spellbound, I walked through the streets beside those determined men who, since there was no news from one of our eminent consuls in Belgium, held up the big-lettered sign with the inscription "Where is Roberto Payró?"[33] Meanwhile, in the vigil of silence and study, I was horrified and transfixed when I leafed through those macabre photographs showing a corpse's rigid fist sticking out of the natural grave among parts of howitzers, or the white face of a soldier half devoured by the rain and the night vultures.

That arm, that face, belonged to bodies that once had a name, a destiny, love affairs, whims, tastes, inclinations, affection, hate and ideas of contrition and of peace. Those feelings, that affection—as Spinoza[34] called it—did they end with such ruins or did they continue to be transformed, beyond death, "into something richer and strange," as is written on John Keats's[35] tomb in Rome? So much pain, so much joy, such instantaneous glory, so much hope, so much daily weariness, so much rest at night, so many desires, so many destinies, so much hardship and so much idleness—does all this wind up in a liberated body insensitive to the rain? Or does it all continue, change, germinate, like the grain that only with death acquires fecundity?

Nothing. Neither the Stevenson nor the Sterne I read clarified this for me, nor my daily conversation with people of frivolous morality. And at the university each morning, instead of finding a teacher, a man whose function is to teach, I found a person or several lawyers whose commitment to teaching was purely budgetary. Empty men, petulant and gray, without any authentic sense of life, some of whom mocked their own course at the Law School of the University of Buenos Aires, preferring to act like a trivial bourgeois witling before his students rather than do something less wretched and more decent. And I remember these men; I don't forget them. I have seen some of them hold positions of authority in our country and raise their cynical perspicacity as profiteers, demagogues and politicians over the head of countless good-willed people and then, terrified with the feeling and afraid to verify it, I sensed that the very country they served might resemble them.

I used to correspond with a friend my age who studied philosophy, an intelligent young man, solitary and ascetic like a mystic, of few words and gestures like one dwelling in mountain retreats. Several times a week we exchanged thick envelopes full of paper covered with small print, with comments on hundreds of books and ingenious and bold definitions about everything beautiful in this world. My only other genuine relationship was with a small group of literary novices—full of ardor and enterprising spirit—who founded a magazine[36] in which, along with a lot of puerile activities, I planted the seed that now begins to germinate. The first meetings, loud and disorderly, were held in that provincial law student's room in a pension, in that humble, gloomy upstairs room on the 25th of May Street, not far from the colorless river and the already archaic arcades of the Paseo Alem, where prostitutes and hustlers walk up and down in the late afternoon. What arguments we five founders had in that room, what passion we shared with one another! We were vehement, sleepless, pressured, under the protection of the name already chosen for the literary ship, whose holds we would load every afternoon with our impatient writings and our edited and measured errors. Yes, everything with us was "counted, weighed, divided." We counted and divided ourselves up into different factions, although we scarcely saw each other: two of us were the rebels, the revolutionaries; two were the literary conservatives and the fifth—always oscillating between two theories harshly defended and boldly acclaimed—struggled not to spoil his decisions as a prudent arbitrator with such and such an exaggerated bias.

At that time almost all of us were law students: the other rebel and myself were very poor students; the others, excellent ones. We two were rebels and poor students because we wanted at all cost to initiate a critical examination of old canons of art and to bring to the fight new criteria, opposition, a new thirst and a new fever, an unsullied fervor. The others, timorous and prudent, feared for the fate of the journal. Thus, the two of us defended living with danger, which is to multiply life; and the others defended living without daring, which is to kill life without glory. We soon had our own small gathering place and others eager to enter the hubbub of ideas joined the original charter members. There was nothing not treated in those hurried pages, a fact or just a notion, incontrovertible or absurd truth, law or fiction, from Croce's ideal system to Oswald Spengler's presciences,[37] from Cocteau's paradox[38] to Logan Pearsall Smith's morganatic triviality,[39] from the theological hierarchy of the angels to the *Travel Diary of a Philosopher*.[40] We were not yet twenty years old and were the first to translate, although rather disorderly as corresponds to our age, Lautréamont's torment,[41] Apollinaire's calligraphic poems,[42] Joyce's labyrinth.[43] And besides, we were ready to enter through the narrow door of Surrealism, shouting, like the guard who sees the express train leave: "To the absolute via freedom of expression! Down with literature, down with composition! To destroy is to create; nothing is erected except by placing the stone on the bare ground!" I became indignant, inflamed, at my prudent companions of that magazine edited by mere boys. I shouted, I said "Enough!"[44] to those who timidly brought to the tiny editorial office the praise of such and such a poet officially enthroned in the pages of our literary history. With what passion, with what candid seriousness, with what exhausting sleeplessness did I live this eternal story of the adolescent rebel!

At the café tables the other rebel and I—do you remember, Louis Saslavsky?—screamed out fanatically against the stupid guardians of tradition and their ceremonious air. There were not enough cruel words to apply to those people who had stayed behind and saw in us with great alarm the ignominious madness of those venturing to live outside the law. My companion was less indignant; he looked at things with suspicion, smiling scornfully, and opportunely released the poison of a bitter and dissembling irony. Soon the editor of the magazine left the smug, elitist majority of writers and joined our spirit of revolt. We then openly steered the prow of the magazine on a course leading to many, many vaguely acclaimed changes. The common notion of necessary biological mutation was brandished in our hands. And finally we savored the victors' pleasure as we saw the long row of people who did not understand and stayed behind, motionless, crystallized.

We well knew that what really made sense was not our stopping to contemplate but our impatience to break all bonds and begin the conquest of a philosophy much more difficult than any contemplative lyricism, the conquest of a territory where thought might grow with uncommon discipline and which one could not seize without injuring one's hands. Asceticism is always involved in youth's rebelliousness. This deep-seated conscious and voluntary penury gladly offered in exchange for a problematical salvation is what is true and pure about that rebelliousness. Unsuspectingly, such was our most violent vocation. For us, "God and his right" meant to think in a disciplined way that became increasingly stripped of formulas and dissembling. We accused the dissemblers of being hypocritical in subscribing to a cause which the perverseness of their very hypocrisy might make dangerous. We laughed at them, but we were furious too.

In the morning my life was spent among the world of books, in the afternoon in the darkness of the movie houses, in the early evening with the endless arguments and nervous commentary on literary works. The nights partook of a certain oneiric wandering and passive retreat in that area of my psyche where my imagination indulges itself, secretly operates and prepares—always tied to the least foreseeable attempts, to the darkest and most secret calculations—the process that leads to the final act of creation. But the daytime was the real field of battle—daytime and afternoons.

Afternoons, winter afternoons, winter afternoons in Buenos Aires. Cold and arid streets, fritted lights on nightfall, deserted northside neighborhoods, old streets near the wharves smelling of fritters and fairs and bric-a-brac, strident sounds of bells announcing cheap shows, large intersections of downtown traffic with the pretentious edges of new marble, almost treeless squares, distant parks with second-rate statues, monotonous voices of countless newspapers, streets with hidden lovers, stiff flower beds, splendid cafés, hotels and restaurants, crowded, tangled avenues. Ah, city, city, vast opulent city, city without beauty, wasteland, valley of gray stone, your three million souls suffer so much deep hunger! In your heart we were like ailing blood, those of us who were less than twenty with an uncontrollable fervor in our souls and minds, those of us who suffered when we saw just causes trampled on, the causes whose objective has an indefatigable, non-spatial beauty, like the whirling flight delirious people imagine around their heads. As a group we were inexperienced, irritable, vindictive; we liked to live a free life, to discuss things, to read avidly; we were proudly jealous, gruff, bristly. After haughtily flaunting all day our projects and opinions and showing our scorn for sleep and food to whoever wanted to see it, we would undo that outright lie after midnight by poking in the family cupboards for some leftovers of cold chicken and then fall asleep with no hatred in our hearts as soon as our exhausted heads hit the pillow. In the daytime we were like district attorneys fulfilling an arbitrary ministry.

How many times have I felt like punishing and humiliating anyone who, at meetings in a café or in the small editorial office, dared raise his voice against a revolutionary principle of aesthetics or against a bold attempt to evade prescribed rules! How many times have I felt full of bitterness and anger against the inoffensive defenders of the "unchangeable laws" of literature! "Imbeciles!"—I furiously reproached them—"Is there a discovery that does not invent its own routes? What you hate is discovery; what you fear is going beyond. Incapable of any daring, you live out of fear and are then sad idolaters of those fears converted into images, sanctified."

My growing metaphysical anguish fused in my soul with fright and execration against impure men, against the falsifiers. I trembled night and day because of that anguish; night and day I grew to hate because of that execration. It seemed to me that the impurity of certain human natures—more than any other systematic social injustice—was always the most deadly poison in the small spheric glass that contains and limits us all. In such impurity lies all injustice, for such an impurity is nothing more than the valuing of cold, self-serving feeling and the consequent rejection of someone in need who knocks on the door or who lives battered by the storm. And this is all there is on this earth: love or the absence of love. But if I knew the sense of that hatred because I also knew its effect, I did not know, on the other hand, the path of the other, of that terrible anguish that awaited me behind each joy, that stopped me on any road to ask me: "If you don't know what you are, how can you know what you are seeking, how can you know where you are going? Does the soul belonging to that fallen soldier's stiff hand know more than I where he was going, what his destiny was beyond the voracious dampness of that earth on which his body was rotting away?"

Suddenly, the tragic sense of man's destiny had intruded into my sleepless nights and my days filled with thinking, aimless walking, and meditating. During such a crisis, how astonishing it was to see a world for whom the idea of its own destiny reveals an opaque an animal-like irresponsibility. How difficult it was to comprehend that betrayal of man's intelligence in the light of his capacity for reasoning! Because all these men around me reasoned—but from what well-spring? From their conscience, from their soul? No, but rather from a certain vegetative focus endowed with instinct, with just the will of preservation.

Since my religious channels of communication were not open—in the midst of personal terrain that was too terrestrial and almost lacustrine—the only thing that metaphysical fever aroused in me was the tragic terror of death. It was then that I began to sense the feeling of the heroic in man. Still ignorant of the moral essence of the saint, even more so of the ascetic or the priest, and also cold to military ambition, I knew that what my instinct began to seek was the heroic in thought; the seed of the glorious sacrifice from which is created a special kind—certainly not serene—of work of art, a special kind of poetry. If I could never learn the ultimate fate of the soul of the soldier killed in battle, at least I wanted to know his destiny as an ordinary man, which is the supreme thing possible in a life that fatally ends in an eternal and nameless rigidity. And inasmuch as before death the most transcendental thing about man is his intellect—since virtue too is basic intellect, for it "understands" in the divine sense of the word—it was the story of that intellect that excited my voracious and cruel appetite.

On presenting the intellectual story of those years, I do not wish to narrate the story of a few books but rather the story of my passions as I read and studied those works. It is the story of the living development of a passion. The passion, first of all, of William Blake,[45] in whose prophetic books and terrifying proverbs of hell, taken from Swedenborg,[46] one cruelly learns how energy—the energy of creation and the energy of faith—is eternal delight and that a thought fills the immensity (and here Blake and Pascal converge). "Joy impregnates, pain carries forward," affirm those books which reveal the ecstasy of a visionary Christian who is not a prisoner of theological systematization. I approached Blake as I would a man in whose family I felt comfortable—and what terrible comfort!—because of his way of considering "well thought out consciousness" as the beginning and the end of all things. Then, the passion of Rimbaud,[47] whom I saw drowned in savage and sublime rapture, wandering, as Valentine Hugo[48] paints him, through the streets of Charleroi, inveighing against established lies, bourgeois conformity, man's moral fraud. What drew me ardently to him was his aspiration to fuse with the infinite by means of an intrepid act of his spirit, unafraid that that intrepidness might mean his own disappearance from all lands visible to the rest of humanity, his escape towards unfathomable worlds in which he never stopped getting lost.

Next, the passion of Kierkegaard, the shepherd's son, the anguished one, the one sentenced to an eternal pang of conscience, the one who had shouted: "My whole life has been a struggle against myself. I don't want to have disciples." Indeed, it was a struggle against himself that acquired the same tragic character, the same desolation as in Nietzsche.[49] Kierkegaard,[50] haunted by the idea of martyrdom, was scandalized by the fact that the visible Church hardly comprehends the true sense of religion and turns it into a system of knowledge, instead of deeply feeling that to be Christian means not only theological knowledge but, even more so, incomparable misery, pain, drama, penury and humiliation. Kierkegaard had such a deeply courageous conscience that he raised his voice in the emptiness of his painful existence to proclaim that being Christian is equivalent to becoming Christ's contemporary. And it was this—for which no one could pardon him, just as he knew that no one would be pardoned for it—that drove him vehemently toward his spiritual abode, buffeted, whipped by constant cold and terrible winds, by the tremendous intemperateness of a soul that had dared to say: "I am like a Lüneburger pig.[51] My thinking is a passion."

And before Kierkegaard's passion, I had suffered Nietzsche's passion, but not in his fits of exacerbated theorization, not in the theory of the eternal return nor in Zarathustra's moral system—for this seemed to me the most German of the ideas in that intellect which paradoxically disparaged the Germans—but rather in the aphorisms arising from the heights of his own horrible personal suffering. I felt I was next to him when he shouted out his heart-rending despair in that sad final document which is the *Ecce homo*,[52] when the man who terrifyingly brandished his fist in a menacing and merciless gesture could not hide the signs of emaciation on his face and the red road of tears, the tragic appearance of despair and human vulnerability, when he said: "Philosophy, such as I have lived it, such as I have understood it until now, is a voluntary existence in the midst of ice and high mountains, the search for all that is strange and problematic in life, for all that which until now has been banished by the moral code . . . You had not even searched yourselves; if you did you would have found me. That is what all believers do; therefore faith is worth so little. . . . Now I order you to lose me and find yourselves. . . . And I shall return among you only when you have all denied me." And after having proudly shouted, "My life is a perpetual victory over myself," he lowered his voice to say, without being heard: "I knew that no human word could ever reach me." No longer is he the victor of former years, but the creature abandoned in existence, numbed, grieved, tremendously lucid and bloodied without blood, the spiritual *Ecce Homo*.

Then the passion of Novalis;[53] then the passion of Hölderlin.[54] The dreadfully serene hymns to the night and the spiritual songs where the agonic struggle between life and thought is played out, where the three central points of Novalis's inspiration (love, poetry, and death), are stirred—what were they so anxiously seeking if not the act of "creating within themselves"? The nocturnal recollection prior to life is born again with each man; divinity eternally attracts while human beings draw apart; the finite struggles against the infinite and hope against despair. Novalis says that "thought is compassion." Unamuno would be quick to define: "Compassion, shared passion." And we are again in our familiar environment, that is, feeling thought as a passion of the conscience.

But that was not sufficient. No, it was not sufficient. In order to attain knowledge of the soul's supreme tragedy, I had to take my eager vision to the scene of the deepest tragedy capable of being produced in a human conscience, that of having destroyed oneself, lying prostrate and burning like coals, for it is no longer wood but rather something mysterious and different. And in this way I felt the cold fright of Hölderlin's poetry. The delicious thread of my journey through moral countries, the diametrically opposite end of which was tied to a Platonic reading, had reached that terrible jungle of destruction, fire and pain.

But those books were not the ones which had shaped my anguish, but my own immanent anguish that had sought that proximity and kinship in misfortune, without which no spirit feels its transcendence.

That kinship in misfortune! What poetic thought does not breathe a bit of tragic air?

*   *   *

Deep concern and uneasiness of mind were constantly with me. For a long time they were my companions, like somber moral dogs stretched out in the nocturnal desert. As I took my daily walks through the city, I did not need to ask myself tragic questions. I myself was those questions and I carried them warm and burning within me, like my blood. What are you in me—humanity? What are you in me—country? What are you in me—nation? What are you in me—ambition, venture, drama, laughter, and future? And when I returned alone toward nightfall through the streets that form the furthermost labyrinth in the north of the city, I saw myself a sluggish inhabitant of that "strange idleness," of that "strange pride" to which that poet of

knowledge alludes: "Après tant d'orgueil, après tant d'étrange oisi-
veté."[55] No text or required study could attract my attention, for
there was no humanity or passion in either. What did I care about a
chemical formula, a geological concept, scholarly facts, a bit of trigo-
nometry, when what was right before me, right before my eyes, not
letting me sleep with its continuous changes and unexpected ways,
was man's disquieting jungle, his very nature, the gulf of his daily
renewed misfortunes, the river of his melancholy song, the mountain
of his raptures, the valley of his morning optimism, his accidents, his
fauna, his roads, his abysses. A lively passage in fiction, an agonist's
shout, taught me more than all those monotonous and uninspired pro-
fessors. And that should not be. What were those men, those teachers
lacking? I could not find out then and only later would a great American point it out to me. The defect these men suffered from was quite
simple: it was the uninspired, lifeless way they lived, learned and
taught. What I had called mortal monotony or insufficiency, what I
found terribly lethal in these pedagogues, was precisely their absence
of life.

Seeing them, I could not tolerate my own ignorance. Listening to
them, I could not tolerate my own inexpressiveness. Observing them,
I could not tolerate the gratuitous and already unproductive quality of
my life. Just like the man who gets set to leap into space, I needed to
go back, to take stock. And this is what no one wanted to do: to go
back and take stock. What they wanted, what really mattered to them
was to move forward visibly, although that advance was a deception
for them as well as for the others. I was alone with my need.

To take stock, to go back, meant to gain a solid footing into greater
knowledge, into basic questions, into the fundamental traditions of
the spirit, and into a clearer awareness of myself as a man and of my
world as an entity that resists and fights, both with and against what
there is to fight. To go back and take stock also means to become
strong in order to face certain adversities, to expose my spirit to all
kinds of climates, to force it to know, to struggle and to resist.

In a few short years, my constant exposure to that literature, filled
with ideal heroes, anguished and sacrificed souls, enraged defamers,
rebels and visionaries, pure souls in a state of divine wrath, had given
me the best that a living "being" could give another, that is, the artic-

ulated lesson of its suffering, suffering that is vanquished and "understood" and turned into that virtue which overpowers it and which we call language. Can there be a better lesson than one coming from a person who teaches us the way he has overcome a passion or suffering, the way he has overcome stupid, cruel, blind natural despotism? Besides, the literature of those tormented souls had given me something else: a vocation involving a still higher intelligence, the desire to ascend one step more, a sudden vocation for religious thought, and the verification, the sudden sense of the purposeful harmony which surely links all created things.

And it was through Saint Augustine[56] that I reached these fervent thinkers. Was there a voice that held more attraction for my self-disputation, for that disputation that had no solution on this earth? Later on, I could understand only the saintliness of one who reaches that state starting from the most horrible existence, of the one who sinks his defective boat and saves himself—but afterward!—with no small risk and sacrifice, like that ex-lover, ex-gambler, ex-Manichaean,[57] that African who before hearing Saint Ambrosio's[58] salutary lesson practiced his theodicy, his natural theology, maintaining that "all things that are corrupted are good, since they could not be corrupted in the first place if they did not have some goodness. Nor could they be corrupted if their goodness were unassailable, for if they were exceedingly good, they would be uncorruptible, while if they did not have at least some goodnesss, there would be nothing in them which might be corrupted."

I dwelled on the *Confessions* for a long time. It was an abode of comfort, but even more than of comfort, of joy. In those books, behind each bush there were food and clear water. In spirit, could I not call my own that Platonic experience after which Saint Augustine, still looking for the incorporeal truth and invisible perfections, found that he himself was full of intolerable complacency? And could I not call my own, too, the feeling that except for a religious principle, "one should lament all the less the other things in this life the more one is wont to lament not having them; on the other hand, one should lament them all the more, the less one is wont to enjoy them?"

At that time I was both happy and unhappy, with my inner self fertile, predisposed to faith, but absent faith. At once a happy state and a great sorrow and disquietude. Loving God without having Him; having a presentiment of Him without feeling Him.

I rushed headlong into reading other mystics, other creative writers burning with the same fire we see in El Greco's *Resurrections.*[59]

Then came the modern writers, Coventry Patmore,[60] Claudel,[61] and Eliot,[62] but not before Santa Teresa[63] and San Juan de la Cruz,[64] not before his *Song.* With these latter authors, I found myself at the very root of Spain without realizing it. With my sleepless body, my eyes enraptured, my whole intelligence captivated, I was touching that tormented nerve and repeating:

Reveal thyself, I cry
Yea, though the beauty of thy presence kill,
For sick with love am I,
And naught can cure my ill
Save only if of thee I have my fill.

O crystal spring so fair,
Might now within thy silvery depths appear,
E'en as I linger there,
Those features ever dear
Which on my soul I carry graven clear![65]

Since I felt myself at the very roots of Spain, I felt I was also at the roots of my land, near my own roots. Neither with Cervantes,[66] nor with Calderón,[67] Lope,[68] or Mateo Alemán[69] had I ever had such a feeling of affinity with my own being and my land. The tree loves its roots when it feels water has reached them; and that love is mixed with its need for growth and fullness. Slowly, within myself, within my walking and living tree, that longing for fullness, that is for culture, took the direction of philosophic theory. But all too often so much dialectical reason turned out to be much too obvious. "Much ado about nothing."[70] Or better, "nothing ado about too much." Too much for too much. Sometimes too much abundance for very little; other times too little for so much; in general much around nothing. Reasonable reason always spoiled by a theoretical and meditative reason. How poorly my reasoning performed in abstract discourse! How I wanted to touch the essence or the substance of things, the living source, without argumentative intercession, without *ergos*![71] In philosophical theorizing—ah, Germanic Kant[72] and Hegel,[73] that old pantheist of Stuttgart!—for me everything stemmed from this obvious reversibility: I think, therefore I exist; I exist, therefore I think. I think in order to exist; I exist in order to think. I think; therefore I have thought. I have thought; therefore I shall think. I shall think; therefore I shall stop thinking. I shall stop thinking; therefore I shall stop existing. So much thereforeing![74]

Of what use is a syllogism except when it is capable of being in contradiction with itself? Syllogism's human virtue that puts it to the test and without which it does not exist because it contains no drama. And what does not contain drama is artificial. How worthy of commiseration is one who believes that a blade of grass knows no drama! And man does not bring the drama to it; the grass already has that drama, in the heart of its perishable being, which does not engender life without dying. Grass already has drama within, in its vegetal destiny.

The frequent reading of systematic philosophy separates me for some moments from the world of the objective, the dramatic and the material, for no other reason than my spirit's lack of aptitude to reduce it to pure essence, to change existence for essence. Deaf to what might be expressed merely in terms of essence, responsive only to what might be expressed in terms of existence, I felt that my deepest commitment was with those men whose preoccupation comes from a state of life, from a conflict or living responsibility and not from a logical discriminitive or argumental state.

After I voraciously filled my head with the most varied books, with the most daring concepts and the most subtle, abstract and apparently harmonic theories, the process of philosophical theory seemed more and more the game of a constant dialectical rectification. For each Hume[75] who made the nature of knowledge lie in the perception of the senses, there always was a Descartes who made it reside in reason. And for the idea that things should be adapted to the mind there was always an Immanuel Kant who said that neither the senses alone nor reason alone could provide knowledge, but both at the same time, since it is things that adapt themselves to the mind. Hume's intelligence is as exact, precise and universal as Descartes's and Descartes's intelligence is as exact, precise and universal as Kant's. However, the three theories are at variance with one another. All this coming and going to the same reservoir, so much improbable and rational dialectics, which was defended cyclically in times past by men of equal ardor and sincerity, appeared to me quite ingenuous in its desire to elevate man, that "thinking reed"[76] to be the arbiter of phenomena and essences, when time after time everything escapes his vulnerable reason. For me, modern philosophy—on turning away from the fundamental questions—continued to be the love for rational speculation, and this love interested me less and less as it stifled me with its incessant rectifications of erudite thought. This deception drew me closer and closer to art, which without ever belying itself, is never equal to itself and is reborn in new, differentiated forms that do not contradict each other when revealing man's contradictions. And I approached this fundamental theology because it is all inherent poetry.

Passionately, I returned to the tormented ones, *to my* tormented ones, to my Kierkegaard, to my Saint Augustine, to my Pascal. To those men who did not forget their state of desolation and their commitments to the eternal. To those men of heaven and hell, of plains and mountains, confronted with the forces rising up now and for all eternity, confronted with man's conflicts and with the conflicts of the infinite. I returned to those men who do not play with principles but with their existences, letting them be numbed or triumphant, fallen or freed, according to what they have risked in real combat and the way they have fought.

In the emptiness of the crowded Buenos Aires, in the big city, in the black-asphalted streets, straight, all alike, endless in the stone steppe, hungry for truths like a young wolf unable to find his prey in the middle of an inhabited area, it was the sense of man's disproportion that tied me most dreadfully to Pascal's dialogue, it was that incessant feeling of being next to the abyss about which Léon Chestov[77] wrote with such anguished intensity in his beautiful "Night of Gethsémani." Afterward, I wanted to bring to the novel that incomparable terror for which there is no redeeming light other than the one we turn on in our own affliction as wandering and loving men, eager to wander and to love, lonely passers-by in the city, beside the gardens, the grass, the granite walls, the bridges, the steel, the ambition, the elevators, the factories, the highways, under the sun, the storm, the clouds. The terrible fear of the abyss. Man's disproportion . . .

Then I grew angry with that thought. It is not enough for me to see it written on his face. I want to see what is behind, to take it apart, to plumb its depths. I want to know how much of it is mine and how much I belong to it, how much it has to do with my nature and with the nature in which that nature is planted. "Because, after all, what is man without nature? A nothing in relation to the infinite, an everything in relation to nothingness, a median between nothing and everything." And then: "Our intelligence has, in the order of intelligent things, the same rank as our body in the expanse of nature." Man needs to keep that center, since all extremes are harmful to him, whether it be of temperature, of wisdom, of virtue, or culture. Extremes either escape from us or we escape from them. Nothing stops for us and we are always floating between an extreme of appearance and an extreme of certainty. And, nevertheless, we tend to know the everything, "we border on everything." It is impossible to know things because things are simple and we are complex in body and soul. And if we are spirit and matter, that is, a compound, how are we to know the spiritual alone or matter alone? And here I found Pascal akin to Saint Augustine when the Jansenist painfully affirmed that man can not know what a spirit is, even less, the form in which a body can be united with a spirit. He can not conceive that when he is that!

And there I was in my city, anguished, aimless, not in contact with anything except those terrible "means" to which Argentines attach so much importance. Always the means. And I found that this abomination for the contemporary Argentine's way of living was also confirmed in Pascalian thought: "It is deplorable to find men thinking only about the means and not the ends." We could add this naked truth: that there is nothing more pitiful than observing those who continue "their parents' way of life" because they have been forewarned it is the best; thus, because he is so admonished, the infidel continues to be an infidel, the locksmith continues to be a locksmith, the soldier, a soldier.

The means! In other words the lack of vision of the whole, that is, of the principle, the lack of vision of living harmoniously and fully. The mistake in believing that there can be an individual, isolated good, in believing that there can be another kind of good that is not a symphonic good, in believing that if we do not prosper by making things prosper all around us, our prosperity may have been more than just appearance and deception. The mistake in believing that there can be life by "representation," by appearance, a life put on for show, that is, a life that is "represented" instead of a life that is lived.

How can we be content carrying within ourselves means and not ends? Means of "getting" things instead of means of "being" them. Harboring such thoughts at that time, I felt I was rebelling harshly against myself. But this metaphysical disquiet never made me want to escape from life.

How can we thwart the thirst for life and experience with the wall of dogma and the reticence of extraterrestrial prohibitions? What long days of yearning! The streets attracted me with their bustling joy as did the misery of the pleasure the joy leaves and the taciturn aftertaste. I went into restaurants. I sat down to hear rather mediocre symphonies in the back of cafés, when it was cloudy and rainy. I approached the people, my compatriots, and saw on their dark countenances the possible presence of a non-social, internal cause that moved them. I saw it also on the foreheads of the ambitious, on the chins of the daring and the impetuous, on those faces full of youthful pretension, where the triumphant future could be read in the shine of their eyes or in the self-assurance of their talk. I went out to the country, to the outskirts of the city and saw the people who have friendship with the sun. In these people—and they were different from the others—at least life came up to the surface fully and honestly in each person and did not hide behind a facade of gesticulating or "representing."

All this means that there was a visible Argentine and another invisible Argentine, silent, obstinate, emotional and hard working in the vast depths of the country, in the rural areas, in the provinces, the towns, the jungles, the territories. And even in the city, but in the inner soul of the city, not on its surface.

But the visible Argentine had primacy, held sway.

What was that visible Argentine seeking? The exaltation of the person, of that amalgam of emotion, intelligence and will. But it was not an exaltation of the authentic values of the person, but an exaltation of fictitious values. It was an exaltation of individualness, that is, of a convenient formula of vegetative and deceitful existence.

I clung more and more to a tragic concept of consciousness. I detested that kind of collective conformity that was no more than a lack of true happiness and the substitution for that happiness of a visceral and triumphant facility for just being installed in the nation, for being installed in life. Such a thing disgusted me.

I needed to search for my Argentina, my Argentina in her true life, in her drama, in her conflict, and not in the external prosperity of the cities, in the daily jumble and in the general confusion of all her happy improvisations. I needed to set out and find my Argentina. But where to begin? In what direction to take my first step? Since nothing can ascend without rising from the land, what I required above all was to implant myself in Argentina differently from the others, not be be lying on Argentina in an adventitious way but rather to submerge myself in her, to penetrate under her surface, to get up only after having lived through the subterranean experience of the rhizome, which rises up almost incorporeally from a rich claustral body.

My wandering was tormented like that of an adventurer behind prison bars. The prison was that struggle to take possession of the country instinctively without seeing it, without touching it, without living it with my own body in its own different latitudes. What essential elements of my country could I capture in the city? Time went by for me in a constant flux between desire and anguish, in a perpetual oscillation between those two violently contradictory tones that my encounter with life assumed. At that time, what drew me away from Christianity, as it did Jacques Rivière,[78] was not so much a feeling of the reality of nothingness as the value it conferred on my despair. Intellectual and passional yearning did not take its ember away from me and in this ember I found dilatory reasons for delight. What slowness of movement on the outside and what vehemence, what passion from within! I spent days drowned in emotions watching the starry heavens and graceful constellations of my hemisphere, as if in that Orion's dagger,[79] in that Centaurus,[80] in that Southern Cross,[81] there were implicit lessons for the faithful observer. I spent days hearing the secret voice of the country's interior, the story of such and such a harvest, a plague, a town that just emerged, woods that have been exploited, cattle successfully bred, a settler who became rich, a colonizer with fortune on his side, a town that multiplied, a region made productive, an Andean river, vineyards, wheatfields, northern sugar cane fields, productive forests, men, women, children struggling against the elements and the indomitable land. My fervent desire was to be face to face with those kinds of people tempered in such an environment. Why wasn't it easy? Why didn't these people appear? Why is it that what appeared on the surface of the country was something else, other kinds of men, other natures, less strong, less authentic, incredibly false.

Nothing I wanted to find appeared. All the workers in my country's powerful living poem were hidden, submerged. That incalculable human wealth was a hidden treasure, sunk many meters below the observable surface of the nation.

I understood then how those two worlds were separated in Argentina, the visible and the invisible world. Like the rhabdomancer[82] who walks in the darkness guided by the forked staff, I walked behind the latter world, excited and with high hopes. But the other, visible world hid this invisible world from me under its surface. And then I became infuriated at that intentional disappearance, at that disappearance brought on by the interaction of human beings, by a culpable conspiracy.

Notes

1. Buenos Aires is one of the largest cities in the world, with a metropolitan population of around 9,000,000. There are large groups of Argentines of Italian, Jewish, German, and English origin. Buenos Aires is the political, financial, economic, and cultural center of Argentina and dominates the nation to an extent that few other capital cities of the world do. To the magnificent harbor of Buenos Aires flows the wealth of the rest of the country, gathered from the rich pampas, from Mendoza, from Cordoba, from Patagonia. This dominance has caused no small resentment on the part of the provinces, which feel relegated to an unwarranted subservient position in all of the nation's affairs.

2. Babylon. The ancient capital of the Chaldean empire, famous for its great wealth and luxury.

3. The rough equivalent of our high school is the *Bachillerato*. It is a six-year program beginning at the age of twelve. After the *Bachillerato*, students may enter the *Universidad*, which corresponds to our college or university.

4. Victor Hugo (1802–1885). One of the foremost figures of the Romantic movement in French literature. As a poet, dramatist, and novelist, he exerted great influence and was widely acclaimed by the critics and the public alike. Among his most famous works are *Hernani* (1830), *The Hunchback of Notre Dame* (1831), *Ruy Blas* (1838), *The Legend of the Centuries* (1859–1883), and *Les Miserables* (1862).

5. Leo Tolstoy (1828–1910). Russian novelist of great psychological insight. His *War and Peace* (1865–1872), *Anna Karenina* (1875–1876), and *The Death of Ivan Ilyich* (1884) have all become classics.

6. Maurice Maeterlinck (1862–1949). Belgian poet, dramatist, and essayist. Among his most famous works, written in French, are *Monna Vanna* (1902) and *The Blue Bird* (1909). Much of his work is fanciful and symbolistic. He was awarded the Nobel Prize in 1911.

7. Billy "Bombardier" Wells (1887–1967). Famous English boxer who won the All-India heavy title in 1909 and the British heavy title in 1911.

8. George Carpentier (1894–1975). French light heavyweight fighter who was world champion in 1920.

9. These are among the principal streets of the commercial downtown area of Buenos Aires.

10. Croesus. King of Lydia (560–546 B.C.). His name has become synonymous with great wealth.

11. Boeotian. The adjective is derived from Boeotia, a district of ancient Greece, whose people the Athenians considered coarse and dull.

12. *Sketches by Boz* (1836). A collection of stories by Charles Dickens.

13. Alessandro Manzoni (1785–1873). Italian novelist, poet, and dramatist. His most famous work is the romantic novel *The Betrothed* (1825).

14. Gabriela Mistral (1889–1957). Outstanding Chilean poet of the post-modernist period. In 1945 she became the first Nobel laureate from Hispanic America. Her most acclaimed works include *"The Sonnets of Death"* (1914), *Desolation* (1922), and *Tala* (1938).

15. René de Chateaubriand (1768–1848). Seminal figure in the development of French Romanticism. *Atalá* (1801), *René* (1802), and *Les Natches* (1826) are novels set in North America. The *Genius of Christianity* (1802) is an impassioned defense of his faith.

16. Alfred de Vigny (1797–1863). French romantic poet, playwright, and novelist. Melancholy and loneliness characterize his verses in such works as *Old and Modern Poems* (1826) and *The Destinies* (1864). *Chatterton* (1835) is his best play. *Cinq Mars* (1826) is an important historical novel.

17. William Makepeace Thackeray (1811–1863). English novelist who depicted upper and middle class English society. He is the author of *Vanity Fair* (1847) and *Henry Esmond* (1852).

18. George Meredith (1828–1909). English psychological and social novelist. His most distinguished works are *The Ordeal of Richard Feverel* (1859) and *The Egoist* (1879).

19. Thomas Hardy (1840–1928). English realistic novelist whose works represent a reaction against Victorian modes. His best works include *Far from the Madding Crowd* (1874), *The Return of the Native* (1878), *The Mayor of Casterbridge* (1886), *Tess of the D'Urbervilles* (1891), and *Jude The Obscure* (1896).

20. Guy de Maupassant (1850–1893). Popular French fiction writer. His sharply realistic stories frequently have a surprise ending, i.e., "The Necklace," "A Life," and "Bel-Ami."

21. Ivan Turgenev (1818–1883). Russian poet and novelist of the realist school. Among his most important works are *Fathers and Sons* (1862) and *Virgin Soil* (1876).

22. Johann Wolfgang von Goethe (1749–1832). German poet and dramatist. His masterpieces are *The Sorrows of Young Werther* (1774) and *Faust* (1790–1833). Goethe's contribution to Romanticism went far beyond German literature.

23. Honoré de Balzac (1799–1850). The great French novelist whose detailed portraits of early nineteenth-century manners and customs are revealed in a long series of works which he called *The Human Comedy*. Among the most widely read novels in this series are *Eugénie Grandet* (1833) and *Le Père Goriot* (1835).

24. Stendhal. Pseudonym of Henri Beyle (1783–1842). Author of *The Red and the Black* (1830), one of the outstanding novels in French literature.

25. Gabriele D'Annunzio (1863–1938). Italian author whose works include the novels *The Intruder* (1898) and *The Victim* (1914), and the plays *The Dreams of an Autumn Sunset* (1897) and *The Dead City* (1902).

26. Aeschylus (524–456 B.C.). Greek tragic dramatist and lyric poet. Works: *The Suppliants* (492 B.C.), *The Persians* (472 B.C.), *The Seven Against Thebes* (467 B.C.), *Prometheus Bound* (465 B.C.), *Oresteia* (458 B.C.).

27. Laurence Sterne (1713–1768). English novelist, author of the nine-volume *Tristram Shandy* (1759–1767), a humorous, witty, satirical account of a boy's early years. Sterne also wrote *A Sentimental Journey Through France and Italy* (1768).

28. Sir Thomas Browne (1605–1682). English physician and writer of the Renaissance period. Besides his famous work *Religio Medici* (A Physician's Religion, 1643), he is also the author of *Vulgar Errors* (1643), and *Urn Burial* (1658).

29. Daniel Defoe (1660–1731). English novelist, author of *Robinson Crusoe* (1719), *Moll Flanders* (1722), and *Journal of the Plague Year* (1722).

30. Revelation 20:10 reads: "And the devil that deceived them was cast into the lake of fire and brimstone, where the beast and the false prophet are, and shall be tormented day and night for ever and ever."

31. Blaise Pascal (1623–1662). French theologian, author, mathematician, and scientist. He vigorously defended the religious reform movement known as Jansenism in his book *Provincial Letters* (1656). In his most famous work, *Thoughts on Religion and Evidence of Christianity* (1670), Pascal writes of the ineffectualness of reason to offer solutions to man's conflicts and problems; instead he calls on faith and mystic revelation.

32. Sans-culotte. The French word means "without breeches." The reference is to those workers during the French Revolution who wore long trousers, while the nobles wore knee-length breeches. The term today is used symbolically to refer to a person who rebels against established social norms or practices.

33. Roberto Payró (1867–1928). Argentine novelist, short story writer, and dramatist. His best work is the neo-picaresque novel *The Marriage of Laucha* (1900). Other works of fiction include *Pago chico* (1908) and *Amusing Adventures of Juan Moreira's Grandson* (1910). Payró's most famous play is *Over the Ruins* (1904), which portrays traditional gaucho life in conflict with the values of the newer, more progressive generation.

34. Baruch Spinoza (1632–1677). Dutch Jewish philosopher, whose pantheistic view of the universe alienated him from both orthodox Jews and Christians. For Spinoza, God can not exist as a separate spirit, but is the universe in its totality. Mankind and all things are a part of God. Works: *Tractatus Theologico-Politicus* (1670); *Ethics* (1677).

35. John Keats (1795–1821). One of the great English poets of the Romantic school. "Endymion," "The Eve of St. Agnes," "La Belle Dame Sans Merci," "Ode to a Nightingale," and "Ode on a Grecian Urn" are among Keats's most enduring poems.

36. Reference to the *Revista de América* which Mallea helped to found in 1923.

37. Oswald Spengler. (1880–1936). German philosopher. In his famous *Decline of the West* (1918–1922), he states his view of the cyclical nature of history and suggests that Western civilization, having passed its high point, is now descending.

38. Jean Cocteau (1889–1963). French novelist, playwright, and poet. Among his best works are *The Terrible Children* (1929), *The Infernal Machine* (1934), and *The Terrible Parents* (1938). Cocteau was also a film maker: *The Blood of a Poet* (1933), *Beauty and the Beast* (1946), *Orphée* (1949). In all the genres Cocteau cultivated, he was constantly experimenting with form, technique, and expression.

39. Logan Pearsall Smith (1865–1946). British-American essayist and critic, best known for *All Trivia* (1933), *On Reading Shakespeare* (1933), and *Milton and His Modern Critics* (1940).

40. *The Travel Diary of a Philosopher* was written by Hermann Keyserling in 1925.

41. Le Comte de Lautréamont (1846–1870). French poet born in Uruguay. Despair is a recurring mood in his poetry, as is seen in *Les Chants de Maldoror* (1868–1870).

42. Guillaume Apollinaire (1880–1918). Avant-garde French poet and critic. Works: *Calligrames* (1918), *The Poet Assassinated* (1923).

43. James Joyce (1882–1941). Irish novelist whose *Ulysses* (1922) is one of the most influential works in twentieth century literature. *Ulysses* is the prototype of the stream of consciousness novel, with its interior monologue and deep introspection. Joyce's other masterpieces are *A Portrait of the Artist as a Young Man* (1916) and *Finnegans Wake* (1939).

44. In Mallea's novel *The Bay of Silence,* the literary journal founded by Martín Tregua and his companions is called *Basta,* which in Spanish means "Enough."

45. William Blake (1757–1827). English poet and engraver. His poems are collected in *Songs of Innocence* (1787), *Songs of Experience* (1794), *The Marriage of Heaven and Hell* (1790), and in the series called *The Prophetic Books,* comprising such volumes as *The Book of Thel* (1789), *America* (1793), *The Book of Urizen* (1794), and *Milton* (1804). Blake's poetry frequently reveals a haunting symbolism and strange mysticism.

Blake is the first of several authors for whom Mallea feels a strong spiritual affinity because of the emotional travail they suffer in writing of their experiences and expressing their innermost thoughts. This suffering is the passion Mallea is referring to in the phrases "the passion of Blake," "the passion of Novalis," "the passion of Hölderlin," and "the passion of Kierkegaard." The deeper meaning is that as Blake and the others suffer, Mallea feels that suffering deeply, is affected by it, identifies with it, and transfers it to his own state of mind.

46. Emanuel Swedenborg (1688–1772). Swedish philosopher and scientist whose writings reveal a mystical, spiritualistic union with God. Among his works are *Heaven and Hell* (1758) and *Divine Love and Wisdom* (1763). His most ardent followers formed a society called the Church of the New Jerusalem.

47. Arthur Rimbaud (1854–1891). French symbolist poet whose works reveal an almost hallucinatory vision of reality. In "A Season in Hell" (1873), an autobiographical poem in prose, Rimbaud reveals his tortured spirit and soul. One of his best poems is called "The Drunken Boat" (1873). An unstable and restless person, Rimbaud spent many years of aimless wandering in France, Belgium, and England.

48. Valentine Hugo (1890–1968). Highly imaginative French painter and illustrator.

49. Friedrich Wilhelm Nietzsche (1844–1900). German philosopher, author of *The Birth of Tragedy* (1872), *Thus Spake Zarathustra* (1883–1884), and *Beyond God and Evil* (1886). He rejected the moral tenets of Christianity and based his negative philosophy on a belief in the weakness of the masses and the superiority of select groups of men. Nietzsche advocated the education of a race of "supermen." Disturbed and tormented from his early youth, he went completely mad at the age of forty-five.

50. Sören Kierkegaard (1813–1855). Danish philosopher and theologian, considered to be a precursor of existentialism. For Kierkegaard, knowledge of God can not be attained through reason, but through faith. Among his books that had a tremendous impact on European and American thought are *Either-Or* (1843), *The Concept of Dread* (1844) and *On Christian Training* (1850). In Latin America, Kierkegaard's religiously oriented philosophy was in consonance with the anti-materialistic, anti-utilitarian thinking of many intellectuals.

51. Lüneberger pig. In his book, *Either/Or,* Kierkegaard writes: "I am like a Lüneberger pig. My thinking is a passion. I can root up truffles excellently for other people, even if I get no pleasure out of them myself. I dig the problems out with my nose, but the only thing I can do with them is to throw them back over my head." From *Either/Or: A Fragment of Life.* Vol. I. Translated by David F. Swenson and Lillian Marvin Swenson. (Princeton: Princeton University Press, 1944), p. 28.

52. "Ecce Homo." Title of an essay by Nietzsche in which he refers to himself as the Antichrist.

53. Novalis. Pen name of Friedrich Von Hardenberg (1772–1801). German poet and novelist of the Romantic school. *Hymns to the Night* (1800), a series of prose poems, show Novalis' strong religious and mystical feelings. Few writers have expressed a more agonizing preoccupation with the theme of death.

54. Johann Christian Friedrich Hölderlin (1770–1843). German poet. His verses, although beautiful and sensitive, are often lacking in real warmth and seem to be out of touch with reality. Hölderlin possessed a great passion for ancient Greek culture and held a "pantheistic view of nature." Besides his lyric poems, he also wrote *Hyperion* (1797–1799), a novel in the form of letters. He became completely deranged in 1806.

55. Translation from the French is "After so much pride, after so much strange idleness."

56. Saint Augustine (345–430). One of the four great Fathers of the Church. His mother was a Christian and his father a pagan. He led a dissolute, hedonistic life before converting to Christianity in 386 through the influence of Bishop Ambrose's sermons. Of his numerous writings *The Confessions* (397) is St. Augustine's most important and influential.

57. Manichaen. Believer in the doctrine of Manichaenism, according to which two opposing forces—light and goodness; darkness and chaos or evil—rule the universe.

58. Saint Ambrose (339–397). One of the Fathers of the Roman Catholic Church. He became the bishop of Milan in 371. Important writings: *On the Christian Faith* and *On the Duties of the Clergy.*

59. El Greco. His real name was Domenikos Theotokopoulos (1541–1614). Spanish painter. Born in Crete, El Greco resided in Toledo, Spain, from 1575 until his death. Famous paintings: *The Adoration of the Shepherds, View of Toledo, The Stripping of Christ Before the Crucifixion, The Burial of Count Orgaz, The Resurrection.*

60. Coventry K. D. Patmore (1823–1896). English poet who frequently treats religious and mystical themes. Works: *The Victories of Love* (1862), *The Unknown Eros* (1877), *Religio Poetae* (1893).

61. Paul Claudel (1868–1955). French Catholic poet who frequently wrote on mystical subjects, as in "Corona Benignitatis Anni Dei" (1914), "La Messe là-bas" (1919). Perhaps his best collection of verse is found in *Five Great Odes* (1910). Claudel was also a distinguished playwright, one of his masterpieces being *Tidings Brought to Mary* (1912).

62. T. S. Eliot (1888–1965). American English poet, whose themes touch man's deepest feelings as he expresses his own despair and frustration over twentieth-century materialism, utilitarian values, and cultural sterility. His many volumes of poetry include *The Waste Land* (1922), *Ash Wednesday* (1930) and *Sweeney Agonistes* (1932). Eliot was very active in the Anglo-Catholic church and some of his poems show deep religious orthodoxy.

63. Santa Teresa de Jesús (1515–1582). Spanish mystical writer, famous for the warmth and generosity of her character. Among her works are *Life* (1562–1565), *Way of Perfection* (1570), *Foundations* (1573–1582), and *Inner Castle* (1577). Her lyrical poems are beautiful expressions of her love of God.

64. San Juan de la Cruz (1542–1591). Spanish mystical poet whose perfect communion with God is expressed in the beautiful lyric verses of "Spiritual Song" and "Dark Night of Love."

65. From *The Complete Works of Saint John of the Cross.* Translated and edited by E. Allison Peers from the critical edition of P. Silverio de Santa Teresa (Wheathamstead/Hertfordshire: Anthony Clarke Books, 1974), p. 420.

66. Miguel de Cervantes de Saavedra (1547–1616). Spain's greatest literary figure, author of *Don Quijote de la Mancha* (1605–1615). Other works are the *Exemplary Novels* (1613), including *Rinconete and Cortadillo, The Little Gypsy Girl,* and *The Illustrious Kitchen Wench;* the play *Numancia* (1588); and the adventure narrative *Persiles and Sigismundo* (1617).

67. Pedro Calderón de la Barca (1600-1681). One of the great dramatists of Spain's Golden Age of literature. He is particularly skillful in the cloak-and-sword plays, such as *It's Hard to Guard a House with Two Doors* (1636). Calderón also wrote many plays in which the concept of honor is a principal theme, such as *The Mayor of Zalamea* (1642) and religious plays such as *The Wonder-Working Magician* (1663). *Life Is a Dream* (1635), a complex philosophic drama dealing with free will, is his masterpiece.

68. Lope de Vega (1562–1635). Founder of Spain's national drama, Lope was the prolific author of over two thousand plays. He wrote historical dramas, such as *Fuente Ovejuna* (1612), light comedies, such as *Lady Simpleton* (1613), and cloak-and-sword plays such as *Scorn Works Miracles* (1617) and *The Girl with the Water Jar* (1627).

69. Mateo Alemán (1547–1614). Author of the Spanish picaresque novel *Guzmán de Alfarache* (1599, 1605), which excessively moralizes as it spins out the succession of adventures that befalls the protagonist.

70. *Much Ado About Nothing* (1599). One of Shakespeare's comedies.

71. *Ergo*. The Latin word for "therefore."

72. Immanuel Kant (1724–1804). German philosopher, author of *Critique of Pure Reason* (1781–1787), *Critique of Practical Reason* (1788), and *Critique of Judgment* (1790). There is little doubt that Mallea examined Kant's philosophy closely and was influenced by the limits he placed on the powers of reason.

73. Georg Wilhelm Friedrich Hegel (1770–1831). German philosopher, born in Stuttgart. One of Hegel's basic philosophical tenets is that the universe consists of a simple absolute spirit or idea. Hegel made no distinction between being and thinking; for him no reality can exist outside of our own thoughts. Hegel's most important works are *Phenomenology of the Spirit* (1807) and *Science of Logic* (1812–1816).

74. Mallea is obviously playing with and extending René Descartes's famous sentence "I think, therefore I am." The French philosopher and mathematician (1596–1650), in his famous *Discourse on Method* (1637), greatly influenced the development of modern scientific thought. His rigorous philosophical doctrines issued from a consciously thought out method that was clearly in harmony with the scientific spirit.

75. David Hume (1711–1776). Scottish philosopher and historian. Hume's idea that human knowledge derives from the senses, from impressions, and

from experience is expressed in *Philosophical Essays Concerning Human Understanding* (1748). Hume is essentially an empiricist.

76. Thinking reed. Complete quotation reads: "Man is but a reed, the weakest thing in nature, but he is a thinking reed." (From Blaise Pascal, *Thoughts*)

77. Léon Chestov (1866–1938). Russian writer and mystic philosopher. Among his essays are: "The Apotheosis of *Disorientation*" (1927), "The Night of Gethsémani" (1938). and "Athens and Jerusalem" (1938).

78. Jacques Rivière (1886–1925). French essayist. He renounced the Catholic faith as a very young man, but after much inner struggle returned to Catholicism in 1913. Rivière played an important role in French intellectual life from around 1920 to his death. Works: *Essays* (1912), *The German* (1918), *Aimée* (a novel, 1922).

79. Orion. Constellation close to the equator. It is known as the Great Hunter. Several faint stars form the sword that hangs from the belt.

80. Centaurus. This very large constellation is found in the Southern Hemisphere. Alpha Centauri, one of its stars, is the third brightest in the sky.

81. Southern Cross. Constellation of four stars in the Southern Hemisphere.

82 Rhabdomancer. A person who practices divination by means of wands.

III.
The Visible Argentina

The naked inhabitant. The invading,
moldable mass seeking a form.
Debilitation of our own form and
therefore of its power to shape.
Substitution and artificial
"representing" for vital living. The
external appearance of humanity.
Enthronement of the means and neglect
of the ends. Contaminated. A
fictitious world was substituted
noticeably for the real world.

When I began to look with real concern at that world whose nature I wanted to discover, to possess in its true condition, in its truth and in its lie, I did not have a career. I was not a politician, nor an industrialist, nor a speculator either—none of those professions was mine. My vocation was not an adjectival function, carried out and completed. My vocation was myself. I did not feel Argentina in any of the possible ways of "doing something in the country." I felt her in a different way. I felt my country "by being my country." Which means that I suffered her, that I made her not from without, but from myself, within myself. And what was I? The least important thing of all: a man with a vocation to create with words, a man of many doubts with a vocation to write.

Thus, what I first noticed was the predominance of the naked inhabitant, Argentina in its humanity. The first thing I looked at was not the State, or the Government, or Argentine knowledge and learning, but rather the Argentine man, inasmuch as everything else should be his product, his kindred offspring. And when I tried to carry forth my plan I had my first devastating confirmation, the confirmation that the function exercised by that man in this country was not, as might be assumed, a prolonged application of certain very human aptitudes and faculties, but rather a tumor, a cancer which denaturalizes and consumes him, a physiological knot that stunts his growth and thwarts his natural destiny.

I began to feel my people in their joys, their amusements, their problems, their passions, their intelligence, their work. I had several million human beings living around me in the vast meanders of the flat city, in the monotonous narrow streets of the capital, on whose coast the river digs out a child's profile to the north and west. And the city has the child's tenderness, the almost irrational cruelty with which it timidly protects itself before giving in. And when the city gives in, surrenders, its heart is magnificent, but until then, what a harsh countenance it turns toward the foreigner! The psychology of Buenos Aires, in its gestures, its caution, its demeanor, its jealous reactions, resembles that of women who are nursing: they all have a certain haughty, almost disdainful and cold dignity, as if in their explicit reserve they already showed their pride in what they have to give. They are the same women who do not yield except after a secret ecstasy, keeping for the man they do not choose the rigidity and distance of an unnecessary aloofness. The capital is like that, glacial, mute, with something inhospitable on the outside of its hospitality.[1]

Don't think that my contact with the city was not painful. Like Captain Ahab's struggle in Melville's beautiful book,[2] my struggle with the city's white whale was a cruel one. I went to the theaters and saw the people; I went to all the public places and saw the people; then I went to the banks, the industrial plants, the lecture halls, the universities, the schools, and I saw the people; I went to the places where politics and government hold session and I saw the people. The initial feeling one got seeing these people was a strange one, because in a very deep sense they did not give of themselves. Their inner mutism seemed to me more and more incomprehensible, for outwardly, in their direct contacts, they were rather garrulous, rather loquacious, while beyond that external energy they clung to an indescribable silence and reserve. This meant that there was something destroyed in those human groups, something unfortunately sacrificed to an attitude, something fundamental and authentic deep down in those souls which was sacrificed to a kind of unauthentic morality. What did that something consist of? What did that morality consist of? How was such a substitution brought about?

It was necessary to penetrate further, to obtain an indirect confession from those men. Direct confession was impossible, since those invidious people closed off—with the sluices of an inflexible taciturnity—their possibilities of communication whenever I tried to have them speak of themselves.

In general, the *porteño*[3] shows a surprising intelligence on first examination and a no less surprising aptitude for assimilating culture. But it is in this organic precociousness of his intellect, in this fundamental aptitude, so apparently positive, where his true weakness lies. Because that facility, which would be magnificent as a means, is nothing as an end in itself. As an end it is a trap, since it wraps the subject in a kind of perfidious net, without allowing him to free himself, to develop, to grow, in short, to have maximum fertility. A man who has a good stomach will laugh before the whole world, confident he has the most enviable health; one day that heart, that blood, which were conspiring in the shadows, become defective, something, in short, explodes in him, and apoplexy strikes him down. It was too good a stomach for sound health. Health is a system and none of its manifestations appears alone; all or nothing.

But added to the danger implicit in the dermal luster of intelligence, there is another one I clearly saw: the danger of the aptitude for assimilating culture. Because if in a living organism there is no assimilation without transformation, without the production it fosters, neither does the culture which is devoured and dies on being assimilated have value in an immaterial organism. And this culture, on not being assimilated, is death instead of life. Culture exists through a phenomenon similar to the oxygenation process of the lungs or the chlorophyll; a wooden box can receive and store oxygen, but it is a dead act. Like oxygen, culture is not biologically spiritual as such, except when its influence prevails through a chemical bond. Without blood, without sap to fertilize, oxygen is no more than an errant body.

And that man, that man with whom I first came into contact in Buenos Aires, presented to all the free currents of culture a life blood with no resistances, with no power of selection or rejection—an empty blood, intellectually speaking.

From this also stems his confusion in believing—so often and so obstinately—that a formally educated person is more fundamentally cultured than a "well-bred" farmer of plain common sense or an Aztec Indian. (This, dear reader, you should not forget; it is more important than it may seem here, because such an apparently insignificant error of differentiation has a lot to do with the problem of the visible and the invisible). It seems difficult for the visible Argentine to think that the cultivation of a spirit is of little value when that spirit is not cultured in the very beginning, cultured in its first cell, that is, in its very constitution.

More than two million souls walked through the same streets as I. They formed two very compact, very strong groups: one made up of those who have their roots in our land and the other made up of those who came from the most remote regions with dreams they formulated in the most diverse languages. However, a common bond between these two groups and not a clear separation was visible to me even after walking in the city just a short while. Was that bond a common ambition, a common will, a common comprehension of life, or simply an illusion of the untrained eye? The question is unnecessary; the bond was clearly and simply the common desire for dominance and power in a world where everything seems easy, where the sky is so prodigiously clear, twilight so varied in its differentiated splendor, the nights so universal, the weather so much without extremes—at times heavy, at times unstable, in the long run clement.

Those foreign contingents are those which have pronounced the word wealth and fixed the terms of the struggle. But such a word is tragic, such a word is pleasant only in its appearance, such a word is the ambitious shout of desertion that wants to appear like something else. Life is a use of man in this tragedy, a use of man in a kind of war that gives respite but not a long truce. Those who escape, shouting out "Comfortable life!" have deserted a mandate and that desertion is avenged. Those men who came and shouted out their aspiration for material riches, let's not forget, came from terrible moral anarchy,

from unutterable poverty, from European systems in crisis and dissolution. With their longing for liberation, what could they bring to
another land? Principles on which to base a harmonic nationality, a
harmonic world? Order does not begin in a flight to comfort, but in an
awareness of a certain sacrifice for a certain goal. What those foreigners could bring was their violent hunger and thirst for bread and material betterment. That material hunger and thirst are human, that is,
just and also moral. The moral part of that hunger and thirst is a will
directed towards action, an aspiration to create, and more than anything else the energy derived from a sadness that wants to be transformed into a joy.

We see, then, that those blond men from distant shores, whose eyes
revealed the suffering of untold generations, brought us an element of
life, of energy in movement. If this energy was not capable—because
naturally it was not its mission—of initiating with its movement the
sense of an order, of a system, it did have, on the other hand, splendid
human resources to integrate something powerfully active and corporeal into that order. Those men formed moldable human material.
But who was going to give them that system, that order? How was it
to be given? What was going to be the matrix capable of molding
them, of giving them a total form, of imposing on them a period of
gestation suitable to the form?

Naturally, that matrix could not be any other but the spiritual
make-up of our people. But something serious had happened. As the
human contingent of foreigners kept nourishing our soil more richly
through every port, railroad and road, our spiritual form, our wealth
of soul and knowledge was *explicitly* being eroded throughout the
country.

(I have emphasized the term *explicitly*. I have emphasized it for this
reason. Because I believe that such degeneration, such weakening of
our spiritual physiognomy has been the work only of the present, persistent state—a spiritual, intellectual and moral state—of the men
who apparently express our country, who have expressed her in this
century, or rather who have taken possession of her expression. It is the
result of a state of decadence in those men—a decadence of those who,
without being Argentina in any way, have shown her in their likeness,
have directed her in their likeness, ignominiously.)

The great legions of people eager for material wealth continued to fill our vast land surface, from the pale moon-covered regions of the north to those regions witnessing endless nocturnal deaths whose red-black blood spills onto the southern canals. But those other legions of people, instead of feeling their ambition programmed to our world's ascending symphony, saw, perhaps disenchantedly, many things, men and circumstances of the new land programmed to an imported route of physical and vegetative prosperity. Instead of finding a new order, and a good one, the immigrants saw the bad they brought over reproduced with but few differences.

Those recently arrived legions did not meet the real Argentina, but only the visible Argentina. Their contact was with the kind of man I grew to detest, at times with wrath, frequently with despair. Their contact was with those men who lived Argentina falsely, who "represented" Argentina.

Never did that term classify people more forcefully.

Of all those who touch Argentina's surface, the worst, the most harmful and the most condemnable is the person who has substituted "representing" for living. We are not dealing with a universally common type, but with our own particular type of social virtuoso of fraud. Behind a learned and cultured appearance, his so-called ideas are numerous and his belief nil. His whole performance is gesturing, acting out a role; even when he thinks, he gestures. If there were something in him about which he could not gesture, he would mutilate it, just as we bring a rotten abscess to the surgeon. His vocation is essentially ministerial, bureaucratic, even when he fulfills only the most modest functions in any public institution. They are not few in number. They are the ones who are quickly noticeable, a real State, from the high official to the lowly neighborhood lawyer or doctor with pretensions of worldly acclaim. These are the people who, in their own words—words that are always abundant, rarely held back, always carefully measured whether in public or in private, in the bedroom or at the banquet—have the country in their grip.

With tragic constancy, with irremediable, widespread appeal, they are actually those who "represent" the country. And one would be mistaken in thinking we are alluding to an incidental and caricatural figure. With unfortunate frequency, we receive from them government, political voice, our body of teachers, proclamations, and we should all be satisfied with what they say of us. They are false spirits, false Emersonian[4] words, strange pragmatists, all emphatic lecturers. Many of them oddly reconcile a violently and solemnly expressed nationalism with the efforts *in situ*[5] of strong foreign capitalistic enterprises. They form such a diffuse and prolific mass that their voice fills the entire country from one end to the other, from the legislative assembly, the rostrum, the university lecture hall, the open letter or the newspaper article whose basic syntax must have been thoroughly corrected, thanks to the meticulousness of those journalists whom they despise for lack of "flashy show." Their style is the speech; their apotheosis, the banquet; their most disturbing seductiveness, publicity. Not always venal, but always submissive, attracted by the medusan[6] tentacles of public exaltation of their person in the most diverse forms (from the precise repetition of their name in the society columns to the impossibility of refusing to serve on the most pompous but vapid boards and institutions).

For these perversely ingenuous men, what is truly essential is what gesticulates, what puts on a show; what is sensible is what is sustained at the top of one's voice; what is decent is what nicely fits into their system of prejudices they loudly call dignity. Incapable of thinking with discreet honesty and integrity, they fear the secret accusation of some sudden burst of conscience, and they live publicly in the street, on stage, apprising everybody of their intelligence, education and valor, because they are afraid to notice, when they do keep quiet, that they lack these very qualities. Imbued with such a great sense of sufficiency, they prefer to learn the least possible number of things so as to continue to believe there is nothing they do not know. But there is one thing they stubbornly seem not to know, namely that they are as much the true Argentina as the madman who thinks he is Henry IV.[7]

This observation amounts to a vehemence, which is the way I first observed that visible human layer of our country. It is certainly true that today I look disdainfully at them, but without anger, because we obviously can not be angered by something we see already bitten by its own worm and soon to be devoured.

What appeared to me very serious was that having gained power through their understandable influence over the most important means of communication of the great educational, political, industrial and textile centers of the country, they were the matrix called upon to mold the immigrant, to shape him, to give him a character structured to their own image and likeness. The serious thing was that apparently the moral inhabitant of our land threatened to receive norms or principles only from those social specimens incapable of authentic normative power and in whom philosophical principles are fundamentally shallow. The racial, ethical and political inheritance of our people was, so to speak, delivered into their hands.

And it was even more serious that we kept on moving along the path of mere show and pretense, in that dangerous quagmire. It was a situation like the one experienced by someone who finds himself in the middle of a swamp whose surface is monstrously enticing, as far from the lights of the stellar firmament as from the land on which terrestrial order is sustained on rock. These men live without belief, without a sense of the sacramental, Christian value of life, with scarcely the feeling to make the sign of the cross, which, as befits their nature, represents more a gesture than real fervor. They lack the sense of unity, the sense of an organic way of living to which all living bodies must be tied in order for their deepest essence not to perish. These men in whom the most terrible betrayal of the spiritual was carried out, a betrayal which consists of an unscrupulous and constant exercise of a kind of luxurious Pharisaism,[8] these men exclusively subordinated to the coefficient of their personal prosperity, were in themselves just appearance. Not life, appearance; not health, joy, progress, but the appearance of joy, the appearance of progress. Not humanity, but the appearance of humanity.

There was a false sense of refinement and aristocracy in that whole world. But this refinement and aristocracy—persistently cultivated and demonstrated—did not have their origin in a true refinement or true aristocracy, but rather in the apparent transmutation, in the improvised and apparent refining of an intrinsic barbarism. It was a barbarism that was a mixture of instinct and nebulous ambitions developed in utter disorder and firmly restrained, just when they began to emerge, in order to make them look like something else, then repressed and immediately externalized under the appearance of distinction that at times was grandiloquent.

What was important for this world was the outward sign—the gesture. One buys one's way with the gesture, one lives with the gesture
and the gesture was what one had to put values on. Even when the
men of that world spoke, their words acquired the value of a gesture,
even silence had the value of a gesture because those who kept it, those
who persisted in a game of opportune mutism, reserve, reticence, only
wanted to avoid the risk of having a possible personal defect judged by
others. Developed beyond all belief, fear of being exposed had become
an inhibition whose external form was extreme discretion.

And these men whom I met daily, who filled the professorial staff at
universities, the science laboratories, the art-supporting institutions,
the school auditoriums, a considerable number of schools and acade-
mies, who scattered about and ran around like a thick wave flooding
Assembly seats, exclusive clubs, federal government offices—these
men had an adjectival and not a noun function in our world, a function
in which the important thing above all was to "represent," to appear,
not be be. They shed their vital humanity and became transformed
into a conscious and clever reflection of that humanity. They ceased
being men and became derivatives. An industrious and successful
lawyer derived from a nonexistent man; a politician, any sort of professional, derived from a need to act in function of, in representation of
that social role. And these men had begun not to live like men, not to
love like men, not to suffer like men, not to hate like men, not to have
passions like men, not to have devotion like men, but to live, love,
suffer, hate, have passions, have devotion in accord with what they
wanted to appear.

Visible Argentina was infected by them. But, what did such a state
of existence have to do with the tradition, with the authentic soil of
our country? What did such a false kind of life have to do with what
springs from true roots, with what is raised according to the same laws
of development as a seed, a stalk, foliage? Nothing. It had nothing to
do with the national monad, with the beginning of life which springs
from a unity and develops or grows organically. And the kind of person who suffers from this defect may give the appearance of life and
progress, the appearance of prosperity, but he lacks real strength. He
is somewhat spineless and carefree and, when called upon to multiply,
can only produce the germ of some poorly directed, disperse instincts,

his only future salvation being that after so much chaos there may finally arise—by dint of horror and uneasy conflict—another organism hungry for authentic and not false life.

In the end, that dissolvent illness has contaminated our songs, our dances and our cultural activities. I could no longer hear a voice without feeling the ill-fated counter-song, the delirium of appearing falsely. I could not approach one of those soapbox orators without fear of finding that exacerbated and vast desert, just as full of pretension as of emptiness. I could not read a book or an article without finding the same struggles in a character after the conquest not only of his somatic happiness and his physical comfort in the sense of possessions and wealth, but of everything that resembles the spirit without actually being it. And if this caused me alarm, it was because I judged that evil even more dangerous and dreadful than the flagrant deficiency marked by critical thought in the United States regarding its own destiny. It was more dangerous because if the deficiency in today's United States is only a temporary one (a condition characteristic of early childhood in which instinct is dominant, with its particular kind of behavior, its peculiar greed and its natural philosophy), our own deficiency is greater since it is more than the sign of something immature; it is the sign of a will to see only the disfigured and superficial part of a destiny, to accept only the least integral, softest and therefore the least grandiose and heroic part of our world's destiny.

That constant need for pretense, for atomic and personal exaltation (even more than personal, individual; worldly but not functional), for subordination of all eternal principles to a kind of divinely inspired and all-powerful self-worshipping knowledge, expressively inclined to exaltation and eloquence; that need to impose the appearance of culture on each day's events; that tendency toward mistrust and mockery of the genuine intellectuals and scientists who took refuge in their cell; that systematic smugness of criterion and judgment before all manifestation of art—as if the mere circumstance of their hunger for well-being and comfort and information mechanically placed them on a level superior to any man-made work; in short, this idea of judging the most by the least, to use a formula St. Thomas[9] probably liked, could hardly be considered as the mere resultant of immaturity. These things were definitely a sin and a persistent sin against the spirit in that society where eyes are open only for sins of the flesh—as if these are the ones that really mattered!

I believe that our lack of maturity differs considerably from that of the North American as regards the origin and hence the future of the two peoples. By this I mean that our instinct comes from a different kind of formation, it follows another kind of evolution, a different road so to speak. The differences between the puritanical Quaker[10] and the Spanish conqueror were too great for us not to think they rested on two essentially different value systems. The cornerstones of the first churches of the North and the first churches of the South were placed in accordance with two unequal forms of devotion; the cornerstone of the Quakers has its soul tied to the ascendancy of a moral theology, the cornerstone of the Spanish conquerors to a mystical theology. The inhabitants of the North and the South thus knew different kinds of freedom. In the former, spiritual impulse was conditioned by austere, rigid precepts; in the latter, that impulse was raised more daringly and more ardently toward God. The former were confronted with a Book; the latter with the infinite. If the Book is a fact, the infinite is a pure aspiration. From a sense of the fact is born perfection in a system of facts, but from the other flame emerges *the* fact, the fact *created* more than *constructed,* the fact raised to the category of an expression of a sacrifice, the supreme and heroic fact: the deeds of Hernán Cortés[11] and Joan of Arc[12] and the symbolism of Chartres.[13] Such is the blessing of our inheritance from Spain rather than our debt to the Latin character. And, in the light of these things, how are we to accept the degradations that are not even the blind consequence of instinct, but the criminal indulgence of intelligence in its own deceit and of creative freedom in its inactivity, in its inertia disguised as movement and in an apparently fruitful sterility, which is the sterility of the man who functions in a world whose organically immutable dependence on values has been replaced by the exercise of apparent values?

Instinct does not lack objectives; they are elementary, but objectives just the same. The fickle human tide that constitutes the visible Argentina enthrones the means exclusively. The men who make up and stir that human wave are means themselves, means that multiply without losing their condition of being means, means seeking to have more means. An artist is an end in himself, a saint is an end in himself, a hero is an end—these three are examples of the humanization of an end, because they are masters of their own end or destiny, in the sense of having given their life the will to act determinedly. Destructive of true Argentine values are those men who think and function only in terms of means, those who can not abandon the imprisonment of wanting to attain without transcending themselves, the imprisonment of the end that remains just a means.

I wanted to find humanly responsible men and I found only the appearance of humanity, the representation of humanity, the show of humanity.

Every creation is an end, not a means. What else could the visible country be but a country built in thin air just as long as it was made up of men concerned about means and not of men who are creators?

All our national resources that stem from a strong and true culture appeared contaminated—oh, how I saw it!—but such an anomaly. What happens when the goals of an organic state linger on as simple means is that, besides the debilitation of all the constructive, maternal or germinative strength of the soul, culture and art, there is also a debilitation in the fabric of the nation's collective life. And although the trunk artificially survives after the roots die, language and speech, that is, the very expression of the people so corrupted, become weakened and denaturalized.

*   *   *

I hated those culpably false people; I would have wanted to hunt them down, to beat them, to reduce them to silence, to clear the air of their presence. And day after day the only thing I accomplished was to feel myself resembling them, contaminated. Their ways took hold of me: their wandering through newspaper notices, the same self-esteem, the same sophisms to appear informed to the fool, the same spirit of irony and mockery at the expense of the candid person, the same smugness and self-importance, the same basic stupidity, the same complacency in the omnipotent value of how I appear to others, in my external appearance, in my vanity, the same worldly ambition, the same outspokenness and the same pride, the same frenzied stamping in igno-

rance dressed up as information, the same incapacity to analyze intelligently, the same desire to judge everything from above, the same
foolishness of criterion, the same conventionalism, the same hypocrisy, the same howling Pharisaism in the pool of personal resentments,
the envies, jealousies, personal ill will. Not even one trait of true freedom, not even one trait of intelligent and independent will. Nor a
burst of real pride—which consists of having it without showing it
off—of real dignity, of austere dominance over circumstances and
men, of serene inner, not external confidence.

Contaminated. That's how I felt. And I hated those deformers,
those traitors, those bourgeois, asleep in the bed of a certain venal negligence. I hated myself. I could not stand myself. I left my books,
went out to the street full of anger against myself, full of acerb deception, of cold bitterness. I walked through the streets, reluctantly
drank the liquid from a black cup in a café, looked at the city with
innocent wrath and despairingly began to wander around with no
stop. Finally, I entered a movie house to shake off my bad mood in the
adventures of one of those products of the Yankee dream factory.

And after I left the movie house, wherever I went—in the streets,
in the clubs, in the literary salons, at gatherings with highbrows of
both sexes—I once again met those people, adulterated, denaturalized
men, insignificant islands adrift with their own myths.

There were moments when it was no longer possible to endure such
an atmosphere. America, promiscuous land, a land without salvation!
That thought was my companion. I wandered around the city until
reaching the harbor. Under the refuge of the nocturnal solitude, on
the dark coast, with my face offered to the breeze coming from the
river of almost motionless waters,[14] I felt rescued for a moment. There
I saw the free water, the free night, the free stars—the universe. Nothing stirred up, nothing constrained, everything exact, everything
true, everything—star, wind or tree—applied to the fulfillment of its
function, everything subject to the austere joy of the fundamental system, each one for the whole and the whole for each one. I was the
imperfect one.

In the most cultured as well as in the most intellectually impoverished places of the capital, in the rear of private homes, on the theater
stages, in the audible voice in the street, on the lips of the great and

the humble, of the master and the servant, of the pseudo-cultured and the dull, in that visible population that controls the power of the country and its physical resources, in all these places I heard the same language spoken, the same corrupted language, not yet turned colloquial—which would not be that bad—but above all hybridized. Even our pronunciation was almost lifeless, anemic, without that coloration, without that vital pigment a vigorous climate gives to everything born in its region. In the visible Argentine our language had become white, pale, hybridized, falsified.

If this visible Argentine were genuine and had roots, these roots would have a lot of the Spanish soul. He would then believe in extreme or absolute values, which in fact are those I was referring to when speaking of ends. "The Spaniard," a wise Spaniard once said— "either believes in absolute values or stops believing entirely." Dostoyevsky's dilemma[15] applies to us; either absolute value or absolute nothingness. But of course the absolute did not exist for our visible man. There was always a certain constant fluctuating at midpoint, a certain exaltation at any cost of the no-risk median glorified as much in the order of material things as in the order of moral values, that is, if such a category can fit into that latter realm.

Thus we see how a false world had brought about this substitution for the true world. This deception in which everybody seemed to take part was a deception for each individual person, because on impoverishing the human circle that surrounds us what we impoverish is our own life, whom we impoverish is ourselves. And this visible world, seemingly prosperous and rich, was deep down a world in the process of becoming impoverished in the saddest possible way, which is by believing that one is growing and becoming rich. Indeed, this is the most lamentable process for a man, a people or a cause.

When I saw, in this land I loved with unruly passion, the image of that disorder moving ahead, clothed with the ornaments of a strict, safe and almost ritualistic order, I felt the need to escape from myself, to avoid that contact which could corrupt anyone in its likeness. Since we were a people of sturdy stock, authentic, of quick and prodigious intelligence, fundamentally unselfish, facing all the universal winds that reached us in the form of human beings or happenings, it seemed to me that, through a certain self-satisfaction in a premature defect, we were heading for unknown clouds, unknown destinies, unknown grave errors. I needed to sink into the other world, into the non-ostensible world, into the one that lay submerged very far beneath our unconscious disguised as proud-spirited superconscious.

Everything I saw lost in those men in command I needed to discover in others, to see it recaptured. But above all it was necessary to define the origin of the visible ills on the surface of the country. Did these ills have their origin in the spirit, in the soul, in the intellect of those Argentines with influence and power? Evidently in none of the three. It was not a crime of the spirit, of the soul, of the intellect—although these three things were spontaneously involved. It was a crime of conscience. The crime of those men who had disregarded their own roots and kept the country removed from its real values was precisely this kind of aberration. The merchant's moral aberration is the same thing.

It was as if the magistrates, officials, civil servants, professionals, industrialists, all important people and visible Argentines, were selling the adulteration of a natural product at a good price.

Flagellation, flagellation for them? No, not that. But they should be left with their "means" in their hands, while we continue on alone our own way, our solitary way, our ears turned toward the inner song of the earth, toward the inner song of men. To walk alone, until finding other solitary souls, for the torrent that clears away the mud is made from these solitary people. The torrent of those who have faith, of those who do not lie to themselves, of those who do not agree to or want a sinecure. The torrent of the truly honorable people in their loneliness, of those who in their loneliness perfect themselves to be good company for others.

It is not when we make the greatest effort to open our eyes wide that we see the furthest. When we want to see still further, an incalculable distance, we close our eyes for a moment, the eyes of the flesh. That is when our vision becomes the spirit. The one who sees further is not the eagle, but the blind man. Thus, we tried hard to see, straining our vision to keep attentive to the adjacent landscape, but what we saw was the eternal deformation of a people, its characteristics distorted by that abnormal growth developing in its physiognomy.

It was necessary to look with other, more reliable, more demanding, deeper eyes in order to see the other form considerably more consistent, incalculably more honest in its physical and moral resistance: the inner form of this country, the invisible Argentina.

Notes

1. Mallea likes to juxtapose words with similar or related etymology, either forming a contrast or strengthening the expressiveness of the phrase. Thus, the adjective "inhospitable," in contrast with the following noun "hospitality," apparently forms a paradox; in reality the proximity of the two words reinforces the idea of the coldness and anonymity of the capital.

2. Herman Melville (1819–1891). American novelist, author of *Moby-Dick* (1851), which relates Captain Ahab's obsession to hunt down the symbolic white whale.

3. The inhabitants of Buenos Aires are commonly referred to as *porteños* because the capital is a port city.

4. Reference to the American essayist and poet Ralph Waldo Emerson (1803–1882). His philosophy emphasized individualism, responsibility and basic optimism. Together with others, Emerson founded the movement known as Transcendentalism. Books: *Nature* (1836), *The Conduct of Life* (1860), *Society and Solitude* (1870). Essays: "Friendship," "Compensation," "Self-reliance."

5. *in situ*. Latin phrase meaning "in position, in its original place."

6. medusan. The medusa is an umbrella shaped jellyfish with very sensitive feelers. These tentacles seize food and carry it to the mouth.

7. Henry IV. Common reference to Henry the Great, King of France (1589–1610).

8. Reference to the frequently held belief that the Pharisees, an ancient Jewish sect that adhered excessively to relgious laws, were hypocritical and pretentious in their way of life.

9. Saint Thomas Aquinas (1225–1274). Italian philosopher, theologian and teacher, author of *Summa Theologica* (1267–1273).

10. Quakers. Reference to the members of the Religious Society of Friends, founded in England in 1648. Many Quakers came to America in the 17th and 18th centuries and settled in the Northeast, especially in Rhode Island. In 1682, the Quaker William Penn founded the colony of Pennsylvania.

11. Hernán Cortés (1485–1547). Conquerer of Mexico (1519). Born in Extremadura in southern Spain, Cortés first participated in the conquest of Cuba in 1511. In 1519 he became commander of an expedition to Mexico and defeated the Aztecs on July 7, 1520.

12. Joan of Arc (1412–1431). Heroine of French history. Called the Maid of Orleans, she was accused of heresy and witchcraft by the English and burned at the stake.

13. Cathedral of Chartres. Built between 1195 and 1220, this Gothic cathedral is especially noted for its impressive stained-glass windows.

14. Reference to the Río de la Plata. One of Mallea's early volumes of short stories is entitled *The City on the Motionless River*.

15. Fyodor Dostoyevsky (1821–1881). Great Russian novelist of extraordinary psychological insight. His works were widely read by Hispanic Americans and Mallea was deeply impressed by Dostoyevsky's introspective techniques in character delineation. Among Dostoyevsky's best known works are *The House of the Dead* (1861), *Crime and Punishment* (1866), *The Idiot* (1869), and *The Brothers Karamazov* (1880).

IV.
The Invisible Country

*The authentic land, the real land and
its people. The severe exaltation of life.
The spiritual struggle of the creators.
Work devoid of illusion. Creative
discontent.*

If there are two psychologically, ethically, and socially different men
in the world, they are the inhabitants of the Argentine hinterland and
the inhabitants of the city. It seemed to me that in the measure of that
difference lay the measure of our possible growth toward the positive
integration of our destiny. If such a difference were an illusion, the
invisible Argentina would also be an illusion; but such a difference is
real.

Any one who crosses the country free of illusions can verify the contrast between the expectations of the plodding worker from the north
and the expectations of his city relative from Buenos Aires, Rosario,[1]
or Cordoba;[2] between the moral system of the Andean man and the
greed of the small industrialist from Mendoza,[3] between the laborious
life of the Mediterranean tenant farmer and that of his urban exploiter;
between the light sleep of the man living close to the soil and the
heavy, covetous sleep of the man who vegetates in the air. The ambitions, longings, and preoccupations are all different. Even the country's countenance is different.

I travelled along many roads, to many inns, through many cities.
The things I saw filled me with reflective emotion. Even the most insignificant things—just a person's name, the way one listened in a

conversation, a certain natural culture, a certain rudimentary hunger for wisdom—revealed the presence of a very rich, moral hinterland in the unknown depths of our land.

Jujuy[4] resembles its people in a natural way, as does Buenos Aires. I once saw the dawn and the nights of Jujuy, the sky deeply arched and distant and clear in its smooth and intense blue. And under the straight, flat, vast ellipsis lay the white city, the humble house that neither lies nor impresses one except with its great dignified serenity, with the simplicity of a wall or the discreet art of an entrance hall or the cleanness of the rustic roadway stones or the extraordinarily pure classicism of a whitewashed arch or a simple market. Another time, at noon, I saw etched before me from a hotel window the full profile of the Tucumán[5] mountains, at one side of the almost yellow, graceful and wooded city, from the beginning of the plains to the very top where the foliage spreads out and grows thicker, as if we saw in that gesture the continuous enlargement of certain images in our nightmares.

I saw the uninterrupted surface of monstrous ferns. And afterward I walked through the tranquil streets of the village lined with houses, observing (almost without hearing a distracting voice) the calm steps of those people whose expectations for the future corresponded to the attitude of the natural landscape in the face of the sun's mutations, to the changeable clouds and to the marvelous eternal sky. At still another time, one night, feeling good about the warm country hospitality I received (it could have been anywhere in that more or less deserted flatness), I saw some men who had happily left for work that morning return in silence; in a few short hours, the plague, the swarms of locusts had left only the skeleton of the mountain, only the dried branches of the woody thickness, only ruin of what was once cereal. And with a heavy heart I had supper with those men and then went out in the open with them and saw them become happy once again with the friendship of the familiar star and nocturnal hope.

Another time, I lived for days near the irrigation ditches at Cuyo,[6] whose sound at night was like the sound of the famous fountains of Rome, which one hears from nightfall to dawn as a counterpart to one's own thoughts in the hour of recapitulation before sleep. I lived in San Juan,[7] a city typical of the Argentine provinces in the broadness of

Ancha Street and in the twin-domed main church that has a certain modest baroque extravagance in the front part, from the ground to the gable, and nondescript pews. In scattered places, I saw the Spanish, colonial, Jesuit tradition, still not changed or disfigured by a barbarous, confused, abominable, and chaotic invasion, lacking in original inspiration but revealing efforts to preserve the already lifeless vestiges of the most disparate architecture. I saw the man of the province and the man who works the land; I saw the Argentine who is really Argentine, the true Argentine. I saw the uneducated—who, nevertheless, have an innate virtue of which we shall later speak—and I saw the educated, who in the rear of farmhouses, country estates, and shops do not disdain the book but accept it as food and as humanity, useful in the first case and comforting in the second. (No one will offend us by believing we are referring to the puerile meaning of book as the formal printed word; we allude to it as a source, as an always creative spring not only of new learning but of living sensibility).

I learned to see our rural areas, our flat rivers, our calm rivers that moved slowly and whose waters had an unusual color. Clear waters that were at times somewhat turbid as if they had just passed through slime, waters always slow and sad like the movement of things eternal.

I learned to decipher the earth's articulated monologue, which has a strange, different, and meaningful voice. In the mornings, out on the open field, one can see a thin stripe of sun shining through, a thick resplendence on the edge of a long row of hills, and little by little the reflection takes possession of the infinite green extension and makes it white—an extension interrupted now and then by a hill of dark trees. Solitude, sun and animals, grain shining in the sun; suddenly the noise of a gallop resounding on the earth, as if dry, isocronous blows were struck on the taut ground with the hollow palm of the hand. Solitude, sun and animals, grain shining in the sun; then, hour after hour, in the sun or in the rain, the flat desert, the plains, the ground of burnt grass and the horizon all fall under the lash of the sun's red claw. Slowly, as afternoon approaches, everything starts changing its torrent of joy, of joy that breathes, and the atmosphere becomes slightly heavy and the horizon recedes and the land leaves the bed on which it rests and appears high and gravid in the hours preceding nightfall.

The earth, passive before, now becomes active, gets up, "sits up," no longer serves as just a floor for the colt's gallop and man's tasks; it breaks out of its docility and pursues both colt and man in the enormous free space of the night. The earth touches them, seeks them, hunts them. So high is the land that the moon itself appears to be scratched by the hand of the plains.

During the moonless nights, there is one hour in which the only horizon seen is the island of incorporated land on which we are standing, on top of the world. And the land, which in the morning was stretched out, given over to our laborious furor, at night hunts us, surrounds us, threatens us. But the day's work is done and the only thing to do is wait. The night rebel will again be submissive in the morning. Meanwhile, we hear the ceaseless croaking, letting us know the proximity of the pond or the lagoon. We look at the firefly's fleeing spark. In the shadows we fear the bat's flap of the wing; in the darkness we feel the ground trod on by stealthy species, the toad, the newt, the rattlesnake.

And our meditation is saturated with humanity, almost as close to the heavens as to the trickle of water that runs underground. In the presence of nature, we can think only that that world surrounding us is too large for our hates, passions, base dilatoriness, for everything that is repressed feeling. An immense sense of nature is surrounding us and, rather than restraining us and closing us in, communicates with us, extends us to its own measure. It puts us as close to the high starry field as to the low, firm field below, as to the deep water, as to other men, women, and things. What we long to do is shout out: "Lord, Lord, with each second we are being born, we are being born again. Universe, we touch you! Earth, we touch you!" And what we have of the earth is not only the earth, but the way it takes us to the absolute.

Before midnight, when we come home to go to bed, a rhombus of milky moon still accompanies us in our solitude. Our shadow bends as we approach the whitewashed wall of the house, which appears blue. And only at dawn are we and the earth perfectly peaceful, both inert, both recumbent.

*   *   *

And there is, to sum up, a man who lives in that land, who savors it, who wounds it, who works and fertilizes it; a man who one rarely feels lives in Argentina, a man almost submerged in the secret of his labor. The vast plain has given him its basic substance, which is a prodigious fertility. This time, fertility of soul and heart. It is the man behind whose actions, feelings, passions, and intelligence lies the horizon: a possibility of mutation, of extension, that is, of progress, beyond the purely physical. There is manliness in this inhabitant of the land; that is, substantial humanity, human substance in freedom. Even his hands are roots, as well as those tranquil, deep eyes in which a new state of love seems to be born at every moment. And if in the other false and citified being into which the country is being distorted, there is rarely revealed a strong, firm, spiritual vertebration, with this other type of humanity in a pure state, even when taken in its most primitive form, that ethical element which Ganivet[8] saw so deeply ingrained in Seneca's words[9] is always on the verge of coming true: "Don't let yourself be conquered by anything foreign to your spirit. Be aware that even with life's vicissitudes you have within you a basic force, something strong and indestructible, like a diamond axis, around which turn the petty things that make up the scenario of our daily living. And whatever things may happen to you, whether they are those we call favorable or adverse, or those which seem to degrade us through contact, remain strong and erect in such a way that at least it can always be said of you that you are a man."

Am I alluding to the gaucho, to the peasant, to the farmer, to the rancher? No, I am not alluding to any of those "professions" but to a special state, to the ethically well-defined state of an Argentine, a state that resembles the very climate, the shape, the nature of the Argentine land, to the point of being astonishingly identified with them. I repeat, a state that resembles the nature of the Argentine land and its timeless projection, its projection as history and as nationality. Because, and I think this is very important, this Argentine whose projection is presently invisible, has had and will therefore have in the future, a predominantly active role in the course of our history, in the forging of our nationality, in our becoming Argentina.

What I call the invisible Argentine is not, in a simplistic way, the rural man as opposed to the city man. The difference lies in the fact that there exists one kind of man whose moral physiognomy is that of our cities and another kind whose moral physiognomy is that of our unspoiled nature, of our natural nature. It does not matter that one who exemplifies the qualities of this latter group may live in the city, nor does it matter that a person who has the moral physiognomy of our cities may live in our hinterland. This may be a fortuitous circumstance. What is important is not where these people are, but what they are like.

There is a beautiful poem by Walt Whitman[10] called "Me imperturbe," which says:

> Me imperturbe, standing at ease in Nature.
> Master of all or mistress of all, aplomb in the midst
>   of irrational things.
> Imbued as they, passive, receptive, silent as they.
> Finding my occupation, poverty, notoriety, foibles,
>   crimes, less important than I thought.
> Me toward the Mexican sea or in the Mannahatta or
>   the Tennessee, or far north or inland.
> A river man, or a man of the woods or of any farm-life
>   of these States or of the coast, or the lakes or Kanada,
> Me wherever my life is lived, O to be self-balanced
>   for contingencies,
> To confront night, storms, hunger, ridicule, accidents,
>   rebuffs, as the trees and animals do.

Is that imperturbability an attitude, is it a posture? No, but rather a form of "being" which may exist unmanifested, a form of "appearing" which may remain implicit in man; unknown but natural, which may also be explicit, but never an "adopted" attitude.

It is that active imperturbability, its essence, which immediately and vehemently attracts me toward the invisible Argentine—let us still call him that. Of a strong and at the same time very sensitive nature, he lacks, however, the physical attractiveness of certain heroes mistakenly exalted by popular imagination, but his inner strength is what has lasting spirit and quality. A moral quality, an inner quality, an immanent more than physical value, conditions on which rests the will to create solidly, with a firm foundation, and not with a weak transitoriness like everything created by that other Argentine group whose moral fiber vegetates in the air.

Joyfully, I thought I had found the living heart of my land when this invisible man became visible to me, when in the capital city and in the provincial cities I began to sense his bearing, his character, grave without solemnity, silent without resentment, happy without being overly so, active without being greedy, hospitable without expecting any return, naturally generous; friend of the stars, the plants, the sun, the rain and inclemency, quick to accept friendship, loathe to have discord, humanly solitary to the point of the unexpected and sudden sacrifice; full of accurate prescience and the sap of wisdom; simple and without a display of learning; basically fair, more disposed to doing good directly, to displaying heartfelt equanimity than theorizing about injurious ways of action, virile, tempered in his vehemence, so moderate in life; and moderate in his desires that death does not frighten him with her gesture, for death does not take away from him anything he has not offered before with human dignity. When I approached this man—and I always saw him alone facing a land which disproportionately surrounded him and caused him not only material suffering but suffering of the spirit, as Pascal expressed it*—I thought I found Argentina's true heart. It was an experience that can be compared only to the strange joy of suddenly finding the object of a vague and until then missing love. All anguish yields and leaves a living organism in place of its tumultuous emptiness when it finds an incarnate force in which to put our hope and our erring, waning confidence.

I saw those men, I spoke with those men, I listened with emotion to those consciences that had not foreseen their real relationship of mutual fertility with the land and with other men. I found nothing un-

---

*The abyss and the infinite (that is, the infinite space considered as an abyss) of his infinite terror.

predictable in them, for the inner impulse of our formation as a nation had the same chemical strengths as that which this precipitate gives now. There remained in them an eminently Argentine spiritual cause, a sense of existence. Exclusively theirs, belonging to them and authentic. And I called that feeling "a severe exaltation of life."

That exaltation is characteristic of the genuine Argentine, of the true Argentine, of the Argentine who is the human root and not the foliage, not prattle or mere show. The greater care we take in thinking about who we Argentines really are, the clearer will be our conviction of the intrinsic content of these words.

I have stubbornly followed along the path of that thought and each time it appears to me more laden with a truth on which I would like to reflect. Exaltation, severe exaltation, and severe exaltation of life. I do not know which one of the three words seems most worthy or which one most important in the unity of its movement. The three might be the norm for those times when norms served men a little more than as mere verbal expedients and when each man incorporated these norms into his very being as he incorporated worry into his forehead, when the norms were "normal" and incited a sword, bent a knee in the atrium, kindled the moment of martyrdom or led a man to live honestly and die without the inner death rattles.

Exaltation in itself is an act of elevating, perhaps the power of being exalted through an idea, an experience, or a faith. Perhaps the power of being exalted is the category that most distinguishes the human condition from that of the rest of living species. To become exalted is generally a spiritual act and if to this is added the condition of severity—that is, of the mind that avoids triviality and acts accordingly—it is thereby saved from being a lower kind of exaltation, which is exaltation through rapture or elation, and becomes transcendent exaltation because of the fact that all true morality transcends man by dignifying him, by making him master of himself, that is, more than himself, possessor of himself, free to do what he wants.

These men of the provinces, whom I could observe in the most unexpected places throughout the country, carried within themselves like a sacrament that Argentine trademark, that severe exaltation of life. And I recognized that exaltation on the faces—the human face, not the statuary, stupid, and documentary face—of some of our most illustrious men. I saw that exaltation come like a glorious brilliance, descending from the dawn until it passed over land and sank behind the mountains leaving a certain austere splendor; or like a river, flowing across the bed of things and time, from man to man; from the one who won America with his hands and whose horse, in the words of Avellaneda, had covered more land than any other except Alexander's,[11] to St. Esquiú,[12] not to mention others—including Martín Fierro,[13] the moralist—whose patronymic enumeration would only sever the unity of this current, of this active, subterranean flow, of this undisturbed march, of this fluid, spiritual course through Argentine history.

This severe exaltation of life consisted of man's special position in space that includes all of earthly reality, all eventualities and aspirations toward God. It is an eminently worthy position in that space turned spaceless thanks to the human bond stretched between the two ends. That exaltation is also seen in one who exercises the real power he has only to demonstrate to himself that even if he squanders and loses it he will still preserve something worth more, and that is his spirit of communion as a man who has a deep feeling for the things that in turn make *him* feel. That exaltation also consists of the situation of the man who knows the names of the trees and each star's special gravitational pull and for whom this elementary wisdom is a form of riches, in the same way that riches for a musician are the exact arrangement of certain notes that relieves him from his previous anguish and fulfills him. That exaltation is found in the very special, easily defined condition of a person who performs an act only if it has an immanent objective, which means then that he belongs to the kind of perfectly pure humanity whose hands, intelligence, and soul move according to a universal movement and thereby are less sententious or abstract. Exaltation of life is seen in the conduct of a man who has a sense of community. All of this comes only from a natural religiousness, which means a sense of man's position not only with regard to other men, but also in relation to the stars, the plants, the stones, and the general form of all that exists.

This kind of corporeal purity, as we may call it, is not far from Puritanism. The bad thing about the Puritan is that his ethic is experience and that the origin of this experience is external and literal. What leads those who live without losing their footing on earth to practice this severe exaltation of life is the strong man's courage in the face of a primary, unleashed opposition of nature. A kind of mystique, a form of heroism.

The history of America is the history of man facing the rebelliousness of space. And since this space is nature, which means form, it is the struggle of man with the unleashed form, with the strong, primitive form, with the uncreated. That man has to create it all, spiritually, materially, and politically; he has to reduce it, to leave it constructed by an act of dominance and—like all dominance over matter—of creation. His method of conquest is the most terrible of all. His tradition is that of horrible efforts and a few triumphs, but, unlike the European man, he cannot live on these laurels. This situation deprives such a man of possible false arguments when looking at his work. The reality he has before him is unedited. Each new situation invents its lever and this man has to invent his own instrument. And for this reason, his effort is double, since it requires intellect and physical strength at the same time. The tragedy of the Jesuit missionary in his work with the Indian is revived daily in new forms from Cape Horn to the northernmost parts of an America that still has ice and death in its jungles, besides the daily hum of industries in its monstrous and austere cities where plants either grow abundantly or never flower. I have seen men bent over with grief as the devastation of their fields is suddenly revealed to them after the plague, the devouring locusts, had done their job. I have seen men in an obstinate dry spell raise their pleading faces to heaven, and the following day an irate grimace, and then again a supplication. I have seen men with a handkerchief tied to their neck as the only outer garment go out to the fields in winter enduring their ulcers and the approach of death to plough the earth on time.

I have heard of doctors in unpopulated regions who were thwarted in helping dying patients because they lacked good instruments, and I have known how my experienced father once in an emergency cut open a woman's stomach with a sterilized jackknife right there in the wilderness, overwhelmed with great pity and threatened by the patient's husband at the height of his desolation and despair. I have seen lonely scientists wandering in our desert. I have seen poorly paid, hungry teachers longing to teach in freedom harassed by high public officials. I have seen unknown cultured journalists correcting the prose of eminent men who the next day would be lavishly congratulated for the splendid style of those articles. I have seen troubled men in the sad streets dragging along their great anxious consciences among the Babylonian lights, their hearts full of grief and the need to create and express themselves. I have seen noble spirits stifled by the sullen treatment of those who controlled them. Towards morning, along the avenues of the great city, I have felt the traces of intelligent sleeplessness on many emaciated and lost faces. And I have anxiously waited and many times even listened to the almost imperceptible but intelligible and one might even say articulated awakening of all those people whose eyes reveal the universal image of a new Argentina.

And the men who built our country built it in that way. Just like those men I have seen. And the spiritual impulse of all these men was one and the same. It was the severe exaltation of life in the midst of misfortune, in the midst of the bad or the good found all around, of failure or joy, of the sudden contingency, whatever the disaster or the success might be. I have seen them silent and fearless, still filled with emotion, severe with themselves and exalting life. Courageous. I don't know whether they are better or worse, but they are authentic.

I have seen them. And these are the "invisible" men of Argentina, the men whom I have seen create without deceit, live without false show, survive without resentment, carry on without that influence and "pull" which the apparently "great" men, the Pharisees and the Philistines,[14] flaunt at us at every turn.

Man's effort at the painful creation of a world has no comparison except with the effort of one who exposes himself to danger, who risks sacrifice and anger in the conquest of an art form, of a process of creating, as he laboriously confronts another material that is as indocile and hostile to him as the material of the physical world. But the risk to which that sacrifice and that anger whose purpose is the fact of creating are exposed is in no way a fruitless risk. From that marriage under the most difficult circumstances comes forth a new climate of sensibility. And that indeed is the climate of the true Argentina, of the genuine Argentina, of the Argentina I should like to reveal in all its ponderous and hidden force. In a dead atmosphere here we have a living climate, one pushing forward, the fresh wind that makes its way through the corridors and pushes in the doors. That wind nourishes two things: work and men's dreams.

There is no creative work that does not have its origin in an impulse of unselfish intelligence. There is no creative work that does not have its origin in an illusion, in the process of a fantasy capable of being transformed; without that recourse there is no work that does not wind up being the tedious repetition of a physiological effort and a vegetative routine. On the other hand, since the will to create is of divine origin, it imposes on the created product of an intelligent, applied tenacity that incorporeal, animated, absolute element by which it transcends the rules regarding the concrete and relates to the nonspatial, the sublime and the eternal. The act of creating is the most essentially spiritual act. More than four centuries of infinite aspiration is what brought about the miracle that stones of medieval architecture have less weight than any other building stones, except those from another, even more primitive age when that same creative unction moved all mechanical devices. There is always a spiritual element that fundamentally defines the greatness of a piece of architecture, although that element in its most basic form is merely the human risk involved in the work. Perhaps that primary spiritual element is all that remains of the skyscraper and the bridge, but if one of them comes to possess something imposing, its greatness will rest on that element. This is so because there is no greater dimension than that in which a person has transcended his human condition either through aspiration or peril, that is, just by faith and the way he has dared, and nothing less than that.

Ever since the period of national organization, the work of visible Argentina has become more and more a work without a dream, work devoid of spirituality. Physically, in the sense of a comfortable civilization, what has been accomplished is enormous; spiritually, in the sense of culture, what has been accomplished is nil, what has been done is to regress, to regress immeasurably, to lose ground daily. The more we deepen our observation, the worse our disappointment will be on verifying it. But it is not necessary to go very deep. The illness is at the surface and is recognized by its most obvious symptoms; just see the men who govern us in all spheres of public and academic life. They are infinitely duller, more mediocre, trivial, plebeian and individualistic than the men in the formative years of our nation, and if we were to examine their inner being, we would be repelled. More and more, Argentines have been working without a creative dream, that is—in a profound sense—without life, negatively, tellurically, with the obsession of quickly getting something in return. Such and such work for such and such utilitarian object, not for a purpose, but for an object. For these existences move, as we know, in the limited world of the means.

In this state of apparent order there is a repressed moral anarchy. Any one who approaches the places where the visible Argentina is at work will see the external signs of a prosperous and apparently fruitful industriousness. But what a devastating emptiness we find in all these teachers, in all those bureaucratically oriented people from the sciences and the arts, in all that ambitious falseness exalted to gain quick power, in all those industrial money lenders and magnates, in that whole group of loquacious and progressive-minded bourgeois! No flame stirs them, no unselfish faith accompanies them, no sense of organic development of the country as a spirit and as a body, as an entity capable of transcending itself by acts of creative intelligence lies within them except as the vague incarnation of vague ideals, in which the rudimentary positivistic concept of "well-being" and "progress" is always hidden. In no case do they feel that need for self-contradiction, for self-negation, for active doubt, for head-on conflict, for bitter and dramatic hostility to the circumstances of their life, without which no life is created because no life can be created except from cruel conflict, since there is even a struggle to be integrated among those elements of the body which, according to Zohar,[15] strain in the final hour to remain united, to be united even more before the ultimate separation.

Of what can we accuse this injurious Argentina with greater certitude than her lavish complacency? Giovanni Papini[16] was right when he wrote: "But I tell you in truth that there is no more certain sign of an impoverished spirit than being satisfied with everything." His words are even truer in our case, because this country has lived on that specious contentment, this country has fed on that contentment as the core of its well-being. It could almost be said that the visible Argentines are made of that contentment and for that reason are always ready to give up everything in exchange for it. Contentment? But what is contentment? Is it pleasure, happiness? No, it is a satisfaction that is satisfied with the satisfaction itself, rather than with its object. It is not pleasure or happiness because these emotions are essentially movements which elevate the spirit, while the kind of satisfaction we are alluding to here does not go beyond itself. It remains within itself and dies within itself, arid and without any continuation. A higher joy and ordinary happiness belong to the people, to humanity; satisfaction is a decidedly bourgeois state, a condition of class, a state of convenience after the possibility of risk has been averted. It is really a state of "no-risk," of living without "extensions," except the monetary ones, which, rather than extending man, gradually reduce him as do certain pathological formations. It is contentment without glory, the contentment of conformity, the contentment of those who are bored in a form of monotonous dissipation. It is the contentment of an animal of a lower species, of the mole or the alligator that lies in the sun and, as its basic function, just assimilates. It is the contentment of the wretched satisfaction that does not become happiness or take one further step to become joy, or run the risk of losing temporarily to win out eventually and become better and exceed itself.

How different are the invisible Argentines, the true authentic Argentines, the subterranean Argentines, those summoned to a tragic existence at the bottom of the well reached only by the star, a solitary barren well, with its vast abyss under the starry arc, with its alternation of night and sun and bad weather, deep dark well, permanent well! One group, garrulous and content, the other, on the plains at night or in the creative darkness of the city, or at the wooded edge of the mountains, or on the temperate coast or in the cold south, spinning its persistent silence, devoid of bitterness, all through the Argentine days.

One group, rich in its solemnity; the other group, solemn in its proud poverty. One group, shallow and trivial because life was too docile; the other group, shackled with the alternatives of a perennial resistance, resistance of earth, rock, climate, knowledge. One group, giving the appearance of things; the other group creating. The greatest difference was that when one of those small universes began to die the other began to live.

Notes

1. Rosario. A city of 755,000 on the west bank of the Paraná River, about 180 miles northwest of Buenos Aires. It is an important port, as well as a railroad hub. Its principal industries are oil refining, meatpacking, sugar refining, and the manufacture of beer.

2. Cordoba. With a population of 586,000, this capital city of the central province of Cordoba is the third largest in Argentina.

3. Mendoza. Capital city of the central Andean province of the same name. Population: 270,000. The city's diversified economy is based on manufacturing, petroleum, corn, fruits, and many other products.

4. Jujuy. City in northwestern Argentina with a population of 305,000. The entire province of Jujuy is extremely mountainous and has large mineral resources.

5. Tucumán. Province in central Argentina with a total population of 765,000 inhabitants. The western part of the province is very mountainous. San Miguel de Tucumán is the capital city. Sugar, alfalfa, corn, fruits, and tobacco are extensively cultivated. The University of Tucumán is an important educational and research institution.

6. Cuyo is an Andean region of Argentina, occupying the provinces of San Juan, Mendoza, and San Luis.

7. San Juan. The capital city of the province of the same name in western Argentina. Population: 110,000. The economy of the entire province of San Juan centers on agriculture, for which extensive irrigation is needed.

8. Angel Ganivet (1865–1898). Distinguished for his deep psychological insight into the essence of the Spanish character, Ganivet wrote an important essay entitled *Idearium español* (1896), which attacks Spanish lethargy and "lack of national will."

9. Lucius Annaeus Seneca (4 B.C.–65 A.D.). Born in Cordoba, Spain. Latin philosopher and dramatist of the Stoic school. Among his well-known tragedies are *Hercules, Troades, Medea, Phaedra,* and *Oedipus.*

10. Walt Whitman (1819–1892). American poet, whose verses praise the spirit of the common man, individualism, and democracy. One of the outstanding 19th century literary figures in the United States, he exerted a great influence on several Latin American poets, notably the Colombian José Asunción Silva (1865–1896). Among Whitman's many collections of poetry are *Leaves of Grass* (1855), *November Boughs* (1888), and *Good-By, My Fancy* (1891).

11. Alexander the Great (356–323 B.C.). The empire that the King of Macedonia built through his military conquests stretched from Greece to India. The reference here is to Alexander's famous horse Bucephalus, which he rode as far as India.

12. Fray Mamerto Esquiú (1826–1883). Argentine religious orator and dignitary.

13. Martín Fierro. The hero of José Hernández' epic poem *Martín Fierro* (1870, 1872), which treats of the struggle of a simple but proud gaucho against the central authority that tries to destroy his unfettered way of life.

14. Philistines. An ancient Aegean people in conflict with the Egyptians, the Canaanites, and the Israelites. The term has come to refer to an uncultured, unrefined person, lacking in artistic taste and sensibilities.

15. The *Zohar.* The most sacred book of the Kaballah or Jewish mysticism. The *Zohar* was first published in the 13th century and was written in Aramaic.

16. Giovanni Papini (1881–1956). Italian critic, essayist, and novelist. He was a leading figure of Italian Futurism. In 1921, a year after Papini converted to Catholicism, he wrote *The Life of Christ.* He is also the author of *Prayer to Christ* (1926) and *Saint Augustine* (1930).

V.
Scorn

Recognizing our own position toward the two worlds: Resistance and aspiration. Disdain for one kind of humanity, hunger for the other kind. Diffuse feeling will be swept away by energy emanating from the spirit.

I lifted my spirit and opened my eyes to that reality. I felt strangely full of anguish and rage. I was full of both hatred and love. I thought I had reached a fertile moment in my life, when the storm in our soul tells us which are our deep hatreds, which our deep loves, what it is we carry fragilely within ourselves and what is the unshakable rough and lasting part of us; what there is within us that has been destroyed and what there is of an invincible nature. And there I was surrounded by the two countries. One was the country I rose up against and refused to live in, the one I stubbornly wanted to avoid. And the other was the true, creative country, the country of mine, my country, much stronger than the other, in the same way that the deep undertow currents are much stronger than the surface waves.

It is delusive to believe that our loves and hates originate haphazardly. Those elementary feelings make elementary creatures out of us all, shelter us, and then return us to our own passions with greater strength, to the shores of our own being. And the closer we are to ourselves the more elementary we are. One neither loves nor hates instinctively or infantilely, and even in the least sentimental lover those stirrings of the soul are all storm and nothing by way of reflective continuity. To love is a dark storm and to hate is a dark storm, just like everything in the child who cries and laughs according to secret humors is dark. It is dark and instinctive but certainly not haphazard. As in the child, everything is tied to immanent laws in each organism. What we hate and what we love are the fruit of the strange flowering of our seed once it has died, the kind of good that can finally grant freedom to the confused, complex, and contradictory tangle of our social ills. To hate and to love are finally to know what we want and are perhaps the only means man has to clear the way within himself and get outside, a method by which he one day escapes his intricate jungle.

Rebellious on the one hand and deeply moved on the other, I recognized myself both ways in my resistance and in my aspiration regarding that world to which the more tied my destiny was the more extensive the universality of my thought would be. Indeed, there is nothing more accurate than André Gide's statement[1] that a writer is universal in the measure in which he penetrates deeply into the specific, and that Shakespeare or Gogol[2] or Rabelais[3] belongs to all mankind only because one is so very much English, the other so very much Russian, and the third so very much French. And besides, our anguished need to break away from our quagmire-like spirit and seek deep roots keeps us in an instinctively tentacular and investigatory penury until, at rest, we feel we are in the region whose terrestrial substance is what is best for our blood and what quenches this thirst for belonging to our land. What I would accept, what I would reject from these people, *that* I myself would be.

There was always a turbulence burning within me when in the presence of restaurant Boeotians, pedantic intellectuals, militant students, and other perplexed audiences I would inveigh against the archaic resentments of certain aesthetes, against literature in general, and against all forms of retreat from life's terrible daily reality. And I felt that this same turbulence had turned into deep scorn for all those traitors who with an air of cortical superiority—a higher consciousness, a higher civilization, a higher way of life—carried along their sick germs until undermining the lot of the authentic people, the lot of that other sacramental existence, that of those who lived with the severe exaltation of life, naked and natural before the object of their creation, exposed to the country's inclemency.

But this scorn soon began to be more than hatred; it came on after hatred and then it was no longer a blind rage but a conscious, furious opposition whose drama and consequences could unfortunately be played out only in my mind. Nevertheless, although it was no more than an apparently individual feeling, I wonder how many other individuals carried that feeling secretly, quietly, in the submerged country, in the country of the silent and the obscure within the larger, visible country?

These are the people who began to interest me, these silent, discontented people, that creative discontent. In what areas of Argentina did they live? In what physical regions? In what moral latitudes? What interested me now exclusively was their conversations, their faces; to read in them Argentine discontent. To feel them suffer, desire, think, judge, hate, and work. To acquire in a very tangible form the personal knowledge of what they could create in common, in a concerted effort, as an extension of their powerful fervor.

In university corridors, in centers where art is exhibited and literature discussed, in the newspaper editorial rooms, in theaters where one uncomfortably hears Johann Sebastian[4] or Pergolesi,[5] in all places one goes to in quest of pure exaltation, there I finally found many of these men who had a new ardor burning inside, a gravid fervor, an ardor ready to explode. Although not timid, they had a discreet and quiet appearance. They were strong, with a vehement and youthful strength. They felt restrained to speak out in an atmosphere where the word might suffocate. They were not taciturn, but in their whole manner there was a faintly perceptible joy. They were very serious, with a certain introspective repose, which is the internal process of the forming of a body. And they were not larval, but already formed in the sense that they possessed the form of their fundamental vocation. They were somewhat inhibited and for this reason even susceptible to a possible neurosis of frustration, by virtue of the difficulty in adapting their inner world to the world around them, to the tangible world. And all the while they were Argentines by nature, strongly Argentines because of the weight of years they carried within, because of the weight of the rich blood and the dense strength of the soul. And now they are soon to possess the way to give those invading and diffuse powers, elementarily formless, the form and will the spirit imposes on them.

The appearance of such a sense of intimate order, thanks to which a person's dark thoughts and actions find an exit through the small but lucid window out to the supreme air and the supreme clarity, is the most transcendent event of American existence. With such an appearance, in that sudden spiritual dawn, this world, overly subjected to the primary mandates of instinctive men as regards life and feeling, acquires its real liberation. Man tied to the water wheel leaves that heavy wheel and begins to walk, to make progress standing up straight, his eyes looking into the space he consumes, his mind busily engaged in forging his destiny, under the bright American sky. I approached the road these men travelled.

Once their work was externalized and articulated, once their action acquired coherence and consistency, these "new" men were to bring potent spiritual energy to a diffuse sentimentalism, to an overly vague and merely instinctive creative impulse, to a chain of disordered emotions. Without this primacy of an inner structure, neither man nor country can entirely fulfill its destiny as living, suffering, and thinking organisms, its true creative destiny.

Each time I saw this youth—men and women holding the new form of a destiny of which they were necessary atoms and which they were glorifying by simply living differently—I felt relieved of a terrible responsibility.

The collective crime in which I was involved—a crime of chaos, comfort, inertia, and falseness—appears to become absolved in the guilty and redeemed in the new, honest, inalienable, growing inhabitants of a country that seemed devoured by its own visible content.

Each time I saw them, I myself seemed to have gone on to something better than myself, to have suddenly been relieved of my anxious vigil, suddenly face to face with new men, with intelligence and valor written on their faces, in whom I could trust and to whom I could surrender my arms confident that just as long as I took refuge not in sleep but once again in concerned vigil and tireless meditation,

I would hear the isocronous sound of their steps, the sound of their being awake on a land asleep.

Notes

1. André Gide (1869–1951). French novelist and literary critic, awarded the Nobel Prize in 1947. Works: *The Immoralist* (1902), *The Counterfeiters* (1925).

2. Nikolai Gogol (1809–1852). Russian novelist and playwright of the Realist school. His fiction includes *Taras Bulba* (1842), a historical novel set in the 16th century, and *Dead Souls* (1837), a humorous novel dealing with a scheme to acquire land. *The Inspector General* (1836), Gogol's best play, deals with corrupt government bureaucracy.

3. François Rabelais. (1494–1553). Author of the monumental *Gargantua and Pantagruel* (1532), a long, irreverent novel satirizing French society.

4. Johann Sebastian. Reference to the great German composer Bach (1685–1750).

5. Giovanni Battista Pergolesi (1710–1736). One of the principal composers of the comic or light opera.

VI.
Kinds of Consciousness

A new world moving ahead. Inner freedom and consciousness of that freedom. The capacity for suffering as a virtue in a people. Need for resurgence of the various kinds of Argentine consciousness. Foreign thought. More than logic. The country does not grow by force, but with the growth of each person. The search for the authentic world continues.

I have known of some men whose concept of greatness did not go beyond the purely individual, but those men were not truly great. They were supreme egotists, confirmed cynics, eternal self-worshippers, illustrious neurotics who in spite of themselves sometimes succeeded in moving the collective spirit with the echo of their monstrous lack of human warmth. The others, the really great ones, the humanly great ones, have never sought to fill a desire for self-aggrandizement, but rather to be able to see contemporary reality, which always falls far short of their dreams, raised to a pure and general concept of the species. These men have not thought, lived, and felt for themselves but for all mankind, in the sense that they have aspired to make living less painful. They have dreamed of a less suffering and freer humanity, a humanity more closely resembling in earthly things what it can conceive of intellectually. The others, those who think only in more or less metaphysical terms, wanting nothing to do with the temporal destiny of men and their happiness in the valley of life, have always seemed to

me the worst Christians, the worst men, the least able, whatever may
be the level of their logic and the theoretical scope of their intellect.

As far back as I can recall, I always felt an affinity to those who feel,
think and live in terms of humanity. At first, I thought there were
many in this group, but I soon realized there were very few. Mankind
tends more and more to think in personal terms and less and less to
extend its ideal dialect beyond that radius. But out of that minority,
out of that quantitatively more limited and qualitatively more extensive way of thinking there will finally emerge whatever the best group
obtains for the worst group in all collective arrangements.

There was something deeply rooted in the world of America and in
my preoccupation for man's inner self that made me conceive of greatness not as a possible individual ascent, not as a small eminent island,
but rather as the progressive and symphonic march of a whole entity
consisting of the greatest possible number of human units. In this
concept there was something as clear as a graphic image—the image
of a world which by ridding itself of its ballast, previous bonds, instinctively animal passions, anger and resentments, deeply ingrained
hatreds and spirit of vindictive persecution, might progress in such a
way that everybody would participate with equal consciousness of his
fundamental part in the whole. Always the image of marching ahead;
that same image that so many times has made me see my own life as
something too motionless, too static and inert with respect to what
the contemporary world needs by way of proper direction for each
soul, by way of a clear, vigorous commitment.

But deep inside me, where my passion lay, there was no inertia. My
whole spirit was moving ahead, eagerly moving ahead. I was like a
prowling and hungry gray wolf, my eyes inflamed from seeking so
intensely, lightly brushed by the vigilant and eternal light of my longing.

This longing had no limit. It pursued me, it lived with me, it
hunted me down, it did not let me live, it was with me at every moment, the whole day. It was that desire for unity that the several parts
of an organism feel when they are mutilated in body and suffer from a
lack of wholeness. How are we to live in a world that rejects us not
because of our deep differences with it, but because of its basic anarchy, because of its link to fatal necessity and not to the function which

may make out of that necessity something subordinate to a greater will, not to the will of living with a potent and natural fullness? What was my world of America but denaturalized islands, islands sick with the illusion of their own personal dominance, removed from all integral and creative concepts of life.

Where was the origin of such confusion in that world, of such anarchical character? It was not hard to answer. That external world lacked freedom, that external world lacked consciousness. In its visible exterior, it was a world of freedmen, not of free men. And in its deep interior, that is, in its hidden and good part, it was a world that still had to struggle tenaciously against that other world in order to clear the way and live something more than a hidden, embryonic life. The vast sun and the unfettered space of America covered their best merchandise with a false pavilion. These men passed off their best merchandise as contraband. The pavilion was the proud, haughty, vain, materially powerful, and despairingly vacuous life; and the merchandise was what it carried hidden in its mother's womb.

What this world needed, then, was growth—growth is birth incessantly renewed. What this world needed—and how great that need was!—was to grow in the direction of its inner freedom and in the direction of the consciousness of that freedom. Harmony is not possible, or at least lasting harmony, even between two mere human beings, except when those two senses are developed. And no other process is needed: the harmony brought to a spirit because of the presence of these two senses continually places that spirit in harmony with the real world, with the world of surrounding reality. When that harmony is missing, man experiences his own disintegration, although he hides behind a glimmering show.

But to say harmony is to say growth, because harmony is maturation. And maturation implies, in the organism where it is produced, a development of pain. The cells become distended, the tissues suffer vegetally. When man matures, his capacity to exist and to learn is what enables him to endure suffering, to sustain the effort to conquer himself in order to go beyond one state and reach another higher one, to go from the particular to the universal, to multiply and add to what he already has, to exist and to learn from knowledge. And in Ecclesiastes, "And he that increaseth knowledge increaseth sorrow."[1]

Knowledge adds sorrow because essentially it is sorrow, because it is maturation of knowledge. Like men, nations that have not suffered know only limited greatness. And this sorrow is what confers on man and nations a heroic sense of their destiny and a state of potential greatness. Nothing is attained without passion; the quality of some men's passion is what accounts for the greatness of nations. We should be suspicious of America's happiness; let's not look far for our proof. As far as Argentina is concerned, only during her periods of hardship and suffering has she shown her real greatness: the prolegomena of her emancipation, the internal building up of her national organization, the years of America's emancipatory campaign, and the age of tyranny have been the open doors solemnly ushering in a corporeal and forward-moving greatness.

It would be foolish indeed to deduce from this that we must rush forth in search of sorrow, as if it could be found on the outside. But the capacity for suffering—and I am not saying the vocation—is fundamental in a nation, and that capacity is so inherent in human consciousness that for it to exist requires only that consciousness truly exist.

Therefore greatness is engendered in conscious suffering not only because, as Gide says so well, "suffering makes us greater; when it does not bend us it molds us and hardens us," but because that suffering is consciousness in itself, consciousness of existing and consciousness of the transitory drama that each of us performs on the tiny, finite state we carry with us from one side of this earth to the other.

The rest is triviality; the rest is feeling that we live in the most grievously frivolous atmosphere. It was the way I felt I was living as long as my life's journey did not reach the grave and reflective zones of invisible Argentina.

I carried this Argentina in my own sorrow. And the more suffering that reality afflicted me with, the closer I was to Argentina. In the moments of greatest uncertainty and torment I touched her; like me, she was all consciousness in those critical moments. Consciousness, what we needed was consciousness.

There is consciousness when a man leaves home at dawn with God's newborn light to harvest the fruit of his sowing, and knows what he has planted in his fields and what he wants to reap and with whom he will share that fruit in summer's favor and winter's adversity. Consciousness is when a man of the city who knows both joy and sorrow restrains both with worthy exaltation and without triviality. There is consciousness when a man accepts for his work only what is good for his work, for his art only what is good for his art, for his business only what is good for his business, for his craft only what is good for his craft. And he practices all of this without committing the crime that threatens to be perhaps the most heinous of our time and which can be designated most appropriately with the words "invasion of humanity." There is consciousness when a man grows without invading, without material or spiritual transgression, caring only about a principle of authenticity.

Our people would not again match its historical greatness as long as its growth toward a more creative nature was not again active. The great living contingents remained paralyzed; the only thing in motion was the monetary mechanism involved in purchases, in large financial undertakings, and in the fluctuation of the products on which the country speculated. But at the heart of it all was just a lot of words from some and a great silence from others.

It is out of this silence that we shall see the different kinds of Argentine consciousness emerge: the moral consciousness, the historical consciousness, the intellectual consciousness, the human consciousness. Ask an average Argentine—I used to insist—what his land is. He will scarcely be able to stammer about a certain valor, a certain nationalism, as if any kind of nationalism can exist without historical consciousness. Ask an average Argentine about his literature. He will speak to you about some vague books, about a "national literature," as if a national literature can exist without a consciousness of literature "being lived" rather than literature "being made." The most he will utter is some isolated titles, names of books, words. Ask an Argentine about human values and he will barely answer you by mentioning the social status with which he usually identifies himself.

It is when all those forms of consciousness leave their embryonic state and take shape that we then shall begin to grow from the part to the whole, from potential matter to the form, to use Aristotelian terms; in the same way, when there is consciousness of a feeling of love the desire to unite with the loved object definitely begins. Not before.

What happened before was this long, long wait to bring our consciousness to fruition.

*   *   *

Our city was too big; I found few people. Once, I came across some men from a small provincial town who seemed preoccupied and worried. With the same insistence I asked each of them some questions. With the same persistence, they gave me answers that were not always explicit and clear, but which in essence contained the same things: the worthy, severe, human exaltation of their vocation, of their discontent, of their worries and their desire not to incorporate a personal lie into a universal reality.

Harsh and at times intolerant people, like the yet unformed bird that an egg carries inside, to which it must give life and for which it struggles and bleeds. Our history, our geography, our real wealth as one of the largest and most powerful countries in the large and powerful continent contained the fundamental essence of our nation and this essence was unknown to most Argentines. However, our history, geography, and wealth constituted the matrix of life and in that matrix was the seed of an incomparable future, the future of that world of consciousness and freedom which I returned to hour after hour in my deep reflections. When and in what way was this world going to leave the matrix?

I saw and spoke to a few foreign intellectuals who were passing through. They were men of high intelligence who had come to our region to say pretty words to us, but their knowledge of our inner being was no better when they left than when they arrived. They were philosophers, thinkers, and writers who, because of an inevitable weakness in their intellect, proposed to fit our moral landscape into the dialectical prejudice they brought with them. They were all brilliant men who held professorial chairs, but how trivial they were in the way they comprehended humanity! More than once, in short, feverishly hurried encounters (the fatigue of intelligence brought on by their hastily made trip, the sudden disorder caused by mental stress and strain in the life of these thinkers and lecturers) I tried to explain to them the sense of our subterranean nation, of our invisible humanity they did not reach. They looked at me as if I were a dreamer, because what they understood here with their merely logical instruments were only pragmatic circumstances, external anodyne, modes of being without any interest.

More than logic was needed to understand the "other" Argentina. More than logic was needed to know the inner soul of an Argentine province, to sense the real values of life among those simple, humble, slow-mannered people beside a colonial church, next to the sound of the streams, under the nocturnal darkness in which the heavens descend and everything expands, grows, and dilates in the humanized space, in the recumbent and timeless space, suddenly flooded by the tide of that dense, corporeal collective feeling that has the same form, the form of the vibrant and vast plains; in the space from which there arises, like the humus of the ground, an incalculable aspiration, a striving from the ground upward—something that will rise up without losing its own extension, without losing universality, humanity.

More than logic was needed to understand—that is, fuse mind and object—the struggle of those youthful Argentines who study and make honest mistakes in their desire to give themselves what the country without teachers, generally without historical consciousness, practically without religion—outside of certain books which are not read but just alluded to and certain old, insipid anecdotes—has not given them, namely knowledge of its own destiny, knowledge of its roots and its growth. Yes, more than logic is needed to understand the tremendous burden borne by that vast youth that wants to accept only the roads of truth, an authentic and free existence in the midst of an odious tangle of prejudices, false values, empty idealism and enthroned pretension.

More than logic was needed to reach the point a few of us had already reached. To see with all of the body's eyes, the eyes of the blood and the skin, painfully, the ascent of those spirits toward their own integration, most deeply dramatic stages that can be witnessed in a person's innermost being. And those foreigners, those thinkers, those men committed to a life of reflection, were fundamentally only men of logic. My contact with them, however, was a valuable experience in another sense, too, since, without their help, without their direct presence, I would not have been able to perfect, define, and extend a general concept of history, and what is more important, of racially, historically, and socially responsible man face to face with the problems of today.

Another concern deeply troubled me. Generally speaking, nothing that exists around us exists except according to our own measure. In the measure that our perception is small, so too will our vision of the world around us be small and our landscape small. When our view is full of wisdom, the landscape becomes larger and multiplies, the detail takes on an instant richness, the blade of grass not only reveals its coloring to us, but also instructs us in the universal form of things and urges us to meditate on everything created. Likewise, as regards human relations, the greater is our knowledge of a person's secret expression, the greater is our faithfulness to that person. Nothing is truer than the truism "Love is blind," but it is so very true not because of its quality of being a truism, but because there is no one who sees the world better than a blind man, since what he sees he sees by feeling it, that is, by "being" it. (And besides, there is nothing that sees more than love, because love sees so much that it manages to see even what does not exist; thus, not only the sublimation of another human being, but also jealousy.)

And I said to myself: "If my land is small, it is small to my own measure. I am so insignificant that what surrounds me is also insignificant. As a few of us grow, the existing and inner invisible Argentina will grow along with us because its apparently undefined present state will be defined in us. We must know what this invisible Argentina contains better than Argentina itself. We must know fully what it has that is different in its different parts."

I made up my mind to increase my erudition, my formal knowledge about America, in all possible ways. Yet the term erudition has always been repugnant to me because the sin of the word is always close by. And besides, what I learned from reading so many theorizers on Spanish America was just lyrical lessons, an idealistic body of information in a larval state, mere notions, bits and pieces slightly swollen, hyperbole.

America's destiny will not move forward by words alone, but by the hope and desire of human beings—I assured myself— by a particular way of existence made of pure life directed from the inside out, just as the trusting man and the prescient man go through life without any sort of inhibition. America's destiny is a progressive incorporation of free souls, but the acts of those free souls can not live in an old world, which would be against nature, but have to live in the world those people are to create with the deeds of their free living.

How can the limits of that world be set beforehand? The frontiers, the irregularities of terrain, the horizon?

The space I moved in was already quite inhabited by the owners of that world in formation. I had left behind the whole ostentatious collusion of the visible Argentina, but that was not enough. In each case, it was necessary to inquire into the deep concerns that lay hidden in those silent consciences behind a sallow Argentine face, behind an attitude devoid of gestures.

Day after day, I myself was surprised on that journey towards the essence of new, unknown souls. It was a moving journey. I threw out my books and demanded new, human verifications. Neither the landscape nor any other form of nature except mankind held my interest. The streets were small for the image of that daily journey.

I saw a man and endeavored to capture the real meaning of his words, to see through his external attitude, to do away with the conventional, to reach that fire, that passion which must be lodged in the most protected corner of his person, to discover the failure beyond the apparent satisfaction, the anxiety beyond the laughter. The desire for love, the heavy and stately look that the women had—what secret story were they hiding, what feeling for the humanity all around did they have? Did all those men of the city meet these women's needs or deceive them? I compared some foreigners, Europeans, women I had known before, attractive women of fine character, with these Argentine women, with these reserved, very beautiful Americans, who speak little but are prudent in what they say and intrepidly curious. The difference was in explicitly knowing or not knowing what they wanted. Knowing what one wants is the only triumphant liberation from the larval state of one's being. When a person knows what he wants there is joy and action in him. The human response was scattered throughout the city—in the theaters, parks, hotels, libraries, museums.

Previously, on other occasions, I delighted in awakening in the country, when the dawn sent its first red legion to attack the night. Other times, too, I looked forward to spending long hours in deep reflection—along the rural roads, walking alone beside the high fields and large ponds of still water. All of this was now replaced.

At this time I had absolutely no interest in anything except human destinies in their incessant variability and changeable manifestations. I knew that these men had new attitudes about their country and I wanted to incorporate them into my way of living. This could be possible only if I incorporated them personally into my deep anguish. At times, many times, I returned home without having encountered anybody of interest. No such student, no such talented actress, no such dabbler in esoteric philosophy had showed me anything worthy of being picked up, thought about, and loved. They were sad days. On the other hand, when I finally met through an unexpected third party a person of deep passion after waiting the whole day, I suddenly became emotionally excited. I felt I was not alone in my loneliness. I felt happy; thinking of my country became tolerable to me. I felt that the very best of my country was cumulatively becoming part of me in a very human way.

I felt I was in a new country. I returned to my study, content but no less anxious. Those destinies must be united, must form one body, must make themselves felt in the nation's soil. With the knowledge I gradually gained from those I met, I began to know the nation in all its living strata. But since I did not have the makings of a boss or leader, the taste of failure was already on my lips. I couldn't help in anything. And besides, however strong my feeling was about this nascent world and my experience with its isolated, scattered symptoms, what I could give them of myself was far too little. In no way could I add ingredients to those they already had. The most I could pass on to them was their multiplied and extended presentiment of a truer world, the re-finding of the great destiny as a nation which they had seen lost all around them, as well as a fervor, a fervent love for their cause.

The most I could give them was that. But, considered in the light of such an urgent necessity, that and nothingness were one and the same. My impotence and my grief because of that impotence then became overwhelming.

Notes

1. Ecclesiastes 1:18.

VII.
America

A house in Vicente López[1] and its
unexpected inhabitant. A vision, a
man's work. The symphonic whole.
Reflections in the street. Working to
understand the thought behind the
truth of America.

At this time a writer[2] from another part of America came to Buenos
Aires. His reputation was already established and many people listened to his words. But the real sense of his message was scarcely understood and soon forgotten. It was not an easy message, but a very
difficult one. Yet it was not his language that was difficult, and his
overall conception of the problems was, in the words of one of Juarès'[3]
biographers, as diffuse as it was exact. What was difficult in this message was not its external content, but rather its assimilation, and if one
was not willing to live that message fully, it was totally useless, for
then only the isolated words would remain.

Before this man came, I knew a book of his called *Salvos*,[4] which
contained valuable critical essays on the French theater of the Vieux
Colombier and on Charlie Chaplin. I also knew particularly well his
Our America. This book and a recent reading of some other works of his
would have been enough for me to marvel at the outstanding qualities
of that man. The morning he arrived I was at the dock and he already
knew something about me through a third party. He told me he was
going to live in a small house in the Vicente López suburb and that I
should go to see him there that very morning. I did. After a few hours

he confided to me in general terms his fundamental system of thought. His thought was important in this respect: it was a completed whole. In spirit, his thought was ecumenical. And that same morning I resolved to work with him on a Spanish translation of some lectures he would give in Buenos Aires. The theme of those lectures was not abstract; the theme of those lectures was America.

He was a man of small stature, with a young and brilliant light in his clear eyes, a loose lick of hair, small snub nose, and the slow walk of those on whom the permanent exercise of the intelligence imposes a harmonic and unhurried rhythm, the tranquil walk of the sowers in the North American meadow. He took pleasure in what was all around him and by just seeing him one could tell that his instinct, his mind, and his senses worked constantly to give him a quick understanding of things. The house in which he immediately took up residence on the morning of his arrival belonged to a fellow American who had had it built on the outskirts of Buenos Aires, in a secluded spot, among high eucalyptuses and bead-trees, in accord with the architectural principles of the Southern United States. In that two-story house—the first, ground level, the second, with a garret—with dormers on the red roof, one could breathe the fragrant atmosphere of Louisiana or South Carolina, with the triangular-topped door between the thin temple-like columns. And through the windows, which allowed tongues of white muslin to escape to the cool morning air, could be seen the buttresses of the large comfortable rooms, constructed for a harsher climate than that of this Argentine suburb where the trees were abundant and the sun shone daily with great regularity.

What that man had suffered, toiled and lived through, what that man held in a state of inalienable and solid purity was simply enormous. Born in New York, he forged his own basic character with such austerity, with such rigorous discipline and steadfastness, that he seemed to be a figure out of the Italian renaissance, except that to that humanism of exclusive aesthetic and vital transcendence—that is, the form—that man added the compassion, the profundity and the religious fervor—that is, the essence—of one of the holy warriors of the millenium. And I should add that there is no hyperbole in this, but that, on the contrary, even that literary praise seems too inert, too verbal to describe an intelligence so alive in its comprehension of uni-

versality and in its tragic and constructive sense of things and events
and their interrelationships. Of course he was a very naive person, but
like most just people in the eyes of cynics, all spiritual creators are
naive people. Those who are able to understand Pascal's Thought
#687[5] know this all too well.

Contact with Van Wyck Brooks,[6] the polemic with Orage,[7] and
the literary proximity of the great revolutionary creators of the new
art of the United States—whom Frank brought together and directed in his magazine *Seven Arts*—nurtured this intellect, in which a
present and also a provident consciousness of the American problem
seemed for the first time to take full shape, since in turn this consciousness had been fed on a highly defined, sensitive conception of
the medieval Catholic community. The effectiveness of a man lies in
his knowledge of the hidden order in all diversity. Such hidden order is
what is called "sense" and the one who discovers the sense of the surrounding disparity will be the only one not devoured by it. As the
scope of Waldo Frank's work grows, that is, grows in diversity, at the
same time it summarizes, concentrates, purifies and perfects its inner
unity. The larger in scope he has made his culture, the more that culture is one. The more things, circumstances, peoples and countries he
has studied in their fundamental structure, the more exact is the analogy in which he discovers they are all linked.

Frank's moral explorations into the inner soul of the motherland
Spain and the tropical jungles of America, far from being antagonistic, are elements that abound as a very powerful reasoning process in
fashioning his personal concept of the New World. I once had to in-
troduce Salvador de Madariaga[8] at a lecture he was giving on Argentina. He perhaps had read and repeated that expression "New World"
many times and held that it was a somewhat artificial designation,
somewhat false, coined by American youth. That is not so. It is obvious that the expression does not belong to American youth; it belongs
to the spirit of the Conquest and to the Spanish frame of reference from
which it emerged. Originally full of meaning, the expression today is
devoid of meaning. What is important is to develop and rebuild the
original concept and assure the continuation of its original meaning
and spirit. Waldo Frank, the newcomer, knew what the two words of
New World contain: new spirit, American spirit.

With what emotion, with what gratitude do I recall those days, those fresh mornings in Waldo Frank's transplanted house! We were two men committed to the American cause: one, distinguished, older; the other, unknown, younger. One great, the other insignificant, but both aroused by the same devotion. How well I remember the many conversations we had along the cobblestoned road in the town; the streets of shiny pavement among slopes of recently watered grass; the afternoons of hard work after returning from the city at my prescribed hour, meticulously examining the words I was to translate from English to Spanish at the same time that Waldo Frank's typewriter was feverishly tapping away in the nearby room; the nights of vehement conversation under the stars! His whole vision of the American world (our universe succeeding the European universe, the germinative sense of the Indian, the one and indivisible power of the great masses living between Bering Strait and Cape Horn) seemed to be summed up and miraculously diagrammed in the Milky Way. And he spoke with his precise, emotionally moving method of argumentation; his lucid ardor, his harsh obstinacy over the problem of replacing the effete, European order by a recently created order, by an order about to be articulated, uncontaminated. And I listened and looked at the same stars in the September sky. The voice I heard was an American voice; the night was American. Nothing impeded the course of those two ambitious imaginations: one, firm in its wise and guided projection; the other, full of illuminated delight before the greatness and truth of the concept I was listening to. Finally, not one unnecessary word, but much caution, a sure, cautious progression in the way that man spoke, as if the testimony of the cosmic world, of that sky, those stars, that beginning spring night, all imposed their admonitory and watchful rigidity on the possible boldness of two lips. And what he said was expressed with just words, because he was fundamentally a just man.

This man longed for an orderly and joyful world. Son of an old bourgeois family from the United States, he grew up in a disordered world, where order was replaced by a handful of simple "traffic rules." As a reaction to this, Frank believed, thanks to his acute hidden sensitivity and to the integrity of his creative genius, in the possibility of establishing a world in which the primordial harmony of things would be set up in accord with the structure of the medieval Christian universe, when each living particle existed without being restrained or denaturalized simply because each one adapted itself to the other and the balance saved the whole. "Theoretically, man has had power in proportion to his responsibilities toward other men." And each human being's happiness was limitless because it was directed to God, just like each thing was directed to another thing with which it had an interdependent relationship, and God is not the limit of anything, but rather an extension. He imagined himself remembering May Day in happy pre-Shakespearian England, when circles of children played around the phallic-shaped pole, in the shadow of the cathedral and next to the huts and tents of the acrobats and merchants—children already carrying within themselves the fate of future men whose needs would be totally fulfilled between religious aspiration and the desire that life inflames both in the sinner and in the righteous man. But what he asked for was not a smooth and simple return; what he asked for was the appearance of a civilization that would originate in the same way that the culture of the Mediterranean people did, the culture of Egypt, Judea, Rome . . .

I observed the sensible, judicious, prodigious, Christianly sensible way of speaking of this man who possessed above all other talents the ardor of a mysticism that was not fanatical, not rapturous, but truly profound, grave, and unwavering, pure in the implicit purity of its honesty. Frank dressed simply and had a sober and informal appearance, somewhat sportive in his lightweight, light-colored tweed suit. But that inherent valor, that non-abusive, balanced handling of the idea, that deliberation in which there was at the same time a great capacity for logic and a sharpness of mind and intuition, that essentially poetic condition characteristic of his deepest reasoning—all this combined to give this New York artist that wisdom that religious men of seclusion exercise over the worldly and the secular by uttering just a single, very elementary word. And not in vain does this monastic image come to me, for there was definitely something ascetic about that man of thirty or so because of his deeply felt contemplation and the truth of his character.

Frank soon began the tedious part of the work he was to develop in
Buenos Aires: the days in which he had to finish in eight hours an
eight thousand word lecture. In the new house in Vicente López, the
typewriter keys clicked ceaselessly and the noise died away in the indolence of the great drooping locks of the willow tree, and in the
haughty branches of the eucalyptus, in the patio, the middle of the
archipelago of flower and green vegetable beds under the summer sky.
With the ink still fresh on the pages, I took the recently finished essay
home with me at night, and after eating in the silence of the city
around midnight I began to work on the translation until dawn. More
than once, when the thirty-odd pages left me sleepless, I got up from
my work table on noticing that two lights were already falling on the
manuscript: the light from the lamp and the light of dawn. Then I
went to the open window, put my elbows on the window sill, my soul
full of that American song that went from one language to another and
in which there not infrequently appeared references to Thoreau's
thought,[9] Melville's myth or Walt Whitman's solemn and abundant
charm:

> Once I pass'd through a populous city imprinting my
>   brain for future use with its shows, architecture,
>   customs, traditions,
> Yet now of all that city I remember only a woman I
>   casually met there who detained me for love of me,
> Day by day and night by night we were together—all else
>   has long been forgotten by me,
> I remember I say only that woman who passionately clung
>   to me,
> Again we wander, we love, we separate again,
> Again she holds me by the hand, I must not go,
> I see her close beside me with silent lips sad and tremulous.
> Before me lay the nocturnal city, the river. The calm.

Before me lay the nocturnal city, the river. The calm. The night.
Without the constrictive urgency present during the day, the dream of
all those destinies moving ahead pounded in my spirit: the capital city
held those destinies and further on, to the east, to the west, north and

south, the whole country held them. This silence was Argentina, this purposefully directed deliberation and not the daily shouts and noises of a stupid and vain bourgeoise. This silence was the state of aspiration, the other was expiration, that is, death in the form of empty words, death brandished on the sorry gestures of angry clamor. To aspire to is, in itself, to live; and the people sheltered in the deepest layer of this nocturnal metropolis never ceased aspiring, continuing in their aspirations toward a more complete life in which art, faith, joy, culture, vocations, responsibilities, and obligations, when they became broader and more manifest, would raise everybody's existence to a higher level. Is it possible to describe the sensibility of certain kinds of youths whipped at the same time by all the winds of anguish, aspiration, uneasy hope and desire?

I then returned from the window to my desk, turned off the lamp and continued working in the growing light of dawn. I still discussed the text, got up, re-read a paragraph, gestured with my head and mouth without speaking, entangled in vehement disputes with myself over some parts of the message I was translating which hours before ceased to be a dialectic text and became the magical touchstone that explicitly opened up before me the history of the United States, from the epic arrival of the Mayflower to Huckleberry Finn's[10] slowly riding up the wide, mighty Mississippi. The whole process of America's slow growth seemed grandiose to me, in a way crucially different from the acts of integration and disintegration of the great historical European empires, from the inordinate and cyclical violence of a Caesar or an Asiatic Genghis Khan;[11] America's strong, deliberate, immense development, those millions and millions of leagues of land which stretched out before the men moving west—all of this was undoubtedly different in meaning from those other heroic deeds. The heroism of America had a different rhythm, and in this rhythm was a fundamental essence that had to do more with holiness because of the imperturbable, ascetic, and permanent quality—its sense of eternity—of the courage displayed. It was the simple rhythm of man's work on earth. I not only felt this; it was an image before me. I saw it, I saw it even as an hallucination. It touched me, it made me tremble, it moved me to tears with that simple, emotional stirring that even the most humble workers must have felt when they built the cathedrals.

When I finished my work one early dawn, unable to sleep, I went out and began walking along the long drive that turns sharply at the Retiro[12] and then goes up toward the beautiful vegetal gulf of San Martín Square.[13] I walked up that ruinous street toward the English Tower[14] under the row of yellow arches, and then I walked down along the gray street that in a sudden, short movement continues on towards the city's vast flat area along a green hill bordered with second-class lodgings and restaurants. I felt absolutely alone with my land, walking in the awakening moments of the deserted streets. In El Retiro, a bird started shouting out its song with a cold throat, then was silent. There was no wind, only that daily mist that gathers in front of the sun. The moment of dawn and the whole atmosphere invaded my being. And as I walked with my eyes full of distant visions, I could touch my country's different boundaries: the jungle north, the uninhabited mountain ranges, the frozen south, the ocean. I was a different person. I was made of such different parts that, when they all joined together in the depths of my being by dint of their will to unite, there was just one resonance. And both the joy and the suffering of this humanity giving birth to itself were mine at the same time.

When I reached the square I saw a young woman dressed in black come through one of the side streets. Her face was very white and her body trim. As she drew closer to me I saw that she had intense black eyes, encircled by a dark area, the sad, timid eyes of many Argentine women. She had a cautious look. Instinctively, I followed her for a few steps. The great Argentine dream would perhaps be materialized in those grave and suffering eyes, in that rhythmical and rapid step that indicates a haste to arrive. What is certain is that I saw her pass by, disappear, become lost from view along Charcas Street behind the square. In that same way, at once corporeal and fleeting, our country went by unknown before the eyes of most Argentines. I thought again about the lethargy of some and the insomnia of others. That woman was perhaps a harlot because she had not found her destiny, or perhaps she had found her destiny once, intensely living one minute, a few immortal moments, just like the woman in Whitman's poem. I felt all around me the vegetal presence of people in the center of the square. What a city! What a civilization! How imposing and vast was all that construction over an area that fifty years before was just flat wasteland. A universe now, a stone cosmos.

In a half hour or so, all this ground would be invaded by the active masses, the work regiments, and later on in the evening those same regiments would return home. With what feeling? A feeling of fulfillment, of well being within, a new desire spurred on deep down in their heart? Or nothing more than the habit of construction, not of creation, of construction, the material habit? Were these people given the freedom of their own joys, were they permitted those joys, did they allow themselves such joy? Did they allow themselves a sadness that was more than physical? Or were they a people nostalgic for their songs, for their music, their dances, a people nostalgic for another life, for life? Ah, I knew that deep down in their physical well being these people made the same tragic conjecture that Schura Waldejewa, the Russian peasant girl, would later make, that tragic conjecture that Astrow relates and Unamuno repeats: "What does it matter that I am seventeen years old and they call me a girl?" The disillusioned worker Schura Waldejewa says, "What they should explain to me is what I lack; I don't know. The young people say I'm rough and evasive. Perhaps. What I do know is that my character is bad. But where does this come from? If I knew I could correct myself. Courses in political science? Yes, I attend them. And if it's socialism? I know, the subject has been dealt with. The fact is that distribution is made not according to needs, but according to capacities. What I would like to know is for what reason we are really living. Now we go to work, return home, go to meetings or whatever. And afterward? What is this all for?"

Yes, that is the tragic question, that is the sickness of the conscience. "And afterward? What is this all for?" And this illness does not have to appear clearly for us to suffer from it. We suffer from it when we obstinately close our eyes to what occurs within us, to what the unique particle of each person demands, claims, wants to bring also into existence. The worst is that these people who in a few minutes were going to invade the city, the square I was walking through as I was thinking, continued obstinately to insist on not recognizing their inner road, in not recognizing that they came from somewhere and that it was necessary to know from where. Because if not, what is the purpose of placing one stone on top of another, when the only person giving orders is an inept foreman? Who guides that immigrant who comes here—what does he know about what his children will become? How many know this? Ah, the question, Schura Walde-jewa's tragic question! How many know what they are, what they want to be in the visible, functioning, dominant Argentina?

I headed back home. This bright American, Frank, knew our way of life, our destiny. Many—yes, now many others—knew it. And when a certain knowledge is propagated, it becomes a state of natural science. What I longed for was not any different; it was this state of natural science with reference to what we are without resembling others. We are diametrically different from a Frenchman, a Finn, a Rou-manian. Why? In all those works, in all those writings I was translat-ing, the answer was clearly stated: that we are a new world. But that was not enough, it did not seem to me a sufficient answer.

There was something else to know. What part of that new world are we? I wanted to tell it to this North American whose passion for the whole was revealed with increasingly disquieting religiosity. I wanted to tell him about the powerful forces of nature on which our possible adherence to a new human order is founded.

When I returned, Waldo Frank was already waiting for me. It was six in the morning. Together we looked over the translation. A noun or an adverb gave us reason to speak of this or that recent discovery relating to the theory of style. The books he published as well as those he had written but then destroyed had given this great artist a clear, definite idea of his vehicle of expression. Each verb or adverb was mea-sured carefully and given an exact meaning in the overall construction of the sentence. We spoke about what he had written, about his North America; I still was not mature enough to speak about what was really on my mind. That maturation came later and it seems to me still con-tinues. But at least at that time the important thing was his message and I applied myself with all my strength to assimilate it. Of course there was something more transcendental in Frank than the intellec-tual concept of an American civilization. With this concept, flesh and spirit became body in him; and in this way the concept could not be false, theoretic, or capricious, but vital in the same way that the movement with which we dodge danger, sing a song, or compose a poem is also vital. One of the most potent instruments of his creation was the metaphor. When the metaphor is a good one, there is no form of thought equal to it in its preciseness, in its appropriateness, and above all in its function as a necessity, because reasoned discourse may not have, and does not have "necessariness" in most cases, but a metaphor always does.

Therefore, the excessive pretension of the logicians is laughable because the greatest moments in the life of universal thought have been produced by means of the metaphor formula. And Waldo Frank's whole creative system, his whole America, is a living metaphor, that is, a reality resolved in the form of beauty. And the accuracy of this is provided by merely stating it, without other verification, without even giving in support Spinoza's aphorism, according to which reality and perfection are the same thing. And since to say perfection is to say beauty, to say perfection is also to say metaphor.

I admired his beautiful and confident America, his beautiful metaphor of America. I admired his warm, moving speeches on the artist's mission in his country.

I admired that spiritual leader's tremulous devotion, when, before a frequently difficult public won over almost always by the persuasive charm of his wise, harmonious flow of words, he would explain his sense of the real meaning of America and of that transcendent destiny by which a chaotic splendor—that same chaos against which the "gold theory" of the first prophets (Hawthorne,[15] Melville, Poe,[16] Thoreau, Whitman, and others) unsuccessfully struggled—would gather the elements of its constructive newness into the bosom of its turbulent instinctive life. In short, I admired the extreme clarity with which his mind organized and classified historical data. Thanks to this clarity of mind, the spectacle of New England's tiny theocracies, the neo-Greek sense of slavery in the southern states, the basic inclination toward physical and industrial expansion, the puerile democratic gropings, in brief, the whole conglomeration of small anarchical systems, ceased to give the appearance of chaos and disconnectedness and seemed to us to have a healthy unit of purpose from which we could learn and benefit.

After his lectures, we would frequently go outside with Frank and slowly take in the fresh air of the new night full of myriads of electric lights and luminous advertisements. The white dust was the aureole of the sprawling city erected on the vain continent. We entered Florida Street's narrow channel and the tiny streets off it. But if those streets were narrow, the city's breath was the breath from an enormous mouth that opens in a gesture demanding nutrition, the breath of a limitless, rough surface. Frank was at my side and I felt that he stopped, looked down the interminable street, thought a little and then said to me, putting his hand in my arm, almost without supporting it: "If these two terrible poles, if these two great metropolises of America should one day unite their incomparable strength in one culture . . . , if for once their synthesis were the solution to our progress in this world . . ."

His eyes shone in the crowded street, lit up magically. The halo of shining power surrounded us both when we again walked toward the southern part of the city, toward the wide diagonal avenues. But what was missing was not this ostentatious and material hegemony, what was missing was the other power, the true one.

Both of us were there, however: two men, two masses consisting of cells, viscera, vegetative needs, senses, skin, hands, eyes. We were two organisms fundamentally undifferentiated, barely differentiated in form, two bodies equally inept to resist the inevitable disintegration, physical dissolution, and death. Yet those two organisms were going beyond pure matter through their will: one of those organisms was tied to the other by thought and conscience. My concept of things rose hierarchically on touching that other man's thought. In turn, his thought was directed to the thought of other, higher categories. Our two organisms were two atoms in different states of aspiration, but each organism was necessary to the other in order for there to be living dialogue. And if we touched on some point by which we might overcome biological need, it was through that act of understanding that spreads out and ascends and is finally the true victory of the species over other vegetative classes.

The American problem was simply the spontaneous outcropping of the conscious essence of its human foundation, and the accommodation of what one human being is to what another human being is, without any pretense. A community, a country, a culture, are good only because of the wholeness of that established harmony. All naturally created forms are attained through that harmonizing of the component parts, from the most common flower to the exaltation of the liturgical song, and the most important thing, then, is that each part have an adequate idea of its quality as a part.

That night, on that street in Buenos Aires, I would have fervently wanted many other men to join us, thereby giving us something and also taking something from us. The great man walking by my side well knew the will he aroused in some of us. He knew that an army's morale is ultimately no more than the morale of a few men. And since he understood the nature of the emotion he had aroused in the spirit of some men not only in Argentina but also in Mexico, in Peru, in Cuba, and also understood how that emotion could be spread, he was quite certain of not erring in heading his message with the names of four young Hispanic American authors, for he was convinced that they had created more than a mere literary work by translating their wide readings into Spanish.

Notes

1. Vicente López. A suburban area of Buenos Aires, named after Vicente Fidel López (1784–1856), neo-classic poet of the independence period and President of Argentina from 1827–1828.

2. Mallea is introducing Waldo Frank, American essayist, novelist, and critic whose sympathetic understanding of the Latin American spirit greatly impressed the Argentine writer. Along with several other men of letters, Frank founded *The Seven Arts,* a monthly liberal journal of ideas and literature. Frank, with Van Wyck Brooks, edited the journal. Although shortlived (1916–1917), it was very influential in its time and included among its notable contributors H. L. Mencken, John Dos Passos, and Theodore Dreiser. The liberal social philosophy Frank expounds in his essays also appears in his novels, such as *City Block* (1922), *Chalk Face* (1924), *The Death and Birth of Daniel Markand* (1934) and *The Bridegroom Cometh* (1939).

3. Jean León Jaurès (1859–1914). Orator and socialist leader of France. In 1904, he founded the journal *L'Humanité.* He is the author of *Socialist History of the French Revolution* (1901–1907).

4. In 1924, Frank wrote *Salvos,* a varied collection of twenty-one essays on literature and the theater. The longest of these essays, "The Art of the 'Vieux Colombier' "(48 pages) deals with a French theatrical troupe that visited New York in 1917.

5. Pascal's Thought #687 reads: "I do not say that the *mem* is mystical." *Mem* is the thirteenth letter of the Hebrew alphabet.

6. Van Wyck Brooks (1886–1963). American literary critic and historian. *The Wine of the Puritans* (1908) explores the conflict between material and aesthetic values. This theme is continued in *America's Coming of Age* (1915). *The Flowering of New England, 1815*–1865 (1936) is a brilliant study of America's cultural and literary traditions.

7. Alfred Richard Orage (1873–1934). English journalist, publisher of the socialist newspaper *New Age*. Orage was a staunch proponent of theosophy, a religious and philosophical doctrine whereby a knowledge of God is sought through intuition and other processes.

8. Salvador de Madariaga (1886–1978). Spanish author, diplomat, and cultural historian. He served as Spanish ambassador to the United States and France. His disagreement with the policies of the Spanish Republic forced his resignation from political office in 1936. Madariaga took no active part in the Spanish Civil War, but during his residence in England in the 1950s and 1960s he openly attacked Franco. With equal facility he wrote in Spanish, English, and French on a wide range of literary topics. Works: *The Genius of Spain* (1923), *Englishmen, Frenchmen, and Spaniards* (1928), *The Rise of the Spanish American Empire* (1947), *The Fall of the Spanish American Empire* (1947).

9. Henry David Thoreau (1817–1862). American essayist, poet, and naturalist, born in Concord, Massachusetts. He wrote the classic *Walden* (1854), an account of his two-year retreat at Walden Pond in which he extols the virtues of individualism.

10. Huckleberry Finn. The vagabond protagonist of Mark Twain's famous novel which bears his name. The work was written in 1884 as a continuation of *Tom Sawyer* (1876).

11. Genghis Khan (1167–1227). Notorious Mongol military leader whose conquests stretched from India to Russia.

12. El Retiro. District in the northeastern part of Buenos Aires, near the Río de la Plata. It contains the Plaza de San Martín.

13. Plaza San Martín. Beautiful square in Buenos Aires at one end of elegant Florida Street.

14. The English Tower. Prominent landmark in El Retiro, near the railroad station.

15. Nathaniel Hawthorne (1804–1864). American fiction writer whose works express the Puritanical spirit of nineteenth-century New England.

Works: *The Scarlet Letter* (1850), *The House of Seven Gables* (1851), *The Marble Faun* (1860).

16. Edgar Allen Poe (1809–1849). The American poet and short story writer is widely read and acclaimed throughout Latin America. Poe's poetical works include *Tamerlane* (1827), *The Raven and Other Poems* (1845), "Annabel Lee," "Ulalume," and "The Bells." "The Gold Bug," "The Pit and the Pendulum" and "The Purloined Letter" are some of his best-known stories. See John E. Englekirk's *Poe in Hispanic Literature* (New York: Instituto de las Españas, 1934).

VIII
Meditations

*The Baltic philosopher. South
American meditations. A
non-philosophical terror. The
American world lives by recreating
itself. The emotional order.*

And it happened that at about the same time another spectator[1] conceived among us his spiritual counter-song to those attempts at harmonization. Nothing positive, this time, but a kind of crazed intransigence, a kind of delirious howling denial of our continent, a kind of absurd mental terror like the fainthearted man's cry in the desert night. This Baltic count who flooded his life with torrents of champagne and devoured the whole menu in one of the main salons of a certain luxury hotel in the city, was a giant of a man with a thin beard, Mongolian head, and small, cold eyes of steel who had established his School of Wisdom in a German town and now traveled around the world in a drunken rapture, affirming that one of the pillars of the creative "motus" in the consciousness of the Spirit was the way in which his imagination transformed the Universe.

And no doubt he did transform it, just as the demented man twists the sensitive relationships among things by an act of his liberated genius. Just as this giant pointed an accusing finger at our continent's self-struggle in an atmosphere of telluric apathy, and the world did not tremble but rather his tremulous index finger, it was that very spirit he was defending that virtually came out the worse for it, because the Baltic count stormily argued dangerous issues solely on the basis of the most elementary intuition, decked out—let's not say articulated—with the most skillful and astute rational techniques. Let us see how shortly afterward the philosopher from Darmstadt was to formulate his already artificially matured ideas, his Hispanic American experience, his "reptilian" world of South America:

> The frenzied and reptilian sexuality of the South American is also one of the reasons for South American melancholy . . . *Post coitum animal triste.*[2] What predominates here is the state of mind of the exhausted male frog or female frog swollen with eggs to the point of bursting. Just as in the virgin forests of the Amazon man feels he is being devoured, here he senses how he is sinking in the slime of his own abysmal world. The exuberance of South American life is never found under the sign of joy. I have defined Argentine life as a muted, secret life. At night, the streets are submerged in darkness, the faces are impassive, every one speaks in a subdued voice and a laugh is considered a lack of tact. The most extreme decorum is observed in everything and everywhere. And all of this to cover up an internal wasteland.

The Darmstadt philosopher continues:

> "The South American is the totally and absolutely telluric man, the man of the earth. He is just the opposite of the man who is conditioned and transfixed by the spirit. It was not possible for me, then, to face him with the organs of comprehension I had; new organs had to be formed in me, not without painful difficulty. Just as the Bolivian puna[3] threatened to dismember my body, the vibration I felt in the rhythm of Argentine life alien to me put my psychic balance in danger for a long time. This circumstance found its expression—inasmuch as the body is always the quadrant of life's clock—in prolonged attacks of 'perpetual arrhythmia,'[4] as symptoms of the interference of two incompatible melodies. But in effect such danger hastened the formation of new organs. During their development, I gained a new perspective from the Earth itself. From that point of view everything takes on a very different aspect from the one it has when seen from the Spirit . . ."

Had I read these things at that moment, I would have considered them indifferently. But they were written afterward and then read by me not in a moment of affirmation but of doubt concerning everything around me. At that time I needed to revitalize my faith not only in my own existence but also in its relationship to the existence of my natural surroundings. Thus, that revitalization could not be achieved except by bringing about an act of affirmation through an act of hostility from which I would bravely save something. And I fought against that unjust and precarious thought which an insufficient stay in Hispanic America and a very vertiginous contact with our animal and vegetable abundance had aroused in the Darmstadt thinker, in that remote resident of Prinz Christiansweg Street.

I have never reacted to books except by treating them as persons, and on finding myself with Keyserling's *Meditations,* the answer reached my lips from deep within me, just as quickly as the red, sharp pain that certain flagrant injustices bring to children's faces. There I was before a man who appraoched brilliant purity when he touched on general truths, and stammered, became crazed and frightened when he touched down on earth. The abyss attracted him, as it does certain airplanes, reducing him to the dreadful falling of a leaden mass. The one who believed he had transported his spirit to the highest degree of supremacy, that is, to absolute dominance over fear, was truly terrified when he came face to face with naked nature where good and evil live unintimidated by that very civilization which had made him lose himself along the road of fantasy, in the abstract tangle of symbols.

Everything in our America frightens him: a reptile, the sight of the jungle, the very color of the vegetation and the earth, life in its free explosion. And a puna that attacks him in the Bolivian meseta causes him in his delirious terror to set up the false dialectic by which he reduces a part of the universe to primordial and telluric laws of the third day of creation. This man whom I had seen drunk from champagne—sunken in a sofa at the Friends of Art with all the weight of his voluminous body—his mouth full of saliva, wide-eyed, his forehead soaked with sweat like a priest in the most barbaric ritual, suffers before the violent truth of the American land and before the almost magical phenomenon of a world structured on a slow and progressive union of its separate parts, the most unforeseen of horrors. His serenity characteristic of philosophers is disturbed, his spirit raves, and he becomes terrified and barely logical before the symbols his terror suggests to him to express that world which he feels corresponds to the darkest regions, to the most fearful abysses of his own being. For him everything on this continent seems to be in a mineral and inorganic state. According to Keyserling, the only function his imagination should have is the specific one of transforming the universe, but this imagination, instead of transforming what it finds into creative feeling and spiritual justification, examines it, rejects it, abominates it, trembles, feels a turbid repugnance, and fights to reduce that reality which escapes from him through all his pores to the primary intuitions of his predisposition and delirium.

The pullulation of medicinal herbs in the jungle, the wild, uncontrollable unleashing of the plant kingdom, lead this frenzied philosopher to reduce everything that grows around this vegetation to mineral and vegetable terms. He extends such condemnation to the whole continent and incorporates the surrounding human sign into the sign of the reptile. And his attitude is that of the mountaineer who becomes terrified at the vision of monstrous species in the dim halls of a museum of natural history. Why this abdication of knowledge, since there is no knowledge where a panic occurs? Actually, the term "terrified" would define better than any other the true psychic condition of this interpreter of worlds as he came to confront ours. He reduces his entire interpretation to the land, to the telluric, for the simple reason that the land possesses him and he loses the possibility of subjecting it to a "non-terrified" examination.

On shouting out his horror before so many human beings imprisoned by the land, it is he who reveals how he is suddenly imprisoned; and only from time to time, when he himself is liberated, does his spirit confer on the Hispanic American people the hope of their own liberation. He himself is a victim of the condition he imposes on them, since the more authentically improvident and generous a person is, the less able is he to conceive of a zone of humanity dedicated to prejudice and sordidness. And so the philosopher from Darmstadt deceives himself; the world he sees is not what his imagination in a state of purity would produce. The telluric world suddenly surrounding him is only the reflection of his own telluric fright. The world the fearful perceive is full of fears.

Keyserling acknowledges that "freeing oneself of the land is indeed the goal of all efforts at individual perfection." But it is the term "freeing oneself" that is used mistakenly in the definition. What he should have said, instead of "freeing oneself," is "to raise oneself from." All effort to attain spiritual perfection should tend to raise us up from the earth. (Indeed the spirit says: ". . . from the earth we come and to the earth we shall return," that is, destiny which transcends the earth without rejecting it). And this act of rising up consists precisely of ceasing to be in dread of the earth.

Only a thought overwhelmed by fear, terrified and confused, could see in our America the image of a wasteland. America's gesture today is that of lifting herself up; indolence is an original experience already surpassed on this continent. Whom can the grave, silent march of a new world frighten but someone who trembles from his own unsuitability before the conditions of this world, someone who suddenly sees the floor he believed firm suddenly crack and tremble under his feet, someone who shouts out?

This earth is Creation in its mobile, eternal body. Earth is what is created; compassion and mercy are rooted in the earth and therefore we can not unbind ourselves from it without having nourished even spiritually our roots in it. The man possessing the highest spiritual perfection, the saint, has done nothing in the course of his life except lift himself from the earth, but with his feet always in it, just as the tree has its root in the soil. He has lifted himself from the earth only in the measure in which his roots were strong, for the terrestrial absorption of a Saint Francis[5] or a Saint Augustine was indeed very strong.

Perfection comes to a person through the way he has freed himself from the terror which the telluric danger produces, the same thing Keyserling calls the reptilian quality, the jungle's blind and cruel voracity. A person ought to be on earth without becoming frightened. This is what the Darmstadt philosopher has obstinately wanted to forget.

All powerful impregnation of life and humanity comes from a profound feeling for the land, because what this feeling determines is co-possession with the object toward which it is manifested. Color, essence, substance, come from the land in different forms; the powerful impregnation of life, the spiritual anguish and the feeling of cosmic grief also came to a Tolstoy or a Dostoyevsky from the land.

And all that exists on earth is in a state of regeneration—in a state of growth and incessant multiplication.

When I read Keyserling's *Meditations,* I was struck by the contrast between the truth of his objective observations, the vast and exact sense with which he treated the loftiest human concerns, and the misleading quality of his theorizing on Hispanic America. At that time I tried to discover the origin of this anomaly and noticed that it lay in that dark recess of his soul (at once rancorous and terrified, resentful, not without a strange and remote indignation) from which the author could not free himself when speaking of South America. And that fundamental terror and rancor, and the hatred that comes later, certainly recreated a world—according to the theory of creative fantasy the Baltic philosopher expounds—but in his image and likeness, that is, a world of fright and terror and hatred. It is a world on which the author does not confer in any way the benefaction of mobility, but rather an inexorable stagnation.

But, in spite of that cautious spectator, this world lives on and is recreated in its constant mobility, in constant regeneration. The reptile that terrified the philosopher in the dense jungle, the puna that filled him with indescribable terror, the sudden arrhythmia that seemed to him the terrible claw with which it fatally knocked him down, the monstrous visions that assault him ("an indefinable body, woman, serpent, animal and octopus at the same time; hands and feet emerging like slippery tentacles, like pseudopodia, and a narrow little feminine head, . . . serpentine beings especially resembling eels, that first form of the eel immediately after the larva, except that they are not translucent, but, so to speak, transparent in the darkness," in short, all those obsessions that constituted the essence of his fear of South America are normal, living organisms which, lacking the immodest deformation to which the philosopher's feverish magnetization subjects them, fulfill not only their frightful function of hate in a universe, but also their discreet function of love. Their discreet function of love in the world of jungles and lianas next to the leaf and the fruit modestly suitable to live and be fulfilled as existences beside the huge tree. If this clash upsets the philosopher's psychic balance, the reason is that that soul was inclined toward unbalance and not because the South American world waited for him brandishing its terrible threat. If the vision of a tree carries us to a state bordering on delirium tremens, why blame the tree? It would be better to say to ourselves honestly: the deformation lies in us; should we drag the others in with it?

I found ridiculous and puerile the Baltic count's insistence in ascribing to South Americans, beyond their delicate cordiality, a reptilian coldness. It seemed to me that feverish skin poorly distinguishes temperatures, for if there is one thing in South Americans that is strong and well-defined it is the warmth of their blood. And that unjust insistence seemed to me a flagrant contradiction of his reflections on the emotional order or make-up of South Americans, reflections that are perhaps the calmest, richest and deepest that have been made on this essence of the South American soul.

I found in this meditation on the emotional order of South Americans the important and true axis—that is the point at which reflective power thrown off balance by its own abundance and self-tolerance regained its lost equilibrium—of Count Keyserling's thought. The South American world of desire, of delicacy, the world of emotion, constitutes for him, in short, the state of inertia, an abysmal order prior to the spirit, which is by definition mobility and consequence, intensive concentration as opposed to the extensive concentration characteristic of the emotional order. Before sustaining, and in this way revealing his true comprehension of the transcendence of this order, that the clamor raised today throughout the world demanding a new kind of social community will not be satisfied by means of a "rationalization, nor by a collectivism, nor by social security, nor by a Welfare State, nor even less by means of the extermination of individualism through a Communist mentality, nor through a restoration of the Christian cosmos (for in a universe whose slogan is "once and never more" there can be no restoration of great importance)," before sustaining that the new human community can be restored only through the "apocatastasis[6] of the emotional sphere as such, through the reintegration of the emotional order, which has its roots in desire and is nourished by sensibility," before sustaining such conjecture, he has agreed that the richest and most profound emotional world of our times is the Hispanic world. This confers on our order a destiny which is in a certain way messianic, despite the fact that it is an order not determined by the spirit. But he can not deny the fact that in the greatest periods of Hispanic history there has always been present a feeling, that is, a principle that defines the reason for the goal (something which must be for Count Keyserling the touchstone of the spiritual). And likewise, in the origin of all South American peoples, in the will of their ancestors and in their highest deeds—an already elevated and purified expression of collective inspiration—there exist in their ideal form that will, that principle, and that objective which by their very essence are image, consequence, and spirit.

Count Keyserling* does not seem to know the deeds that shaped the American people, indeed is unaware of the "sense" of its original thought, of its literature and imagination, of its inspiration, and in order to enunciate his general postulates, he has taken the reality of our nations at its point of new pregnancy, in its state of *second* pregnancy. The frequently somnolent and sluggish sight of pregnancy— pregnancy of destiny and therefore of consequence—has been interpreted by him as telluric blindness. He has extracted from Argentina's soul only the image of a life sunk in emotional apathy, in the swamp of sweet and heavy blood, submerged in its lack of inspiration.

It is true that his first error has been in not knowing (in order to see only the characteristics of the undifferentiated mass) the individual expressions of early art and thought in America, since these forms are the highest and therefore the truly symbolic. If that error were the only one in his point of departure, it would still be a very grave defect. But there is more: even in that undifferentiated mass, where he stops and goes no further, what he denies regarding America's inspiration is not something that "does not exist," but something that he has not seen. His intuition is that of the hurried traveller. His inspiration is fecund for itself, but absolutely sterile as regards the world he sees. On the other hand, and I say this in passing, I have never seen an imaginatively richer and at the same time less logical spirit. I have never seen a

---

*It is strange that he has not cited the thought of any of the prophetic men of South America, except a short sentence from Bolivar[7] which was—how could it be from this creator!—a negative sentence.

work in which contradictions and accomplishments are more irreparably mixed. Of course, if this were not so, he would be a man dominated by logic, instead of a creator, an improvisor, because no man so dominated by logic creates in the supreme sense of the word. The imagination is free and manifold, therefore contradictory and beyond logic. But for that very reason, what the imagination should not set out to do except with great precaution is to systematize. The greatest contradiction in the world is a dogmatic imagination.

I don't blame this man. It was difficult for him to see that which is too deep and profound to be perceived haphazardly with a hurried look. That grave sense, that exaltation of life harbored in the deepest recess of the Argentine heart, and which is based on the union of the Spaniards' traditional "manliness" and a certain dramaticism produced by the reality of a flat and deserted land; that consequent will to be superior to the destiny determined by an indomitable and often adverse nature; that having to create everything, even the health of its pain and the light for its darkness, as it is removed from guides, signs, and paths already made; that deep essence of emotion and cordial openness of spirit, that spontaneity of soul, that manifestation of feeling in an active and not a passive sense—all of this could not appear except as a world to which one must surrender or, if not, from which one must flee in terror, a world which puts too many obligations on the soul, too many obligations on the blood, although of course few on the spirit.

But is the spirit anything more perhaps than a conscious and determined drive of the inner man? The nature of that drive is the "sense," to use the term dear to the Darmstadt philosopher. The spirit is the expression of supremacy over mere form, in so far as that expression has supremacy, and in turn expression is related to knowledge as laughter or tears is related to that which causes them. "It was in the form of an image that the spirit burst forth as a new element of Creation." The spirit of America is thus tied to its knowledge (about which I have already spoken in another section), that is, to its discovery renewed in each American. What matters is the American image we carry as a promise to fulfill and an agreement to carry out. The strength of our spirit depends on how much that image is imbued with spirit; spirit of men and spirit of nations. And the sense of that image, its value, will mean the sense and the value of our contribution to the universe.

Notes

1. Mallea is introducing Count Hermann Keyserling, the "Baltic Philosopher," born in Estonia of Russian parents. As a philosopher who tried to bridge the gap between Eastern and Western ideas Keyserling exerted considerable influence in the European intellectual world. At Darmstadt, an important industrial and commercial city in West Germany, he founded a "School of Wisdom." For an interesting commentary on Keyserling in America, see Doris Meyer's *Victoria Ocampo: Against the Wind and the Tide. Op. Cit.,* pp. 49, 50, 73–91.

2. *Post coitum animal triste.* Latin phrase meaning "After coitus the animal is sad."

3. Puna. Arid, cold tableland in Peru and Bolivia, inhabited by the indigenous population. By extension, the term here refers to the icy winds of these regions.

4. Arrhythmia. Medical term for any form of irregularity of heartbeat.

5. Saint Francis of Assisi (1181–1226). Founded the Franciscan order of the Roman Catholic Church (1208).

6. Apocatastasis means "restitution." In Christian theology, it is the doctrine that states that all sinful men will ultimately be restored to a holy state before God.

7. Simón Bolívar (1783–1830). The great military hero of South American independence from Spain.

IX.
The North, The South

*Search for authenticity. The country
as sorrow. A woman of Florida Street.
The Puritan phenomenon and the
Hispanic phenomenon. The moral and
the spiritual. Stroll through the park.
The Argentine spiritual aspiration to
reconquer its rhythm.*

Once again I, I nobody, I all fervor confronting that body of women and men whose laborious sleep—"The embryo's grave and deep sleep"—none of those strange meditations had perturbed. No heroic action, no greatness in me, nor any other kind of concern except urging men to give to others what they carry hidden in themselves. Because of a pause in my life, I couldn't tell for how long, matters concerning my deepest feelings were polarized in that violent desire for human love. Nothing tore at my soul more than that silent march in the desert.

They were eight difficult years. There was no affective human experience I rejected. Men and women filled my life like the human swarm that comes to meet the arrival of the sailing ships in the old water colors seen in books of the sea. It was strange that I should come out of each adventure without any sorrow, just like the one who goes out after a bird and is lost in the thicket, without his prey. But hope went forth in constant sallies, like the famous Manchegan[1] in the dawns of his illusion because "in our mutual dealings with each other, in our human spiritual commerce, we all seek not to die. I shall not die in you, the reader who reads me, and you shall not die in me who writes this for you." And that is what I sought, not to die, because each person I found had in me the possibility of my rebirth in him, the possibility that the parts which were causing my death—through deficiency or absence or illness—could be redone and integrated in him. But in the end, all we do not possess, all we stop possessing and still want, is a deception of our spirit. And when it eludes our will to love it, that is to incorporate it into ourselves, to possess it morally, that evasion is deception, sadness of the flesh as well as of the spirit, even when our motive is entirely spiritual.

And everything in my life happened around that time in a kind of respiratory or pendular rhythm. After the departure, the return. After having become deeply involved in the eager exploration of another nature, I returned and found I could not tolerate my solitude, but had to tolerate it, had to suffer segregation because of my disillusioned anxiety. It was so difficult to find in men an architecture of the soul and in women a certain mobile spirituality akin to the essence of their nature!

And then, the visible country without passions and without God. Because having God is not just going to pray in a temple and organizing public charity associations with the money collected in the exercise of non-charity. To have God doesn't mean just crossing oneself or taking off one's hat on walking by a church, nor having that almost military forbearance, without unction, without faith. There is only one way to have God and that is to carry Him inside. But how does one carry God inside without fire, without passion of the spirit, without the perdurability (not emotional, but even more, passional) of an ardent and lacerated state of consciousness. Because to feel consciousness of sorrow is not to have lost joy in any way, but to know there is no joy not surrounded and contained by an area of more extensive and general sorrow.

For that very reason there is no trivial passion, but on the other hand there are trivial emotional states. Passion always supposes a heroic vocation of the spirit and purely emotional inclinations give a diffuse sweetness to the soul!. By virtue of what grave defect were Argentines always inclined toward this? A simple examination of our basic literature allows us to appreciate how difficult it is to discover the whole, real, living man in the books we commonly read. It is a literature of rather vague emotional experiences, generally undefined, where the inevitable frequency of certain words like *nostalgia, remembrance, sadness, indecision, uncertainty, horizons,* reveal an oscillating fluctuation of the creative instinct. And this reveals imprisonment in the vegetative emotional states, certainly pre-spiritual.

Just as the character in a certain tragedy, in the night beset with grief and floods, wanted to fill with his body all the space occupied by sorrow, so were those eight years of mine full of the desire to be filled with a feeling of exhilaration for my land. But I could not tolerate the absence of passion, the dispassion imprisoned in its emotional cantons, the passion that remained emotion. It seemed to me that I myself was involved in that general inertia of spirit. Again! I would then have wanted to punish myself, to humiliate myself, to destroy all the non-vigilant parts of my body, all the soft parts. I reached the point of crying because of my impotent mediocrity, of dragging myself toward my house from the maze of streets, with a never-ending pain and anguish, in my long purgative night.

More than once as I was walking, some person stopped me, a servant or a grief-stricken woman, one of those humble souls. I stopped to drink with them the cheap liquor of countless bars, away from the urban pomp. And if I could listen to someone's life history, the account of a passion, the living recollection of a great torment, of a tragic moment, or an act of courage or of shame, I felt revived. The yellow breath of the electric bulbs fell on the black pavement and my eyes also walked along that pavement while I strolled and listened to some of the tragic stories. They were stories of truly living life, not of "representing" it, not of posturing, not of non-living, not of appearing to live, like my visible country. Naked life stories. In my anguish I felt a common bond with these people. I would have given my life's blood to redeem one of those obscure and at times banal tragedies and thereby restore health to a human face. I felt torn, flayed. And I would have wanted to compensate for all the cruel hostility of the city gathered in its deliberate and indestructible mutism by never ceasing in my desire to understand and accompany, in my need to have compassion.

Nights, long dense nights of Buenos Aires! Nights of search of souls lying in wait for the truth, whether it be in a stone, in a bit of green park, or in the magnificent rebelliousness of an insurgent, of a malcontent! Disgusted with so much ambient convenience and so much digestive heaviness in the slow-walking people! Nights of facing the city's soul alone, the real soul, with the gradual solemn unfolding of its nights of intense, vibrant living, all of it concentrated in its sky and its ground like no other city, tightly packed in its severe and disdainful dignity, like the men of the invisible Argentina!

Nights of expectation shared in my Buenos Aires with the stardust and the imperturbable sense of time.[1] Painfully crossing sidewalks, intersections, squares, porticos, with no noticeable company except the clouds, the rigidity of the constellations, the turbulent echo of inner harmony! At times, in my pocket, a book with Bunyan's story[2] or Ana Vercors'; other times, with empty hands, a rumpled suit, but my heart, not despairing, my inner feelings in perpetual vibration like the sea anemone's tentacles, all of nature like a hand, alternately inclined to the caress or to destruction, to calm or to fury: ready. Must all those dispassionate people, all those inert men, all those diffuse souls be punished until taking the blood of passion out of them? And how they even seemed to boast of their condition like the Asiatic Philistines! Proud of the somnolence, recumbent, invertebrate! Ah, it was necessary to die in these people in order to reach the others! How to be reborn in one form if we have not died in the preceding one?

But—I thought during those walks—did this land, "our land," belong to them? It belonged less to them than to me and less to me than to those who felt it even better than I, that is, to those capable of feeling it not as it is, but with their own consciousness exalted, in the condition it may seem to them after succeeding in making the land better, after making the land better in themselves. And since drama comes from doing, the land belongs to those capable of feeling it as drama above all other feeling. To feel the land as drama!

All those visible Argentines felt the land ignominiously because they felt it as pleasure. As empty and unsubstantial pleasure, as their own pleasure. They felt it festively, for to feel festively is to speak of it frequently, brandishing rosettes and singing hymns, as if the hymns did not have to be redone to resuscitate them, to make them be more than just words. What they had is a vocal sense of the country. And I saw them pass by and was disgusted, because they were the dead weight, the subspecies, the inertia of progress, the worst of all hindrances.

Around that time I met a strange person. She was an extraordinarily beautiful woman from the United States who had retired very young from the stage and now earned her living painting scenery in the rear of a small shop on a silent street of the city. In that woman everything was expression, so much so that she seemed almost exhausted in her physical appearance because her whole being was overturned, emptied of substance, because she gave of herself in all her spirit and beauty. The most surprising thing there was in that life was its rhythm. In that fragile beauty, in that sleepless spirit, in that life, what there was above all else was rhythm. She was born in a small southern town in the United States, I believe in Florida, and had a negro milk brother. Through what strange contagious process did she acquire from those extraordinarily rhythmical negro people that harmony, that sweet and sonorous-like symmetry of the spirit? She made me think a lot about that northern country, frequently and so many times unjustly slandered. (From Thoreau to Hart Crane,[3] they have a literature with much greater unity than the modern literature of any of the countries that arose culturally in the Mediterranean region.)

If America is a unity, then the first thing we should make clear is our individual difference as parts of that America. The woman I am speaking of, for example, had nothing Anglo-Saxon in her spirit; perhaps she was Anglo-Saxon only in the moral aspect of certain habits, but not in the general harmony of her inner being. But my intuitive and empirical experience regarding the United States had given me different information from that suggested by the case of this unusual woman. However, the point of contrast, like the point of reference, is decisive for certain sudden clarifications. She helped me understand that country of pragmatists and idealists, of pragmatic idealists or idealistic pragmatists, since what is fundamentally characteristic of them is a certain goal that is even more than utilitarian, that is oriented toward manipulative self-interest. This goal involves giving to Caesar not only what is Caesar's, but also a little of what is God's, and giving to God not only what is God's but also a little of what is Caesar's. (Basically, this is perhaps no more than the application slightly more humanized and made slightly more puerile—in the good sense of the term—of the old British principle of conciliation, of compromise, discreetly observed by André Maurois[4] in a study on the character of that nation which was three times conquered by Rome but in which nothing remained of Roman times except for the English themselves, as Chesterton[5] said.)

That woman who resembled the worthy, genuine Argentines (authentic Argentines, that is, those still in a state of purity), carried deep within her all the characteristics that differentiate our people from the people she grew up with. She was like a sublimation of certain persons illustrating this difference. She was certainly symbolic. She was born at the juncture of the two American spirits: that of the Spanish conquest and that of the Puritan settlement. In Florida, where Spanish ambition had reached, after Ribault's Huguenots,[6] in the person of the "cruel disbeliever" Pedro Menéndez,[7] to establish the settlement of Saint Augustine; in Florida, the oldest city of the United States, where fanaticism savagely spilled the blood of Frenchmen and Spaniards. When I learned of this later, through reading United States history, many things in that woman's character became clear to me. The unity of causes and motives throughout the world appears to me more and more miraculous and surprising. The more I extend my appetite for experience and learning among things and men, the fewer seem man's most basic principles. The more woodlands a man goes through the more he discovers that the tree is like himself. What measures the idea of God's unity is in fact the diversity of the species created.

However much one insists, one still insists rather little on the Puritan phenomenon and rather little on the Hispanic phenomenon, the two antagonistic focuses, the two crucial antipodes of America. During the time I spent in Buenos Aires, days of confrontation with the good and the bad of alien ways of thinking, not only did I frequently conceive of such a difference, but I lived the difference, I resided in it, because we do not advance one step in our destiny without having cruelly felt in our own flesh the conflict of the two cells fighting each other, making each other bleed and rejecting each other in the encounter between the essentially moral and the essentially spiritual. The anchor and the high seas. The piece of wood nailed down represents the moral, while the free, consumable space is the spiritual. They are the two points of view of the feeling of eternity that destroy each other.

There was something magnificent in that woman's nature. Since I have never believed in the conventional virtues that give prestige to some men, but rather in the intrinsic worth and quality of certain kinds of individuals, my whole being was anxious and emotionally prepared to observe the manifestations of that feminine soul, even the apparently least significant ones. She spoke all about the land as if in a trance and described the meaning of her dances as something magical and extra-human. She spoke of her life, of her experience, of her passions, of her fortunes and misfortunes, with a spirituality that was just the opposite of rapture but which resembled it because of its quality of weightlessness. And her whole being appeared to be so close to the earth that she had freed herself completely from men. She had freed herself; therefore her being had all the freedom of the universe for her ecstasy and her rapture, her spiritual freedom and the admirable spiritedness of her rhythm. The land was grateful to her for such an act of levitation; and these gifts, this multiplied gift, were her gift.

They were the gift of those who live in perpetual freedom between heaven and earth, unchained, uncompromised, unafraid. According to the Anglo-Saxon spirit? No, but according to the eternal spirit of Spanishness, according to the feeling of eternity that breathes in the original soul of the Hispanic world. And we know that nations are great or small according to their own feeling about eternity. Did not Alonso Quijano[8] believe he was as everlasting as eternity, and did not Juana la Loca[9] and Hernán Cortés believe the same thing? If one of them had hesitated, as Blake said of the star, if one of them had recognized binding chains for his dream, he would have stopped shining, the fate of his impetus would have been the fall. But they were made of self-prodigality and of freedom, and in this measure their destiny had no limits.

Self-prodigality and freedom. Made of rapture and as infinite as the lands, the seas, and the clouds; made of eternal aspiration. And here is the difference between two types of humanity: one group for whom life is a potential "much" between two nothings; the other group, for whom life is a vexatious nothing between two abysses of eternal greatness. I don't know whether the first group belonged entirely to the Anglo-Saxon world, but the second group certainly belonged to the Hispanic world.

I loved this in that woman whose dominance over life had something supremely zenithal, something holy and elevated like the life of certain emaciated ascetics whose spiritual life lights up in their eyes a fire from another world, a beautiful, superhuman brilliance. I sensed strong feelings in her at every moment: she certainly would have known how to die without fear and with her eyes open, just as she rapturously envisaged in her conversation the ideal scenes for the tragic background of her dances. And this condition of knowing how to die, of knowing how to live with a degree of risk by conceiving of one's physical existence as something secondary and subjected to a primordial goal, is not present to the same degree in other countries as it is in Spain. Through his momentous and not-so-momentous history, captured in his Greco or in his Goya,[10] in the mystical flame or in the blood of the bull fight spectacle, the Spaniard is not great because of the way he adores life, but because of the way he scorns it in the service of a greater honor, which becomes the best way to exalt it, to consecrate it.

All of which is the opposite of Puritanism. The Puritan's honor is life itself in his daily actions and his goal is not the search for a perilous way of transcendence with heroism, but the search to justify that life with frugality and one's particular circumstance before God. Frugality and circumstance before God are small gods elevated to God by the Puritan. And St. Peter would say of this that "it comes to be idolatry." Frugality and circumstance are original bonds of the North American's soul. Frugality and circumstances are the opposite of self-expression and freedom that always exist in the Hispanic character in all acts of heroism. Frugality and circumstance are bonds. That was the seed the hundred and two Pilgrims on the Mayflower carried on their tempestuous voyage.

The men born of those Pilgrims were born of that seed. Those men were devoted to their Bibles, but in a violent and at the same time limited way. With their austere reading at dawn and at twilight, what they extracted from the Bible was just an arid and at times inhuman moral code. For this reason spiritual feeling, freely divine feeling many times escaped them. In this way they subordinated their aspiration—essentially free and constantly being reborn like the mystical Phoenix[11]—to the harshest and most terrestrial bonds. Neither heroism nor holiness could flourish in the ruggedness of that rocky land. These people constrained by an immutable morality were terribly unaware that what is basic in the Holy Scriptures is their lesson of constant change, their lesson that everything is a process of becoming. In man nothing is given in a pure state; everything tends to regenerate itself in him; everything is on the verge of becoming eternal and traditionally man is nothing without the road to eternity. Unamuno is right in his interpretation that St. Matthew does not say "Verily I say unto you, except ye be converted, and become as little children, ye shall not enter the kingdom of heaven."[12] Observe: not "be" but rather "become," which indicates change.

*   *   *

One day I was walking with that woman along one of the avenues in the southern part of the city. The slopes of the old colonial park displayed their luxurious green among the small statues stained by the mud from the constant rain. And in the lofty sky, the dominance of a rich sun had lessened after many hours of brilliance. The park's wrought iron fences had been destroyed; the authentically old of the old Argentine park had been destroyed. Only the modest low building of the small museum remained, with its bay window barely rising up from the poorly cut grass, that had a tendency to grow wild. She stopped and looked with astonishment at the typically Argentine resignation of the old park in disuse, at that dignity which survives the violence sown by foreign hands, at that simple solemnity when facing misfortune, at that proud severity with everything, at all this that gave fresh life to that Argentine place.

We renewed our walk in the hot autumn afternoon. I then used all my persuasive force, all my passion, all my true faith to tell her how the best part of our people's nature is made from the silent union of those two spirits: the spirit of giving and the spirit of freedom. The happy vegetating, growing, manifesting of this people are produced by means of that almost exclusive representation of an iridescent optimism. In this country everything appears to be just gloss and well being; but deep down there beats a discreet residue, an apparently distant but real pain, not easy to detect, silent, very much hidden. And this prudent and not very explicit taciturnness is simply the conviction of not fulfilling the creative destiny of its soul, but rather of living limitedly within the borders of its biological destiny. Thanks to this deep need, this people has at times identified itself with the cause of a political party, exalting it in its imagination as the channel offered for the fluvial liberation of that other destiny, the most important one. This people has felt that cause as it would a religion. Indeed, politics, which usually has the appearance of interesting this people especially, may leave it indifferent for long periods of time. And its sudden interest, when it does appear, is only the hope of justifying itself in a movement of faith. But the daily sun sets straight down on that dark suppression; without freeing it, without giving it, instead of a course of faith, scarcely more than a vital confidence in the joy of living, suggesting a somatic satisfaction.

If Argentina has a rhythm, that rhythm is the steady inner oscillating of its deep, unfulfilled aspiration. With its tradition interrupted, its great desire is the desire of a member separated from the body that tries with all its strength to rejoin it. That body, that tradition, is perhaps, humanly, one of the strongest and most harmonious in the world, because San Martín's military feat in the Andes and the whole process of national organization and the people's spirit as a nation have no parallel in history as the express glorification of a people in a fundamental state of love. Suddenly, when this broad gesture of giving of oneself reaches a culminating point, the country's forward steps stop, are stopped. There is not total collapse, but certainly an inhibitory malaise.

And that form of dance which communicates to a whole continent the rhythm of an unusual heroism—a heroism made of pure spirituality and compassion like that of assuming great risk on the most inexpugnable icy areas of the planet in order to bring liberty to other regions—is transformed into another rhythm, into that of a potential aspiration, into that of a passive desire, into passive expectancy. An injurious parasitic vegetation spreads over the surface of the country; it is not that it is going to destroy health, but it does weaken it. And the inner drive, the mobility of the spirit are stopped as far as the country's essential way of life is concerned. The great rhythm is reduced.

She was born among gentle people in the distant Florida soil, and her very nature made her capable of understanding all of this, for everything she attained in life she attained through the intelligence of this passion in aesthetic terms.

Notes

1. Manchegan. Reference to Don Quixote, whose adventures take place in La Mancha, a region of New Castile, in central Spain.

2. John Bunyan (1628–1688). English author of the religious allegory *Pilgrim's Progress* (1678).

3. Hart Crane (1899–1932). American poet, author of *The Bridge* (1930) and *White Buildings* (1926).

4. André Maurois. Pseudonym of Emile S. W. Herzog (1885–1967). French novelist, critic, and essayist. In the 1920s and 1930s, he published many biographies of celebrated writers such as Shelley, Byron, and Dickens. During World War II, he wrote of the German occupation of France in *Tragedy in France* (1940) and *Why France Fell* (1941).

5. Gilbert Keith Chesterton. (1874–1936). English journalist and man of letters. Works: *A Short History of England* (1917), *The Everlasting Man* (1925), *As I Was Saying* (1936).

6. Huguenots. Deeply commited Protestants who were the object of persecution by the French Catholics in the 16th and 17th centuries. The Huguenots belonged to the Reformed Church and adhered to the religious doctrines of John Calvin. Jean Ribaut (1520–1565) was a French Huguenot explorer who in 1562 claimed Florida for his country. His book *The Whole and True Discouerye of Terra Florida* (1563) is an account of his exploits in Florida.

7. Pedro Menéndez de Aviles (1519–1574). Spanish military officer. On March 29, 1565, Philip II ordered Menéndez to drive the French Huguenots from Florida. Menéndez met Jean Ribaut's forces in the St. John's River, but no battle ensued. Shortly thereafter, Menéndez and his men founded St. Augustine, which stands as the first permanent white settlement in the United States. Menéndez' troops were merciless in their slaughter of the French.

8. Alonso Quijano. The real name of Don Quixote.

9. Juana la Loca (1479–1555). The demented daughter of the Catholic Sovereigns Ferdinand and Isabel; mother of Charles V; wife of Philip the Fair.

10. Francisco José de Goya (1746–1828). Spanish painter and etcher. Among his famous works are "The May 2nd Massacre," a realistic depiction

of the horrors of war, "The Nude Lady," and many portraits of the Spanish royal family.

11. Phoenix. The mythological bird that burns itself on a funeral pyre at the end of its life. From its ashes arises another phoenix, with renewed vigor. The phoenix symbolizes spiritual rejuvenation and immortality.

12. From Matthew 18:3.

X.
The Spirit of Giving
and the Spirit of Freedom

Looking at the Argentine capital. The
two fundamental spirits of our people.
Giving, an Argentine virtue. The
nature of the builders. Creative
freedom.

The capital is white; it has the color of new stone. The spectral burst of
its dawn has a steel paleness in which a subdued red scarcely bleeds.
The capital is white by day, steel and blue, and the still white stone,
the new stone, barely reveals its last forms deep in the most immaterial sky in the world. In the city's dawn only the green hues bite the tops
of thick foliage in the remote and sparse vegetal islands in the midst of
a convocation of granite. The cornices and the air unite their still pure
bodies under the crowning arc of a very pure sky that only with the
twilight becomes cobalt color, becomes compact, and has the following elements: green, air, stone, and blue. The capital appears founded
in the dawn of time; everything in it is new today—its reality, its pretension. On its surface the airplane and the building have the same
untouched newness. The capital has something of the cruel and disdainful adolescent next to the senility of a forgotten river. From its
beautiful and diverse northern slopes, the capital at times turns its
eyes to the river, which changes its dirty green for the steel blue of
dusk. And night consummates the marriage of those opposite plains,
that of stone and that of water, in the form of a strong, flat vibration,
very sharp and very slow.

From the last floor of one of the city's highest buildings, I saw the vast spectral spectacle already transformed into night. I hardly needed to bend over the parapet to see below that metropolis of the southern hemisphere, in which, like the northern metropolises ruled by the Cassiopeia constellation,[1] the Americans' ambition transforms the world each day without abandoning a dream oftentimes tragic because of its godless perplexity. Like Harvard Solness,[2] Ibsen's tragic builder, a terrible delirium possesses them, that of ascending to these towers to face that divinity toward which they gravitate in their laborious exacerbation and in their desire to cling to a solid reality: stone. Stone on stone, that height on which I stood had been made by them out of the fearlessness of God's terrible anger that devastates the nights and the days of godless men.

Standing at that balcony in the dark, without leaning out, I saw below the tree-lined square with Columbus's statue in the center and further on poplar groves and still further on the river's inert darkness and the mystery of the space of unending land fleeing toward the interior of the country. I was an island, standing up, alive, surrounded by the night; and that enormous space made me shudder. White sky and calcinated walls were now a dark sea in which the union of light and darkness had a certain testimonial impotence, a certain rigid and emphatic challenge under the infinite cosmic dust, under the handful of stars suddenly immobile in their flight, suddenly crystallized like Lot's wife.[3] Opposite, I saw the two sidereal worlds—night and light above, night and light below—finally mingled circularly in the north, south, west, and east, after having covered so much dark space, in the same whitish dust. And as if it were the rhythmical pulmonary breathing of countless human wills which surrounded the dining table at that hour in thousands and thousands of homes, I felt the breath of the lives withdrawn from the city's fervor until the following day, their vigil, their growth from our land.

Their slow growing, their swarm, their proliferation. Blood of millions of men that will become Spirit in them. Diffuse emotions that will become passions, that will become articulated, that, with their human baggage, will begin to walk less blindly than before, more sure of themselves and of their goals on Earth.

That night there rose up in me the breath of that steady growing like something terribly tangible, something terribly real, something terribly corporeal.

The surface of the country is revealed with its two faces, one looking out and the other looking in, like the god Janus.[4] We can not study it in its spiritual configuration, but in its moral configuration, for in this latter form reside the elements that can reestablish unity in the uninterrupted tradition of those other two configurations. It grieved me greatly to live in a country without faith, in a country where the faithful go to church as if to the intermission in a spectacle one must attend even though it is not entertaining and where one fluctuates between a certain true contrition and a certain convenience to be in God's good graces. I felt anguished at not living in a country where Catholicism was persecuted, because it is persecution and not honors that make men great and worthy. And the countries in which the clergy is persecuted and terribly poor are those which grant man the maximum possibility of austere comfort and true inner health. What I felt myself loudly demanding was something purgative in the heart of Argentina, something that would shake its indifference, that would shake its visible body and make it wake up.

What Aristotle affirms regarding the purgative goal of the soul characteristic of Greek tragedy has always seemed to me a tremendous revelation, not only as an aesthetic judgment, but as a sense of the needs of the soul. It is not possible to conceive of any life capable of transcending itself, and therefore of transcendence, without an awareness of its purgative state, also the first of the theological steps of spiritual life; neither life nor work. And it is in this sense that all reason is tragic and it is in this sense that when that awareness of the purgative state is missing, man is animality, vegetation. And the Argentina we see and touch is the opposite of any state alien to its pride, the opposite of all that is alien to that resplendent pride in which it lies invertebrate.

But this Argentina's bad phase, in reality not her essence. All peoples have a fundamental essence that survives materially, symbolized in their literature and history, and without which nations would become disunited and break up, like the islands of the archipelagos. And in the cohesion of the elements of that essence lies the greater destiny to which a people can aspire, which is having not physical domination over others but hegemony of spirit, in the same sense that an artist's inspiration has hegemony over the devotion of the person who receives him in his fervor.

I have always been moved by seeing in human behavior, whether through individual natures or through collective actions, living movements of the soul that fearlessly come to the surface. And indeed I received a certain sense of fulfillment, a certain proud sense of our destiny as a nation in the midst of an America uncertain of its goals, a disunited Europe and an East in revolt, from the confirmation that in the remote recesses of our actions, where our acts originate and are nourished, those two indissoluble fertile spirits—the spirit of giving and the spirit of freedom—are always present, in constant movements of watching and attending.

These are concrete things, things in which to put one's trust. Those spirits were a breath one could breathe and share in the coldest winters on earth. Was it possible not to feel this spirit of giving and of giving freely as the most spontaneous and earliest manifestation of the Argentine soul?

Heritage of Hispanic people, as opposed to the Anglo-Saxon, heritage of immoderation in passion, patrimony not constrained by the rules of a practical Puritanism.

Strange, strong, generous will to give of oneself, to not withhold; to give, to open up the most generous veins as regards human and material values. All the events of our history—or at least the most noble and consequent ones—that is, the materialization itself of our essence in symbols, are fundamental acts of giving. All the events of our popular legends turned to literature are expressions of this same spirit. Our whole character, the character of Argentineness, is the spirit of giving.

The constant spirit which moves our history is an action alternating between the spirit of independence and the spirit of giving. Even before independence from Spain, communicating that emancipation to other peoples was already on the minds of the first Argentines. Ganivet said that the deepest nucleus in the study of the psychology of peoples is their territorial spirit. Well, our territorial spirit is that of a continent excessively rich for its human content, because of which our destiny can transcend the goals of narrow hegemony or imperialism. In this sense, our real influence in Hispanic America—and in general in all America—will be directly related to the quality of our own builders and not to any spirit of conquest.

The act of giving is the first manifestation of faith, and since faith is the purest expression of the spirit, it is, as I have said before, the fundamental form of man. When man finds faith, he regenerates himself in its form. Even reason takes its true humanity from faith; when this does not exist, reason is a kind of mineral motor. Therefore, religious wars have been the bloodiest, and man has fought in them with his fear at first subordinate to the higher courage of believing . . . Our spirit of giving is the first act of faith, but it has to be articulated, spiritualized, or else it is just emotion that drowns without carrying within itself any really creative initiative.

In this country, humanity gives of itself, plants give of themselves, animals give of themselves, even stones give of themselves in a panorama of offerings. But nature does not externalize. It develops, it articulates that original spirit of giving, if only because it continues to be driven by the same spirit that has created it. When the presence of that higher determination is interrupted, the tragedy of Solness the builder occurs, that is, the tragedy of construction which is carried out thanks to the will to put stone on stone, but which is in the end inanimate creation, sterile and sad creation.

Here again is the tragedy of the means. Here is the tragedy of the builder who holds in his hands the means, the bricks, but does not know what inner force sustains in him that will to build. For what purpose does he build? Only for time? Only for the strangers who will come from far away lands to inhabit the country? What guiding principle moves his hands? What faith moves his hands? Those few words he exchanged with his fellow workers and which serve only to manifest his preferences, likes and dislikes, common sorrows or common pleasures—are they principle and faith? Are those words he utters haphazardly principle and faith? Everything is chance in him: fortune or ruin, opposite poles. It's fine to construct, raise buildings with efficient tools and accurate plumb lines. That can be done—but for what reason? To satisfy that chance?

To deceive onself with false words like these: "I am a nationalist because I want to protect myself, to shelter myself; I am a conservative because I want to subsist; I am a Catholic so that they don't take away my money. Therefore I put that money under the invocation of the cross"?

No, a people ignorant of where it is going is a people without faith, and a people without faith is a sad people. The first movement of faith is not enough, just the giving is not enough. Because when there is no faith behind the giving, man always remains alone and sad.

Then I looked out, without interrupting the course of my thought I looked out, and I kept looking at the light of the streets with greater attention, many meters below, many meters below, until I was able to make out some figures of men walking by. Through the first mass of darkness one could see a whitish mist. This mist gave off halos; and the men were small walking forms in the very narrow passes. I looked at the few men who were walking in the night, down below.

I was also deeply sad, deeply distressed. Although I did not shout it out at that moment, I was locked in dialogue with that humanity walking in the city. And that dialogue, as always, grieved me.

"People,"—I thought—"I want to help you so you may afterward help me. People, I would like to help you to give birth to the truth of your own truth, the truth of what you were, of what you carry within yourself and not of what many shout out you carry within and don't carry. Invisible Argentina, if only you knew the way in which your emotion can be greatness that is well channeled, greatness that moves ahead! And if you only knew how, by simply continuing in your own direction, but also knowing the direction of your future road, knowing your direction, you can go beyond the destiny to which those not knowing that your future is something other than vegetative satisfaction and pecuniary success have tied you. People, you cannot free yourself from your stagnated emotion except through giving, through prodigiousness. People, what you need, what you need among you, is builders, the forward movement of builders. They have given you birth and then have abandoned you, left you."

"Now what you have is Solness, the builders you have are like Solness. They have built churches, but since their faith was insufficient, incipient, they have later remained like him in the marasmus of aridity, which comes after physical work is finished if behind that work there was nothing else, if it was done without inspiration. At the height of his despair, Solness rose up and shouted: "Hear me now, thou Mighty One! From this day forward, I will be a free builder—I, too, in my sphere—just as Thou in Thine. I will never more build churches for Thee—only homes for human beings." And after building homes for human beings, he said: "Yes, for now I see it. Men have no use for these homes of theirs—to be happy in. . . . Nothing really built; nor anything sacrificed for the chance of building. Nothing, nothing."[5]

"People, what you need now is other builders. Those who may not say, 'I didn't build anything solid nor did I sacrifice anything to construct something that could last.' What you need now is men who are different from the Nordic builder in that they can create nothing without sacrifice and consequently they can create nothing that is not solid."

"People, the spirit of giving is so great in you that, since it is only the first step of faith it already seems a complete and well-directed faith. But it is not so; it only seems to be. And your great destiny lies in sacrificing everything to the being, in not wanting now just "to seem" and "to posture," in erasing from your surface the pullulation of those who "seem" without "being." Your great destiny is in being more categorically what you are. In your faith shall be the measure of your affirmation. And this will come as a kind of architecture of the spirit, only with the articulation of your elements in freedom."

I continued thinking like that as the city turned to night before me, the city that would awaken the same way as the day before, apparently cold but with its burning, red, inner inferno, full of secret and restrained ardor.

I looked and said to myself: the other spirit, the spirit of liberty also belongs to this people. Tyrannies are the social forms of avarice. Tyrannies are the species of Harpagon,[6] whose politics was good because he knew how to hoard and have power, whose morality was horrible because of the subordination of everything to those ends. But this is a people of free spirit. There is no generosity conceivable without freedom; everything that assaults freedom is an act of usury, an act of monopolization of humanity to the detriment of the fertile possibility of each human being. Tyranny does not grow in nations where nature is abundant. Even where there are the best practical results, dictatorship is an unhappy parenthesis. Poor creatures in the land of the whip! Poor plants, men, feelings! They may form rich showy tree nurseries, but are probably dead inside.

No generous-hearted man accepts the whip or tyrannical rule, because what else is it but injustice and arbitrariness?

And this people, this people whose broken-off human branches walked through the nocturnal street among electric signs and traffic and universal noise, countless feet below the roof of the building from which I observed them and suffered with them—this people, if they are anything, are a generous-hearted people. Their reaction to rigid rule would be disgust.

I went down the fourteen floors of the building because it was no time to remain in my room. I was full of an emotion which, like that people's, wanted to go out of itself, to be channeled. I started to walk slowly, now at last among those people, my compatriots, my obscure and unknown friends, all those who, without my knowing it or their knowing it, would have aspired with me in the Argentine dawns and nightfalls to many things—dreams of greatness, puerile raptures of immortality. Who knows how many of these people like myself might have often felt the joy of invading hopes and then depression brought on by as many deceptions and then again hope. Perhaps, with this sad and human dialectic, with these cruel alternatives, we were accumulating that wealth of sorrow without which no conscience, no man, no people, can rise a little above its original stature in a small universe within the other universe. Perhaps that same sorrow would some day unite them, in the same unity that all the obscure and ultimate forces, the final inspiration, are united in the soldier who falls wounded and bloody, that soldier whose blood for a moment, a sublime moment, will give, under his body, warmth and life to the earth.

Notes

1. Cassiopeia. Five stars in this Northern constellation, having the configuration of a *W,* form Cassiopeia's chair.

2. Harvard Solness. The hero of *The Master Builder* (1892), by the Norwegian playwright Henrik Ibsen (1828–1906).

3. Lot. Lot accompanied his uncle Abraham to Canaan and together they shared the land. Fire and brimstone annihilated the wicked city of Sodom, where Lot lived, but he himself was spared when an angel intervened in his behalf. As punishment for looking back at the city, Lot's wife turned to a pillar of salt.

4. Janus. Roman god of beginnings and doorways, represented with two faces, one in front and one behind. When there was war, his temple was open; when there was peace, it was closed.

5. From *The Master Builder,* in *Eleven Plays of Henrik Ibsen* (New York: Random House, n.d.), p. 377.

6. Harpagon. The protagonist of Molière's *The Miser* (1668).

XI.
The Country Like Lazarus

Questions to the desert. Trip to a
provincial city. A little town.
Drowsiness. The school, the church,
the cemetery. The parable.

Months, years of real crisis passed. I felt constant, demanding questions violently posed by my spirit—and the desert had no answers. The visible desert continued to produce its emphatic and shrill voices, enamored of their emphasis and shrillness. Argentina was a desert full of words. Emptiness all around the visible men and emptiness inside of them. Full of a luring abyss, to begin; then despairingly empty. And the sustained, brandished, repeated declarations of "We are replete with things; we are rich in everything. We are better than anybody." Within me a shout, only one. "I want to justify the act of living." But the act of living life itself and justifying it with acts of life, justifying it with existence. Existences are justified only by their eminently creative attitude in the most insignificant gesture. But the instrument of the creator is truth; the artist works in reality and his fiction is only the imaginary conveyance of true reality; and even when the novelist lies or the painter lies, he lies in a framework of reality existing in him. In this way his lie is not a sin but rather imagination that he transforms to create a different truth. And I wanted to be nourished at the time with eternal truths—by taking a very noxious drink—and all I found was the fiction of fiction, the lack of authenticity and further lack of authenticity; lack of authenticity of men and lack of authenticity of things in the demoniacal dance of American ambitions.

Everything is rubblework and original poverty as regards creative initiative. The European man has his youth naturally tied to the Giotto[1] on the old wall, to the Manzanares,[2] the Seine[3] or the Vistula[4] of his artist ancestors; here man is tied to a horrendous newness, without redemption. And the authentic Argentina, the real Argentina, appeared to me more and more solitary, more and more silent, more and more overwhelmed by the burden of the other Argentina, the external Argentina, the Argentina of appearances.

I felt an ardent desire to understand the signs showing the beginning of articulation, the beginning of the active expression of those basic emotional states. I traversed the country from one side to the other. It was necessary for me to see the different forms of our inertia in order to understand its enormous danger.

One night I took the train under the glass and iron of the Retiro station—it was the last days of a cold June—and when I woke in my cabin at dawn I found myself in a small provincial city. Ten hours separated me from Buenos Aires. It was a misty morning, cold, sickly, and I quickly went to the hotel, a large building with black walls, as desolate as a prison cell. The old furniture in the room, sordid and dilapidated, was arranged with absolutely no order and the pieces contrasted with one another so disproportionately that the first thing one wanted to do was to get out of that room at once, to be there the least possible time. But hanging from one of the walls, decorated with dreadful floral paper, was a commonplace picture of General Belgrano,[5] with his head allegorically wrapped in the flag. The wakening of the gray day could be seen through the window. I went out to the street and began walking toward the main square to visit the Jesuit temple, crossing that unique, basic and very poor part of Argentine provincial cities: the broad sidewalks, the new asphalt, the monstrously heterogeneous construction, the terribly ornate domes, the original configuration of the large city blocks sleeping its flat sleep. I crossed the square, from which all the trees appeared to have been stolen, the square that seemed neglected and abandoned to its own fate. But, still enveloped in dense layers of mist, the color of the city, its atmosphere, the sidereal reflection on the ground were so pure, so very prodigious in their different hues of gray, that one appeared to be touching the cosmos on one's skin, to be feeling the hand of the air. The temple was a bit removed from the main streets of the city, in a poor and almost deserted neighborhood, full of breaks and holes. The facade was very simple and smooth, like certain Italian church fronts of the early centuries, with a lot of naked wall and on top the graceful belfry. I went in. The only thing worth seeing in that temple was the coffered ceiling, the colorless and almost rotted wood, all that carved work, sumptuous and at the same time humble in appearance and which apparently had never been restored. The broad tiles of the naves were worn out, abandoned and forgotten, and this state of disrepair seemed to be like the sheltered inhabitant among those walls. But my eyes had more than enough to delight in with the sight of those buttresses, borders, paintings, and chancel in which I saw the work of those men whose hand had tarried with love and had transmuted matter, eternally freeing it through artistic expression. I heard the voices of those men, and although I could not climb up to see closely the prodigious architectural and ornamental work in the coffered ceiling, I walked in amazement under the wood construction, which by now had become so spiritualized, so unsubstantialized that its consistency resembled that of certain Asian vegetal fibers in which the trunk flowers from itself and without branches on reaching the furthest point of their cortical dematerialization.

I don't know how long I was wandering through the transept and the principal nave and the apse. Perhaps only an intense half hour, enough for that admirable work to penetrate my being with its subtle message. The only art I have ever felt strongly is the art that comes from the liberation of an agony, not only as a catharsis but as a tangible eternalization of that laborious critical moment by which the small deaths to which the spirit is daily subjected and reduced achieve an instant of unity to become materialized—and thus to be born to another life—in the new body which dematerializes them. Just like the flower becomes the fruit thanks to that virtue, art is death and rebirth of a person before being transcendent because it goes from the particular to the general, to the totality of the other sensibilities. The adolescent artist's agony is saved in the apple he paints. How many hard-ships, what personal anguishes have those coffered wonders saved that in their turn were now becoming dust, but "beloved dust"?

At noon I had lunch with four young men in a Spaniard's prosperous tavern. We were full of critical excitement, of fervor, of provident lu-cidity. But none of us had left the darkness where the new country was being organized. One was an engineer, who had quick intelligence for symbols and proportions. The others were beginning novelists, crit-ics. One had written on Bishop Berkeley;[6] all four were eager, curious men in whom there was none of the usual vulgarity. I heard them speak of many things and I saw that they had not only a real, ill-humored inquietude, but also a sacred candor, which is no small thing in a land of so many sulky, sullen people. And candor lives in the very essence of our people, in our real and invisible Argentina. Candor be-longs to the grave and laborious worker of our land, candor belongs to the man locked in dialogue with the elements. I bathed myself in newness in them, in the fresh and young new spirit of those who carry in their soul an heroic injury, something that will pound on the sleep all around and awaken it with inopportune cordiality, which is always inopportune for those who doze.

And it was later, although that same afternoon, when I saw the incredible spectacle—a kind of visual, revealing, and sudden summation—of what moves about, like hungry eels in a well, in the depths of our omnipresent arrogance, of our omniscient vanity.

I was walking with one of those men, with one of those young fel-lows. He had wanted to show me what we were going to see, and nothing else, because, as he said, it was the only thing with a well-defined physiognomy. How! I don't know if he knew the horror of what he wanted to show me, the true, the transcendent, the signifi-cant horror.

The town we were going to was not reached by any shortcuts, woods, or mountain passes, but by sand dunes and fields in which the only living soul that could be seen for twenty kilometers was a farmer slowly furrowing his land at nightfall. No sun or any light, but a gray-ish paleness at day's end.

Lying as it does on a slope near the river, the small town is reached very abruptly. After a curve in the sandy main road, one is suddenly in

Arcadia.[9] Impossible to imagine more beautiful and aligned vegetation; it isn't the raw jungle, it isn't the green ostentation of the Brazilian countryside in complete freedom. It's neither one nor the other, but the multiplication of wisely and naturally spontaneous small gardens created by God with the minutely prolix and proportioned design needed in the invention and planting of the jungle backgrounds in a Gian Bellini[7] painting, or an Orcagna,[8] with cypresses and orange trees, round, progressive, and concentric boughs, and the fruit's harmonious gravitation, and the segments of grass growing in the soil in just the right amount. And in the midst of that order, everything over there appeared to be deserted. I saw the prodigiously rich farms of that sudden Arcadia; a small central square, the small whitewashed church; and in the square there were trees, beautiful orange trees with fruit in sight, heavy and grave with their hanging treasure; and the surprising thing at every step was the marvelous orderliness of that luxury, with everything there naturally made of "calm, luxury, order and voluptuousness."

I was struck with wonder at what I saw in that town, in that small town scarcely twenty minutes from the capital, but a miniature paradise apparently hidden from the secular world, a miniature peninsula of promise. There was the fragrance of orange blossoms freshly filling the air and the smell of the impregnated, damp land, the strong smell of new leaves. The air around was saturated with these many essences. But, were there men there? Where were the men? We went into the streets of the town. Not a soul could be seen at nightfall, only the patios of the houses, the crowded garden of the estates, and even the interior rooms visible across a wide-open door or a window showed the deserted atmosphere. I asked for those men, I asked for those inhabitants.

Then the man who was with me said: "Everybody is sleeping here. Here everybody lives the eternal sleep."

And soon after, I began to spy the sleeping people through the open doors. I saw some women seated in the patio of the ranch houses, under the orange trees, in the somber atmosphere. One of them held in her hand a broom which she lazily moved around from her chair. Then I asked how all those townspeople could live without working. "They fish in the river," they answered, "and eat fruit." At first that seemed to me just beautiful and also worthy of the physical picture of Arcadia, with its modest houses, with white, thick walls, its decoration of fruits and foliage, with its red-bricked wide sidewalks and dirt roads. But what there was inside that apparent peace was a frightful lethargy.

We finally found a man on a corner. He was in shirt sleeves drinking mate tea. His face was all sunburned, leathery, and his manner revealed a life of indolence. The grocery store he owned was on the corner. We wanted to question him, to ask him something. He then lowered the mate from his mouth, looked at us for a long time with his fixed, heavy, expressionless eyes. After a while he answered us that there were three grocery stores in town owned by three brothers. He uttered that sentence, which must have had no more than ten words, in the same time needed to finish a long prayer. His faltering voice gave the impression of giving out altogether, of breaking all the time, of not being able to continue. Each word seemed to struggle with an invincible opponent, with strange internal obstacles. His earth-colored lips appeared not to move; there were heavy pauses between each word. I insisted, but it was difficult to get a word out of that mass of inert flesh. In the face of this total defeat, we continued on ahead.

We got out of the car opposite the narrow street where the school is. The little school is a shack, a low, bleached clay building, with no jams on the doors. One came right into a room—vacant at the time—no doubt the principal's office to judge by the feminine care with which the picture cards, now dirty and faded, had been put up on the wall. And high up on that wall, painted in big printed letters, in thick black letters, one of Sarmiento's encouraging maxims: "Struggle and you shall live." But the floor was covered with old dust and certainly no one had tried to combat the devouring filth. We came in through a door facing the open patio and the classrooms, the three rooms in a row on the left. A heavy woman in mourning stepped out of one of the rooms and amiably invited us to enter a classroom. We went up the stairs and on going into the first room smelled a disgusting odor emanating from inside. There, twenty or thirty children, with their hands, heads and beautiful faces all bunched together— green eyes in blond heads, intense eyes, mouths curiously half opened—shared the same indescribable filth. Big, bewildered eyes, shocks of shaggy hair. And the teacher who was standing at the large blackboard smiling at us had written: "Our flag was born out of the horror of humanity." And the teacher, upset, hastened to erase and correct. The word "horror" was replaced on the black board by the word "love." As she left the classroom, the anguished lady in black told us that the error was inexplicable, very unusual, because that teacher had been in the school system many, many years.

We said good-bye to each other and then went to the adjacent church, founded in 1823 by Father Castañeda.[10] The sight of that tiny temple was no less desolate. It was run-down, squalid, with broken-legged benches and a few priestly albs lying around, just as stained and unbecoming. A poor woman went with us to visit the church. Her face was sallow and sickly, but it seemed radiant with the halo of a beautiful suffering. She seemed to be the witness in torment of that betrayal of Father Castañeda, she seemed to be the one called on to nourish in her grief the abandonment of and disrespect for this church founded by the man with the "holy fury." Only the rough simplicity of those white walls and the simplicity of the bell gable remained of Castañeda's legacy. The rest had been swept away by negligence. The woman spoke to us sadly of the impiety of the faithful: there was no charity, there was no compassion, and only a few women came to this small temple on Sundays.

We then went to the nearby cemetery, to the old one, for there was also a new one. Almost all the graves were desecrated, the coffins open and empty. There, the breath of the afternoon was a breath of horror. Some local men, whose idleness made it impossible for them to earn any money, went there to look for gold—rings, teeth, earrings, pins. There was a blond woman's head of hair caught on a bramble, and tarsuses and metatarsuses stuck into frightful petrified shoes.

All of these things filled me with sudden fright and at night, when I returned to the hotel, I instinctively remembered the Darmstadt philosopher, who was frightened by the very sight of us. But then I thought it wasn't right—although explicable—to be frightened; it would be better to shout all that out intelligently, to accuse it, to see to it that that death was definitely killed by life. To bring life to this disastrous town.

And I thought—something I am doing now too—about presenting this small scene to those who fill their mouths with the vacuous
verbal proclamation of their verbal nationalism without realizing that
they are the least capable of doing anything for the country, anything
real, anything honestly genuine and without pretext. These people
can not believe that patriotism and nationalism are feelings that sometimes are contradictory, that the former is an essential vital feeling and
the latter a mere attitude. I thought of showing this picture to those
who gather together in vociferous processions, who shout hurrahs
without having in their spirit any better conception of the real Argentina than their outward gestures, their outbursts, their exacerbated
ignorance, their exacerbated deaths. I thought about showing them
this small picture and I'm doing it.

That little Argentine town was a symbol. That little town was the
symbol of a terrible lethargy, the external reverse of a reality, the symbol of a lethargy wrapped up in sham and sheer external appearance,
the clamor, the banquets, the politics, the social farce, the ostentation; that little town that incarnated, among other evils, the betrayal
of Castañeda, was the symbol of the betrayal inflicted on the severe,
conscious, constructive dignity of our forefathers, who do not resemble the present-day visible Argentines but the present-day invisible
ones, who are like our real, authentic people and not like the superficial ones.

That little town was the symbol of stagnated, invertebrate emo-
tionality. That little town, in short, was the symbol of Lazarus's state
before rising up, that is of a state of death, but of redeemable death.

Indeed, the parable of our country is the parable of Lazarus and the
rich Epulon. The rich Epulon dined in his palace, on whose entrance
steps sat Lazarus the beggar waiting for the crumbs from the feast, his
wounds licked by the dogs. And finally the rich man and Lazarus died
and became equal in the grave. But they were not equal in their eternal destinies, because one was buried in Hell and the other carried to
Abraham's bosom. Then, in torment, the rich man asked to be sent to
Lazarus to throw water on his wounds and refresh his tongue. And
Abraham answered him: "Son, remember that you received good
things during your life while Lazarus misfortune; and thus Lazarus is

now consoled and you are tormented. And besides, there is an unfathomable abyss between you and us."[11]

Thus, those who know in our land the severe sense of life, those who don't sleep, those who suffer for feeling deeply a certain sacramental passion, those who are honest with themselves, the invisible Argentines, those whose honesty is almost a sickness, are the ones who live separated by an unfathomable abyss from the rich Epulon, who are not the future part of our country, but the part already saved, just like Lazarus.

Notes

1. Giotto di Bondone (1266–1337). Italian painter, sculptor, and architect, founder of the Florentine school of painting. Among Giotto's most famous works are the frescoes in the Arena Chapel in Padua portraying the lives of Jesus and Mary. He also contributed to the design of the campanile and the facade of the Duomo in Florence.

2. Manzanares. The river flowing through Madrid.

3. Seine River. The famous waterway of France, flowing picturesquely through Paris.

4. Vistula River. Longest river in Poland, rising in the Carpathian mountains, flowing northward and emptying into the Baltic Sea.

5. Manuel Belgrano (1770–1820). One of Argentina's military heroes in the wars of independence against Spain. Belgrano served as commander of the Army of the North in 1810 and won the important battles of Tucumán (1812) and Salta (1813).

6. George Berkeley (1685–1753). Irish bishop and philosopher who held that matter does not exist independently of man's perception of it. Works: *Essay Towards a New Theory of Vision* (1709), *The Principles of Human Knowledge* (1710), *Three Dialogues Between Hylas and Philonous* (1710), *Siris* (1744).

7. Gian Bellini (1430–1516). The leading Venetian painter of the 15th century, famous for the importance he gave to landscape in his religious works.

8. Orcagna. Pseudonym of Andrea di Cione (1308–1368). Florentine painter and sculptor. Orcagna's greatest work is the shrine of Orsan-Michele, a veritable carved tabernacle.

9. Arcadia. In ancient Greek times, Arcadia was the beautiful mountain region in the central Peloponnesus. The shepherd deity Pan was worshipped in Arcadia. From the days of the classical Latin poets, the name Arcadia has been used as a metaphor for rustic simplicity and ideal tranquility and happiness.

10. Francisco de Paula Castañeda (1776–1832). Franciscan friar, Argentine patriot, and educator.

11. The story of Lazarus is found in Luke 16:19–31.

XII.
Invasion of Humanity

Surprised by the various kinds of dawn
in Europe. Accommodating our spirit
to the beauty of eternal objects. Need
for human love. Meeting with men
beside the Tiber. The invasion of
humanity. America, America.

Finally, I don't know when, or how, nor what day, nor in what form—which means that it doesn't matter at all—the dawns of another world became the dawns I awakened to each morning. Amsterdam's theological dawn, the gray and dark dawns of Brussels, Mariakerke,[1] and Bruges;[2] the Italian dawns more suitable to the fortunate humanist than to the era of the Convulsionists and the bonfires, garrulous and happy southern dawns. I could say then like Kierkegaard, "In everything and for everything I lack the patience to live." Patience! Have I ever really felt what this means? Have I ever had time to know what quietude is! Patience, quietude. Words from another hemisphere! My vocation has always been to devour, to drink, to be hungry and thirsty for things, to be hungry and thirsty for humanity and divinity. Not to rest. To sink my roots into something. Yes, but to be able to leave without abandoning, to unite across the constant voyage and not to separate, to know no other dispersion but the last, at the end of everything, when ostentation has vanished with the blood and our blood-drained solitude is alone before God's solitude.

What a senseless, excessive impulse! Oh, life, still mine! On the outside, cold, on the inside, flames. And the inexorable march of time, which scarcely gives us time to seize it and hold it by its sparse hairs. We look at each other's open hands; nothing, hardly even memories, but in us memories fused now into the almost colorless flesh, into those cracked fingers, memories made today, the past made continuous life, life, movement and existence. And one must advance with those hands and fill them, grip reality, not let time escape, fall with it still gripped tightly, grasped. Ah, but time can just as well be the compassion for a suffering and miserable soul as it can be God; it can just as well be the transitory as the eternal. And thereby our hands will be ways, roads. With these hands we shall feel—each one of us!—the act of living the farce and the empty shouts or we shall go forward with them in the way Plato said in the *Symposium*,[3] for it is only with these hands that we shall reflect our forward march as he wanted it, from the love of terrestrial things to the love of beautiful forms and from the beautiful forms to beautiful conduct and from beautiful conduct to beautiful principles, until reaching the supreme principle of the whole that teaches us in a very definite way what absolute beauty is.

But with these hands—when we make them wise—we shall attain another knowledge, more direct and important, namely that of considering human nature as perenially weak and perenially vanquished, of becoming impregnated with its tragic flow, of feeling its agony deep within us and not merely on the surface, and measuring it in a way that is commensurate with its disaster, according to the way it faces disaster. We can thus apply to this Chesterton's words in his study of Geoffrey Chaucer, in the sense that "What one learns is not to despise the soul as small; even when rather feminine critics say that the will is weak. As if the will were ever strong enough for the tasks that confront it in this world. The great poet is alone strong enough to measure that broken strength we call the weakness of man."[4]

Once I left the American world, my own world became like a false rebirth in the north. The joy of the spirit was first. That basic American lack of concern for the recreation of the intelligence, a deficiency for which it had suffered so much, was reversed here, where everything was abundant and prodigious, in a continent where each rock can give testimony to the dead and revived human genius, eternally rebegun. A limitless impatience, that hungry and thirsty and devouring impatience of that time and of all times, left me with sleepless nights after wandering from dawn to midnight with slower and slower steps from the frightening darkness of the Rue Dante—*tu non se' morta ma se' ismarrita, anima nostra che si ti lamenti*[5]—to the terribly lonely nights at the Pont d'Âme, watching the Paris moon fall on so many bones not dead, on so many glorious deeds under the heavens of the city traversed by the reflectors and the motionless milky rhombus. The whole pavement was selenium; at each intersection, some recollection precipitously came alive. From the cathedral walls, the gargoyles jutted out. And it was strange of me to stand enraptured for as many as three hours before Andrea del Castagno's *The Crucifixion,*[6] in the Museum of London, but it was worse, much worse, to feel myself strangely living again in the presence of the apparently dead things of the old cities where Boerhaave,[7] the conscientious, the "Doctor of Europe," and tragic Erasmus,[8] the sick man of Europe, lived at the same time.

In the midst of those putrid waters lying in the muddy canals, in the midst of those gnarled archaic buildings bent over towards emptiness by the years, in the midst of the perpetually gray days and the desolate nights and the cold and sanguineous faces and history's immutable sleep in those countries where people don't seem to be born but die one after the other so that the dead might bury them—what kind of feeling was that whereby the soul did not get mortal breath from the outside except as an intense and invading fullness of living? It seemed almost as though living was not done through the senses but exclusively through the higher and reflective faculties of the soul, although these faculties were not rendered free to their own free will or imagination, but directed, led, oriented by a strange external sense of permanent things. It was this, namely that the spirit accommodated itself to, that is, (from *aequare,* to equal) began to equal those things, to adjust itself to them. And these things were here, existing, surviving, many generations dead but alive in the eternity of the intemporal soul that engendered them.

These things were Dante's and St. Thomas' universe, the universe of the four hierarchical elements when sky, hell, land and man, real as objects, real as things, magnetically drawn together like the points on a compass, accommodate man's spirit to their four essential dimensions. But, did the whole system persist spiritually? I don't know. The daily sight of Amsterdam left me exhausted because it held my spirit delightfully tense. In the Banks themselves, I'm not saying in the ruinous halls where the Rembrandts are watched over, in the Banks of big business, in merchant Bols' establishment, in the old Javanese tobacco storehouses, there was exuded a kind of voluntary submission of a certain order of commerce to another higher order of speculation and of this order to another order and so on successively until making Mr. Bols' establishment appear to accommodate its prestige to the ideal prestige of Rotterdam's gate, in Delft. In other words, since my spirit needed to be arranged in the same way, I found, as I came in contact with all that, the same reality in the world of things as that expounded about the soul and the body of Proposition One of the fifth part of the *Ethics,* written by that same native of Amsterdam where I temporarily resided: "According to the way in which the thoughts and ideas about things are arranged and linked in the soul, the emotions about things, that is, the images of things, are correlatively arranged and linked in the body." Thus, just like the accommodation of those thoughts and those ideas and those images, I too at that time was "accommodated." (Further on, we shall see what was bad about this. The negative importance of the lack of a heaven and hell imposed on Baruch Spinoza's moral geometry).[9]

For the time being, that geometry continued to furnish me with personal fulfillment. The need for accommodation which is the essence of each spirit was too denaturalized in me because of the formlessness and diffuseness of the reality of America. I had then reached such a state of suspension in those distant lands that I barely ate or slept for fear of losing in those moments my relationship with differently shaped matter, with the heart, with the essence—stone and spirit, stone turned to spirit—of the species' creative originality. And everything fitted in well, admirably well, for that relationship, whether it was the proportion of space laid out between the floor mosaics and the ceiling of St. Stephen,[10] a Viennese cathedral dating from the year 1000, or a simple medieval carving of a roe-deer's nape, or the almost lost expression of the last figure of a stained-glass window, in which at times one could make out only a tormented eye or the anguished line of a cheek, as happens with Ambrogio Lorenzetti's four nuns,[11] in which the delicate drawing scarcely exteriorizes the naturally unutterable quality of the inner grace.

And when I entered a royal room, as happened once in a very old chapel of the Hofburg of Vienna,[12] and in the solitary interior, where each piece of furniture seemed to preserve a certain magic of annointment, listened to an antiphon or an oratorio by Handel, what enraptured me was not that "sweet compulsion," as Milton[13] defines music, but the accommodation—once again the accommodation—of my spirit to that precise wholeness, to my dependence on the Argentine man today, as opposed to that other wholeness thanks to which the Pythagoreans[14] found the key to the analogy between the seven cords of the lyre and the planetary system. And I had to go out into the street, for my anxiety was so full, iridescent, prodigious, and walk aimlessly with my eyes motionless, my thoughts almost fixed.

Until then, everything or almost everything had been a form of relationship with things, an awakening to things, in short, to art, but in their tangible and real aspect of revelation. Almost no human presence came to disturb the daily renewed act of accommodating the spirit to the symmetry of the artistic work. I finally left the mist of the continental north and went south to the life of Rome. There things appeared to be even physically united in the succession of time, continued without interruption, for the nocturnal, persistent, uninterrupted noise of the fountains was like a bond in which such unity was achieved. I lived in hostelries, hotels and inns so as not to be stifled too much in the lonely private residences. I lived in relative poverty, with varied tastes, almost always shy and taciturn, ready to provide tenderness toward this or that, always with the voracity of leagues and roads and things, and perhaps, in essence, even after that act of accommodating my spirit to the surrounding beauty, also with the voracity to escape worries, sadness, and cares. And in the end, are they not all ways out?

I rarely spoke with anyone. I would have liked to suppress words entirely, or better still to improve them with signs easier to articulate, with signs that were equivalent to the immediate movement of the imagination, to the tangle of cerebral perceptions. In this sense, I never ceased, for example, during my literary meditations, to be happy with the constant thought that James Joyce's *Ulysses* could one day be surpassed in its own right by a new literary representation of a soul's dizzy and proud monologue. And among all these things, consuming fleeting time with my impatience, groping from city to city, stretching lines—in the precise sense, in the dimensional sense of the term—toward all I saw, toward all I admired, ruminating, devouring, thinking, caviling, awakening to new things every minute, filling myself up with the world, which means to be filled up with perpetual conflict—among all these things I spent my days, the months of my life which started at the shores of the North Sea and ended at the Adriatic Coast.

But then I became contrite. Then the idea came to me concretely that there was a lot of vain exercise in all that. And indeed a lot! Because what my spirit needed, my spirit as a man, not my reason nor my knowledge nor that tendency to abstraction that always contains a vital escape, was not so much to accommodate itself as it was to prolong itself. There is nothing more abominable in the world than man's stagnation in his speculative dilatoriness. After a while it smells. And even the claimed biological necessity for war is only the biological necessity that those pestilences should produce a crisis, should burst out somewhere. I felt I was in that danger, a danger of holding my soul in a sterile dialogue with things, however beautiful they might be, and not going forward, not prolonging myself, not incorporating what is human into the prolongation I was indulging in. Then I felt, as if carried away by some sort of a dream, that I had lost time, a necessary and urgent time, a time I had to recuperate.

I was in a room of the Saturnia Inn. It was night. I felt terribly martyred by my solitude, as if until then I had never felt it, although it had been so great. I wet my head in cold water, closed my books, and began to walk first along Via Mazzini and then through the short and dark Via dei Condotti. Doesn't Descartes relate that he conceived his method in a sweating-room? Nevertheless, his was the method of reason without warmth. A mere epidermic warmth incubated all that abstraction. I saw the philosopher thinking as he was sitting in one of those huge Germanic sweating-rooms that look like Majolica shrines, and that vision horrified me, exasperated me. He said he wanted to get to heaven, *"autant qu'aucun autre,"* just as much as any other person, but what he lacked, as Spinoza lacked, was heaven and hell.

Heaven and hell, within. Fire and charity, St. Thomas' angel and beast. The red and the sky blue. The spiritual abyss—which the great men of logic lack and which he didn't lack thanks to God and St. Augustine—of the flesh and the abysmal flesh of the spirit. Blood and imagination. Bonds and freedom. The act by which the body falls; the act by which it gets up.

But the only kind of union, the only kind of confession, the only kind of meeting in which the two extremes relinquish their own separate or divided vigor, the only way in which man's exact physical relationship with the elements of the universe is suddenly consummated is love. And let's not take this for granted, but let's draw life from this knowledge. We are referring to love and only love which is consummated in the flesh by exalting it or mortifying it, depending on whether it is of a divine or terrestrial kind, but always in the flesh; love which is consummated in the flesh of the spirit and in the flesh of conscience, for God came to the flesh itself to make suffering, joy, and the resurrection be in the flesh.

And there I was thinking—as I was going by the old walls of the Colonna Palace, alone on the Roman street—that the terrible thing that was happening to me, the terrible thing that had been happening to me, was my transitory separation from human love, my change to love of things, a change from which finally the turbulent forces of the stormy heavens and hell wanted to pull me away, to uproot me in order to throw me into life itself, into real, palpable life, into the heart of existing existence, into just the opposite—because of its different fire!—of essence, of the pure idea, of reflective and isolated inactivity.

Ah, how I would have wanted to be an animal of God in the street I was walking along! And not a soul in torment, a phantasm, which we become at times because of using our reflective intelligence so much, that same intelligence which makes us dispassionate when it separates us from all other living things.

How I would have wanted to be an animal, or a being not guided by higher thought processes, something, in short, that was not continuously denaturalizing itself by reason and deceiving itself without even knowing the lie. What greater stupidity than that of the goddess Reason! What greater moral stupidity! That goddess whom they carried with pomp and circumstance and who was killing all those who carried her, without their even being able to reason that she was killing them! But were those men to blame? No, they were not, but reason was, Reason!

Reason, what should it be but a docile servant of the spirit, of the spirit in which our flesh flourishes when it is reborn from its own ashes? But it is necessary to burn flesh for these ashes, because flesh is the core. What a poor heaven and hell it is for those who have never felt in themselves such a fire!

I saw men at that moment, and also women—men going up the street, men walking, men surely full of infinite worries, infinite abstractions! And I loved them all at that moment, as a species, as inner flesh and spirits, as if they were the only object of a strong, mature, inexpressible love! And at that moment, with what strange driving force did this same feeling attract me to God, at that moment when my great emptiness was full of love!

As if nothing concerned me more than to hear human voices and be pushed outside of myself toward others, I entered one of those cafés and sat down and heard the sound coming from the loud conversations. I felt like I was on a great prominence, for my whole being seemed to be dissolved in an irradiant feeling, in the same way that when one is on a mountain one feels dissolved in the abyss that surrounds it. But that was just a popular café in the city, and none of those human beings spoke to me or would speak to me. I looked at a woman's sad eyes and a man's movements as he was drinking, and at the whole appearance of that brief humanity as it is lived. I had something to drink, stayed there a while longer, and then returned to the Saturnia Inn, not with peace of mind because I didn't have it and don't even know what it is, but certainly with a feeling of health which, when linked to my perpetual anxiety, precipitated in my soul the sensation of a thirst about to be quenched.

I once again entered the human continent. I entered that populous universe founded on the Tiber, which on such an occasion and at that time was the same universe whose forefathers had listened to Menenio Agrippa[15] in the Aventine[16] relate the fable of the limbs and the stomach. (The person who related that fable now with fewer symbols was not the Roman consul but a Caesar who had read Karl Marx and then Albert Sorel[17] and who had immediately changed a Jacobian revolution[18] into a hierarchical State. Thus, his original motives were always altered, but the fundamental springs of action do not entirely disappear in their convenient modification. He who has thought like Mammon[19] will not then think like God, but like Mammon in God's manner).

First, they were wonderful days of good friendship with everybody and towards everybody. There was an easy communication with those Latins. Besides, what breathable glory, what dawns of steel, bleeding suns that sink behind the mountains, nights terribly populated by age! During the siesta hour, Shelley[20] and Trelawney's bones[21] seemed to live again in green leaves at the feet of the pyramid of Gaius Cestius.[22] The sun shone straight down on the Ostic[23] highway, the twilights tarried in consummating their union with the virgin night. After a long red struggle, the nocturnal body suddenly lay down, and over that faint body, over that tangible death, over that cessation of suffering and joy, only the ghostly backbone of the aqueducts on the outskirts and the small liquid cascade of the eternal fountains in the town were keeping watch.

And then came the clash. It could not wait. Not only in that city, among those people, but in other European cities where the same impatient steps took me. The clash with their people came: rebellion against an attitude which seemed intolerable to me, unbearable. That attitude was manifested as an invasion of humanity. And this invasion of humanity brutally struck my most sensitive nerves.

It was a depredation against consciences, against the conscience of the person, against the human conscience. It was an assault, a violation of one's moral abode. It was intruding violently into the conscience of another, intent on pillage.

Men attempting to invade other men.

A large part of the European world, the regions of dictatorship and violence, offered no other sight. Terribly angry, irrational men stood armed against free consciences, that is against those consciences in which the act itself is never blind, but passionately just. It is an offensive sight, a devastating sight. It is a sight in which the dignity of the conscience appears trampled on and insulted, the spirit offended, man himself whipped in his purest will. But, what did all that mean? What did all that mean? I wanted to rise up against such a desire of invasion. Caesarian tyranny nauseated me. I was disgusted and felt surrounded by the pressure which the tyrants seek to exert with a gesture of positively stupid arbitrariness on man and on the thirst for justice, on immanent hunger and thirst. "The aims of violence are incalculable, therefore, stupid," says Paul Valéry[24] and he is right. I felt hunted like the weak beast among spears. Indirectly wounded, indirectly offended.

Humanity was the invaded country. Its growth affected, thwarted, its prolongation prevented. And all of this—done in the name of what order?

Certainly not in the name of the order founded on God's law. Certainly not in the name of the order of the Church Fathers. Certainly not in the name of the order characteristic of those natures that are honestly pure, true, and honestly Christian. But rather, founded on an order of violation, of disrespect, of bourgeois values, of fundamental dishonesty; on a purely abstract order, state-controlled, on an impure order.

I stood before a world in dissolution. If once I had been able to accommodate my spirit to the expression of an art that prodigiously reflected the past order of that world, I could not accommodate it now, draw it near, connect it to those attempts at fraud perpetrated by some men on others, to this invasion of humanity. I now felt Rimbaud's[24] holy rebellion close as never before. I now was sensitive as never before to St. John's word and to St. Peter's epistolar text. I now felt the need to rise up in defense against that invasion, not to let my spirit be trampled on, to provide it with arms. Neither conscious act nor conscious word could be pronounced. One could not think in accord with the spirit, but in accord with the rules. And honesty of conscience was reproached in those who had the valor to have it.

This was no order at all; this was dissolution. This was part of a dissolution.

After that, I looked differently at that America which I had forgotten, attracted as I was by the secular pomp of a grandiose but already dead order. I saw America from afar in one of Europe's late afternoons. I saw her wrapped up in the laborious dignity of her towns. I saw her resolute and confident in her destiny with the healthy step of a young body. I saw her a little colder in her geographic head, in the pragmatic idealism of the North, I saw her fiery in Hispanic America, all of her covered by the winds of freedom. I saw her in her prodigious liveliness. I saw her reflected in the sight of her men without human greed, of her multitudes moving forward, sure of themselves, and prodigal. *I utter the word en masse.*

*   *   *

And still surrounded by that other humanity, a tyrannized humanity that is essentially resentful and exacerbated and does not pardon, I allowed myself to walk calmly along that avenue, visited by the rebirth of an old, dormant hope, a native son of a country with a spirit of giving and a spirit of liberty.

The old sun of the Stendhalian panegyric sank behind the mountains, a July sun that dies slowly. I saw before me an esplanade and a café terrace and the last golden and ochre radiance falling on the iron street lamps. Some ragged children came along crying and several men gestured as they stepped up on the sidewalk, teeming with people as far as the top of the street. And it was then that in that religious school the priest could momentarily say his *Kyrie:* "Lord, have mercy." And all those words seemed to be said in vain, because in a country of violence mercy can not long remain. Everything was dark, even this street bathed by the dying rays of the July sun. A great lament seemed to be heard in the air, behind the words of torrential exasperation uttered by the violent lost men, by the violent blinded men. The words were these: "Violence is only in impiety; let us be strong in that impiety. When our impiety is the strongest of all, then we shall be the first." This was called Caesarism. I turned into a less crowded street. Almost all daylight had gone. No. There is another surviving force. As eternal as our skin. Horace[25] had already sang of that force in just and tenacious men—*justum et tenacem*—a kind of man on whom the ruins of the world would fall without moving him emotionally. That's right, without apparently moving him emotionally, but because of the great kinship he feels for other human beings he is not inert, not predatory, but in a deeper, more transcendent sense is certainly moved emotionally.

It was night now. I entered through the open doors, full of sudden joy, as if instead of the impersonal urban hotel's nondescript lobby, I had seen before my eyes the unreal reality of my land.

Notes

1. Mariakerke. Municipality of the Belgian province of East Flanders, near Ghent.

2. Bruges. Old, picturesque city of 60,000 in northwestern Belgium, about ten miles from the North Sea. This "city of bridges" has many 12th and 13th century buildings, including the famous Market Hall and the Gothic Town Hall.

3. The *Symposium* is one of Plato's *Dialogues,* in which several men, among them Socrates, are gathered at a banquet.

4. Gilbert Keith Chesterton, *Chaucer* (New York: Greenwood Press, 1956), p. 28.

5. The Italian words mean: "You are not dead, but are lost, oh soul of ours that so laments."

6. Andrea del Castagno (1423–1457). Italian painter. The monastery of Sant' Apollonia in Florence holds some of his best frescoes, including "The Crucifixion" and "The Last Supper."

7. Hermann Boerhaave (1668–1738). Dutch physician and scientist. For many years he served on the faculty of the University of Leiden. One of his most important books is *Institutiones Medicae* (1708).

8. Desiderius Erasmus (1466–1536). The great Dutch Christian humanist of the Renaissance, author of the satirical *Adages* (1500) and *The Praise of Folly* (1509), works which urged drastic reform of the Roman Catholic Church.

9. Spinoza's moral geometry. In his *Ethics,* Spinoza develops his concept of the universe in geometric terms, as demonstrations of propositions.

10. St. Stephen is the patron saint of Vienna.

11. Ambrogio Lorenzetti (1290–1348). One of the greatest Sienese painters.

12. The Hofburg is the Imperial Palace in Vienna, made up of several edifices dating from the 13th century.

13. John Milton (1608–1674). The great English poet, author of *Paradise Lost* (1667). The line "Such sweet compulsion doth in music lie" appears in "Arcades," 68, 325.

14. Pythagoreans. A group of Greek philosophers and mathematicians under the leadership of Pythagoras (582–507 B.C.).

15. Menenio Agrippa. Roman consul (503 B.C.), conqueror of the Sabines and the Samnites.

16. Aventine. One of the seven hills of ancient Rome.

17. Albert Sorel (1842–1906). French historian, author of the monumental eight-volume *Europe and the French Revolution* (1885–1904).

18. Jacobian Revolution. The Jacobins belonged to one of the most radical political societies during the French Revolution and seized power in 1793. Today the word Jacobin refers to a radical.

19. Mammon. The Aramaic word means "earthly riches." Mammon usually implies the evil of wealth. In Matthew 6:24, appear the words "Ye cannot serve God and Mammon."

20. Percy Bysshe Shelley (1792–1822). The great English Romantic poet composed many of his best verses in Italy, where he spent the last five years of his life. Shelley drowned in the Adriatic Sea.

21. Edward John Trelawney (1792–1881). English adventurer and writer, a close friend of Shelley and Lord Byron. In 1822, Trelawney witnessed Shelley's death at Leghorn; in 1824 he went with Byron to Greece in the War of Independence.

22. Pyramid of Cestius. The tomb of the Roman praetor Gaius Cestius. The tombs of Shelley and Keats are close by.

23. Ostic. Reference to the ancient city of Ostia in Italy, near the mouth of the Tiber.

24. Paul Valéry (1871–1945). French poet and critic. His verses are characterized by extreme intellectualism and abstruseness. Books of poetry: *Le Jeune Parque* (1917), *Odes* (1920). As a literary essayist, Valéry is known especially for *Variété* (1924, 1930, 1936, 1938).

25. Horace. (65–8 B.C.) Roman lyric and satirical poet. Author of two books of *Satires* (35 B.C. and 29 B.C.) and *Epodes* (31 B.C.).

XIII.
The Severe Exaltation of Life

Return. Stripping myself of
everything. The darkness. The road to
Damascus.[1] *Hard, harsh exile.*
Self-betterment. Severe exaltation of
life, the norm of man's creation. To go
beyond oneself to reach the last frontiers
of humanness. Spiritual territories.

And once again I came back; once again I came back to my land. What sustenance did I bring with me to this new world's hunger, made more alive in me by my journey to many foreign lands? None, or almost none, outside of the food which is hunger for hunger. Thirty-three years of life inwardly stormy, tormented, too inactive, full of all too often arid reflection. Thirty-three years of vigil. Thirty-three years of penury, aspiration and inner grief, melancholy and fury. That is, thirty-three years equal to a hard and nervous hand, but empty.

No one could say I had been inactive because, oh, God, what activity, what work, what obstinate obstinacy in myself becoming drama. No, certainly not inactive. But have I been so devoid of transcendent gains, so weak in conflict itself! And have the walls of my abode been so naked! I was little more than a beggar with intelligence in an endlessly rich territory that offers so much.

Behind me the footprint, my own footprint, was not erased and was not the ghostly track of some non-existent steps. I looked at myself and said: "What am I now? What am I at this moment, at this exact moment of passing and passing again through the same point of the pendulum in my room?" I am alive, despairingly alive, in eternal struggle, that is, in eternal defeat and in eternal victory, without the will to rest, having become all grief and resistance and combat. Separated from almost everything—goods, ambition, greed—from almost all men and women except the really lonely people, the really forsaken people.

"Each day more ardent and less satisfied and more joyful?" Yes. Each day more ardent and less satisfied. More joyful, on occasions. Constantly distressed, constantly anguished. On the outside, at times smiling, at times sad. Each day less tolerant of the exploiter, the powerful, the conservative; each day closer to those whose lives are exposed to all kinds of weather. Each day less venal and more disposed to rid my soul of ornaments, to let it be simple, sincere, and natural like the simple, sincere, and natural soul of those always attracted by God's contrition, for they have given all and lost all, except the fundamental adherence to their faith. Each day I learn more and converse less. Each day I am more distrustful of language. Each day less vain and prouder. Each day more certain that the only hierarchies are the hierarchies of conscience and the hierarchies of heart. Further from Torquemada[2] and closer to the constant victims whose names are lost in time. Each day, in short, further removed from myself.

And behind this there was no real worth, no true valor, only steps, vehement steps, difficult steps. I had nothing behind except the gray life of a writer. Without consequences, without creative acquisitions, without heroism of any kind. What I had was just an ordinary life, begun in a city of the Atlantic coast and then continued in the trajectory of my cerebral drama. I had wanted to know, I had wanted to exhaust all possible sources of wisdom—I had finally come to shout out with pent-up fright *La chair est triste, hélas! Et j'ai lu tous les livres.*[3] I had traveled a great deal with small, old books that were dirty and ripped from their binding, marked up with furious red pencil in the margin, next to each familiar phrase. I cried out of impotence before many blank pages, and out of irremediable opacity before many printed pages. I had believed and I had disbelieved. I had learned and I had forgotten. I had found mistakes in myself and in others. I wanted to get hold of a thousand notions and the thousand notions slipped through my fingers. Only a few notions remained, perhaps the least important ones: man is the inexact animal. A horse, a deer, a lion are exact. They know what they want and, consequently, what they are looking for.

My pockets were full of life, adventure, and dreams confusingly mixed. But my life's adventure was the intellectual adventure, the imaginary adventure. And this inclination makes itself attractive, but is very selfish, the most selfish of all the inclinations of the spirit. What I would not have given to make the imaginary trip along the roads we daily traverse, to change this imaginary trip into a real trip, without any wonders! But when we begin to want to become something, we see we are already formed and can scarcely modify to any appreciable degree the slant to which our rigid structure conforms. The purely intellectual wearied me, repelled me. The only thing I could accept from the purely intellectual was the savory fruit of wisdom. But this fruit becomes so lost in the midst of this intellectuality that it is necessary to travel far to reach it, that it is necessary to go much farther than this intellectuality, that it is necessary to reach the land of heroism and holiness. The trees of wisdom stand there, solitary pines laden with pineapples.

I brought nothing in my hands.

From my early childhood, there raged within me a fire, a storm, a flame, and everything I touched I lit up. But that struggle, that constant aspiration to a mystical road, that desperate need to give meaning to my actions, that always virgin appetite—they were all nothing. Nothing either was the bloody fight to kill the mediocrity that took control of the country; nothing the sustained will to spend sleepless nights in the rear of small, cold rooms in complete disarray, filling myself with inspiring dialogues in which the loftiest words uttered by humanity suddenly came upon me to my complete surprise from the heart of those small treatises *de rerum natura*;[4] the obstinacy in learning and suffering, and suffering again and learning again; the decision not to remain in place, to propose constant movement to the soul, to not accept stagnation, or retreat, or rest for our deep concerns. All of this, nothing. Nothing either was the rigid, anguished reflection of many years, the books that grew out of that reflection, the lectures, the notes, the articles, the conversations. Nothing, the days and nights of moral death, sitting before the empty page that takes long hours to fill

XIII. The Severe Exaltation of Life   169

with the free expression of my thoughts. Nothing, the disputes with this one and that one. The sudden alliance with others, my drawing close to still others, the incessant search for those who, as Barrès said, intensify our ardor and feed it with new desires when we reach a certain point of self-sufficiency and fervent deification of the "I."

Nothing, too, the indefatigable plea against vacuous smugness, the deserted men, the politicians, the soul's blood. Nothing, the giving of our blood, our soul's blood, in order to see around us a handful of better people—better in intellect, in spirit, in nature, in conscience. Nothing, what we have learned in a feverish, effusive, intense, ceaseless conversation and sometimes, in a less clear, vehemently human form, what we have taught, taught in the sense of shown. Oh, only in that, only in that sense! Nothing, our hunger and thirst as teachers; nothing, our surrendering peace of heart and peace of intellect. Nothing, our flat "no" to the most comfortable offerings, to the easiest ways, to most envied quietudes. Nothing, our objective to go forward without stopping along all the possible roads toward our creation, along all the roads, all the difficulties; nothing, our objective to pass through the narrow door. All of this means nothing.

And nothing, too, our going out each morning into the newly awakened streets to reflect, trying to place each thing in its eternal meaning: this face glimpsed in the dark, this expression of health or of death, that bough, that sculpture. And likewise nothing, the monotonous and steadfast work of the afternoon, after having spent the siesta hours going uninterruptedly from the warm feeling of enrapture over that Cézanne[5] to this Matisse,[6] breathing in the ink as a worker does the poisonous emissions from white lead, breathing into my nose that smell and into my soul the impregnation of so many impressions, so many memories, so many discoveries, so many false dawns, so many inspirations, shouts, smiles, mutisms, so many revelations, with my head finally falling on my work desk. All of this was nothing. Nothing, the arrival of night over the burden of my aspirations and cares, over those terrible secret feelings in my heart, when time after time we find ourselves, with a certain childish astonishment, full of new presences within our being that are, each and everyone of them, our nonconformity made evident and the human fertility of our grief.

Nothing either, that fertility, because even though it is movement, it does not drag, it goes along in its own track. It is torture that becomes torture. And man's true roads, the worthwhile roads, the heroic roads, are those which some travel without taking tracks or trails into account here below, but instead setting out at most to follow the changeable guide of a constellation.

Nothing, nothing. The dreams, the delightful trips, the unforgettable love affairs, love, shared understandings, plain meals in out-of-the-way inns, the cold nights and amorous pleasure in city and country taverns, the friendly faces, the pleasant words received, the jungle excursions, the confessions made, the secrets remembered, the advice received and given, the friendships cooled off in the hour of personal crisis, the solidarity woven in the hour of collective dangers, the risk run, the wine drunk, the women kissed, the men helped, the individuals combatted, the events dreamed of, the realities brought about, the illnesses cured, the objectives pursued, even the moral assassinations, the miserable dealings with people, the few good acts, justice meted out, the injustices suffered, a day's work endured, a day's work enjoyed, the supreme passion for a woman's image, the lesser passions, the conflicts lived through, the frequently noted human disproportions, betrayals perpetrated, the return of bitterness, the trafficking with our own purposes for other purposes, in short, the whole difficult life as it is lived—nothing, nothing.

And if my existence had been kneaded with the yeast of passion, of ardor, hatred, fury, breath, discouragement, criticism, insomnia, deep thought, cruel taciturnity, cruel joy, hunger to touch the land, to touch humanity, to feel in my words not a verbal warmth but human warmth; and if my existence had been kneaded with the yeast of an impatient and anguished search, of an eternal return to the simple things, of many deceptions, many indecisions, decisions, vocations, loves, raptures, small glory, great woes, pride, idleness, righteous rage, surrender, arrogance, misery, pettiness, foolishness, vivacity, fears, valor, boldness, hunger, always hunger—all of this, however, was nothing.

Nothing!

I didn't bring anything in my hands.

My tremendous despair was that I didn't bring anything in my hands.

* * *

This is so because a mystique, a man's mystique, the true consecration of a cause, the consecration in itself of a truth, demands much more than all that. Much more, many things different from all that. Much more, another world of things. But I am not dead. My whole being is alive. More alive than ever. And what I feel all around me is the step of men in whom I believe. That incessant moving about, so unnoticed and so internal like the movement of deep currents, of those who carry within themselves a great discontent, a great desire, a restless and dreadful ambition of the spirit. The proof of our life, of the certainty of our living, of the dramatic certainty of our living, is that eventually we shall be together. The authentic people and I.

The authentic people! The true people, the worthwhile people, the people who bear the same relation to the external, superficial people as the inner self spoken of by St. Peter in his Ephesians bears to the external self. The authentic people, a state of passion, a state of aspiration, a state of fertile anguish. The opposite of the satraps,[7] the opposite of external, noisy alienation.

It is from this matrix that this new man shall emerge. "And that ye put on the new man," says Paul in his Epistle 4:24, for we are members one of another."

But this idea of putting on the new man is not done with honors, with pomp, is not done with a dream, is not done without heroism. It is not done without a mystique. And what purity of feeling is required for this! What authenticity, what profound manliness! What few things and how much strength in the way we hold them! I felt tragically inefficient for all that. The life of a sensitive man always has much idleness. Too much specious alienation. Too much self-reflection. Too much exile in the borders of allegory and parable.

A state of sorrow spread through the whole world, "of darkness controlled by fraudulent hands," of collective blame and universal anguish, demands something else: sacrifice, perhaps death, a violent, explicit affliction that is spoken and shouted out.

So I resolved to make a clean slate for myself, to take stock, to tell myself that I am nothing, absolutely nothing. I have done nothing, absolutely nothing. I am nothingness itself. Nothingness full of notions.

From everything I have, I want only my aspirations. I throw everything else away, I toss it out. I want only that: my aspirations. With that, one must begin; with that one must go on today. Each person differently.

I throw everything else away. I give it all away for nothing, I leave it: books written, words spoken, stories told, verses learned, literature. I want nothing of that. It's no use to me. If my hands have become full of all that, my hands are lost, unless I do what I have to now and throw away the false burden.

I want to have the hands of my spirit free in this land where I am rooted, installed. I want the hands of my spirit to be those which hear and speak. The hands of the spirit are those of doing, not those of being, because the latter is holiness. The spirit does, must do in this hour, articulating the truth in its naked expression, in its defiant declaration, in its accusation, in its accusing the darkness wherever the darkness may be.

It had been said before. Again, St. Paul in the Ephesians 6:12: "For we wrestle not against flesh and blood, but against principalities, against powers, against the rulers of the darkness of this world." The rulers of this darkness! The governors of the darkness! Against the principalities and powers, governors of the darkness!

Against the ostensible, visible lords of violence and deformation, and physical and spiritual fraud. The Epistle addressed to the man inhabiting the banks of the Aegean speaks against those very people. And what honest heart does not, what honest heart does not rise up against these very same people? What heart, what spirit? I wonder, what heart, what spirit?

I have made my road to Damascus.

At one time I believed in the powerful and in their dissembling court of miracles because my spirit was complacent in its comfort. It was my darkest hour. But what I prefer now is the solitary truth, the equanimity, let us say, of my conscience. The equanimity of conscience is not attained with peace, but with a constant struggle against those who in all fields of human activity are governors of darkness, the despots, the cruel persecutors of spiritual men. That is to say, those who kill according to the only law of their deliberate hatreds, of their systematized hatreds.

*   *   *

I said to myself:

Now, stripped of artifices, false knowledge, notions, literature, I can walk like a man in a state of perfect simplicity. I have nothing, I am nothing, I am an empty organ seeking its nutrition. But this certainty remains with me: if there is something in the world capable of creating as a genius does, it is the power of an aspiration. That is so strong that we can even change a human being's physiognomy by just insatiably desiring it. And in the terrible confines of a monstrous body we can find places full of true grace. Only this have I left within me: an aspiration, a bitter, hungry, and despairingly impassioned aspiration, an aspiration which makes me feel the flesh of humanity in me each day, because that aspiration is a fever of truth. And we know through this fever that we are made of mortal flesh.

But I still had not stripped myself of enough things to reach true simplicity. I was still bristly with defenses, I was still not really alone. I still kept too many tolerated indulgences close by. In that room with the windows open facing downtown and the two sofas standing alone and the green cloth covered with new books, the curtains fluttering in the breeze and the clear air of siestatime inside, I still was not sufficiently alone, not sufficiently aware of the universal outburst of hatred, the suffering, vindications, desire, resentment, fights, deaths. I was still too worldly. People still came to my room who lifted an open book from the floor and falteringly read with a stupid expression on their face and with their nose in the air this or that paragraph from "Ordo Amoris,"[8] from *Paradise Regained,*[9] or from Plato's *Symposium,* and then yawned and went to look out onto the square from the heights of their irremediable stupidity. I still cured my aloneness in interminable obscure conversations. I still tolerated in myself inhibitions and sadness—that luxury.

I still had too much luxury. I still belonged to the visible country too much. I still seriously criticized such and such a play as I left the theater, under the ornate marquis. I was still a part of so much social pretense. I still was not primitive enough, sufficiently naked within, sufficiently authentic and trustworthy. I was still loquacious and artificial. I still smiled when I should not smile, and I lied just to be sociable, and I chatted just to avoid embarrassing after-dinner pauses in the conversation. Still, what is even more serious, for the deepest questions about the inalterable essence of my being, about my pure essence, that is, of my primarily human and at the same time tender and evil essence, for the metaphysical questions, I myself proposed the least difficult answers, the most readily available solutions, the most trivial panaceas.

My entire work of so many years seemed to have resulted in this hopeless exasperation, in this denial of myself.

At noon one day, when I returned from a long trip, I went to my upstairs apartment where I had lived for some years and from which I had seen the city on so many nights. I was very well received there. There was a marvelous brightness around that apartment. I hastily approached the huge windows and saw the sprawled-out metropolis, not confined now in its night, but perfectly clear, imposing and solid in its uninterrupted immensity, emitting its smoke and glowing in the sun above the turbid breath from its own breathing. In the east, in the far limits of the city, it was hard to tell where the river ended and the sky began. It was one infinite plain which oscillated from green to blue, slowly and imperceptibly. Without doubt, neither the Etruscan hills[10] nor the Strasbourg needles[11] nor the memorable Trafalgar column,[12] nor the charming little Jean Jacques Square surrounded by white mountains could be seen there. All that could be seen, other than the bewildering construction, was, towards the far south, a square-shaped bridge of black iron wrapped in the breath of smoke and fog. And seen from that point, powerful and yet dematerialized by the even greater power of air and light which locked together in a grayish union, the spatial dignity of the city was as pure, unobtrusive, noble, and solemn as the little Jean Jacques Square or the Strasbourg towers. It was a special but no less worthy kind of dignity, more rudimentary and coarse but no less worthy because it was man's work constructed with the penury corresponding to such work. And above all, what conferred on it in the distance, from afar, a similar nobility of proportions, was the light, the new breath, life itself, which is after all the great dignifier.

What I carried within me was almost a cry, and this cry was the long and monotonous pangs of birth. I was exhausted from grief. I was all sorrow and reflection and anguish. And on seeing that country spread out, extended, scattered next to me and at the same time so distant, in the same way the object of a desire is remote from the very desire seeking it, I could not contain deep within me a great sadness toward the land in which we have suffered and have divested ourselves of something vital. And my agony was the agony of birth, that small death which is followed by a greater life.

I had lunch alone, among some servants who had received me so well, not really servants, but the cordial company of simple people who on one occasion—everything goes full circle in life—even acted as advisors. We sipped glasses of red wine. I read some letters, from foreign publishers, from friends. I felt free of bonds and isolated in my own universe, like the man who lives in the desert and will not now be bothered by any importunity other than those which time brings in its cloak. I was remote from everything, but there was a vibration in me, as if at the same time my skin were feeling the living contact of many undefined but numerous human presences. I don't know how long I was seated by myself in front of that table, listening with an unusual, lucid astonishment to the deep song I bore within me, that dark final lamentation, that farewell to another life before going to live completely in the inner, authentic country.

It was like knowing that finally the more I separated myself from everything, the more I was going to feel a part of everything. It is through the inner country, the fatherland, that one goes to the other external countries, to the sovereign nation and to the universal country, since the true country, the authentic one, is not created alone, but in conjunction with the inner being of every man. The path I took before, the quests, the need for human warmth, seemed to me now the abjuration of a necessary aloneness.

One does not go anywhere without exiling oneself. The road of creation is the road of exile. And there is a time to reject this exile and another time to accept it. There is a time to choose to stay tied to the fiction all around us, or to exile ourselves. And to be in exile like that, in our own land, is to go down to live with the invisible country, with the invisible sensitivity, to live with the authentic people. And since we shall all be exiled in this way, our essence, our virile mystique, our true valor and our true creative faith will take form in that common exile. Because creative evolution is merely the false name of that creative faith, in the sense that—and each cell of our body knows this— faith is what goes beyond life, beginning with an act of affirmation in life itself. A leopard's health is his faith, the musician's composition is his faith, his materialized faith. Just as the ambition of the ambitious one, of the complacent one, of the speculator, of the bourgeois, far from being faith, is what there is instead of faith.

I felt comfortable in my necessary exile. At last, in my exile. How we love, how we feel, how we think, keep vigil and become exalted in exile's shoreless solitude! In that exile to the authentic country, where we have to build everything: environment, world, air residence, friendships, guests, solitudes. And the more we save from that sacrifice, the more we shall have saved for the other country, for the external country. Happy be the one who lives in a beautiful and unfortunate exile!

Yes, this was the song I heard deep within me, this was the song that burned me, that devoured me, the song of one in exile. What incomparable sorrow and what profound pleasure! What impoverishment and what enrichment! To go away, to be alone, to grieve for a time, to be alone in order to be more with everybody, to be better with everybody afterwards, to be more purely with everybody, to be cleansed when the time comes to return and give of oneself, for indeed all our work is for this one hour, all the hope, the preparation, the tasks, the insomnia, the difficult sacrifice, one's complete betterment from head to toe are all for this one moment. All of this is for the time we return, for the time we bring something in our hands and are not empty-handed, for the time we bring a strong and impassioned note, the state of mind of a mystique, the state of mind of an asceticism, to the world's harmony or general disharmony.

When one goes away, when one has gone into exile, one then touches the other, more difficult territory, the spiritual territory.

When one has cut all ties with the world, then one indeed has become world, then one is in one's own spiritual territory. But, like all things, countries too have two parts: their physical appearance, their outer contour; and their deep, inner territory, their spiritual territory. Then, when a man has created within himself his spiritual territory and joins it to the spiritual territory of his land, what emerges is the true spirit of this union, that is, the pure spirit of nationality, the supreme nationality, the nationality *cum spiritu*. What emerges is the new feeling, the new man, the land's spiritual son.

And how great the pure son of this encounter is! The encounter of spiritual territory with the spiritual territory of our land! Not with the physical and coarse territory, but with the hidden, deep, strange spiritual territory—made of many dreams, so many aspirations, so many sacrificed lives, so many things denied and so many beloved, longed for things—our land's shy, rough, spiritual territory.

I got up, went to my work desk in the huge room and tidied up a bit the books, the papers, all those instruments of solitude. Of small solitude, because it was not yet a question of great solitude!

May each person be consciously exiled in the territory of his particular function in life. The physician in his cures, the architect in his stones, the writer in his papers. May each person learn to be able to defend himself. A writer's papers are blood or they are nothing; semen which keeps creating on touching the air, or nothing. Poor external countries are those of men who can not exile themselves in their sacrifices, in their fundamental commitments, in their essential vocations! Poor countries are those of men who can not exile themselves in their humanity—not in their pretenses—to better it without ostentation, to better it when alone it has often faced nothingness, despair, and death. Poor countries are those of the men who have never anguishedly asked themselves Schura Waldejewa's question: "Lord, for what purpose must my soul live? Lord, to what am I to confer my soul?"

What did I want to do, finally, except to create myself. To create myself! Look, bourgeois, it isn't easy, to create oneself. Because first one must do something very difficult. Because one must first open the veins of falseness, of complacency. Because one must first know how to deny oneself everything, everything, absolutely everything, until only a simple aspiration remains in a simple body; the same with intertwined tree trunks—however much they crackle and protest, only the flame remains. And you, the opulent one, always eating well and then resting well, on top of life always, a gambler in life but a sore loser—are you going to make that of yourself, to have just a flame remain? Come now! I don't think so!

Well and good. But, for that "Come now!" you will be called to account, not by some human power, human faction, human tribunal, but by your own life in the terrible echoes of the long night of sickness and in the claims of your descendants and in the memory of those genuine persons whom you have approached and in your final longing for God.

When one's hands are empty, one feels that claim. Or better still, one feels that claim and hastens to have empty hands until leaving in them only the impotent desire to give. And then after one recognizes that impotence, one has the desire to fill them, the urgency to fill those hands, but to fill them with something true, with something truly important—like intelligence or love clearly made part of faith—and not just money. Because if it were money, Schura Waldejewa's tragic shout would return. And what a shout, what a shout amid the falsification all around.

I set out to work in rigorous silence until night fell. I began to write from old notes the story of a man and woman, whom the false circle of people surrounding them—a Dantesque circle, a viper's nest—has driven to utter deformation, to evil and ruin, to total bitterness from which only the ghostly love that unites them is saved. This is what my work is, this is the nature of my testimony, this is what the creative atmosphere of my exile is, my way of giving truth.

I was alone. Not even a sound, or a voice, high up on that floor, in the lonely apartment. When daylight fled, I put on the lamp and continued writing. Shortly after, I stopped and rested a bit before resuming. I saw the room lit up in one part, dark in the other, where the window with the transparent curtains opened on the blue night, now almost black, now almost strange to the planet. Then I took a drink of water and started my work again. My right hand hurt and I had to put the pen down each time I paused and reflected. All the knowledge I had was still too meager to write that. My prose style was weak; what should have been tightly expressed and precise became protracted and lost power. Concreteness fled and the sirens of the abstract came with their false rhythm. My head suddenly felt tired, my spirit lost enthusiasm and I felt a sort of repugnance for the characters I had started to describe. I leaned back in the chair and kept my two hands on the desk, with my arms outstretched, head thrown back, eyes closed. And I tried to keep those two suffering characters alive and palpable in my mind. Finally, constantly interrupting myself, alternately cold and warm, suddenly surprised on hearing myself speak some words out loud ahead of the normal narrative sequence, I continued like that until midnight, glued to the desk, nervous. I was hungry, tired, and cold. Then I left the papers, went to my bedroom and wet my head in cold water, while my spirit continued to be full of that thought I had been developing and clarifying on those white sheets of paper. And I had the feeling I had done it all wrong, and so, without reading it, I tore up the fruit of nine hours of work.

But such a destiny is our daily bread.

I don't know in what restaurant I ate. When I left, many of the bright neon signs had already gone out. One final, weak lacteous resplendence protected the night from total darkness. I walked aimlessly, for I needed to get rid of nervous strain and let my whole being just relax. Two noisy groups of tourists crossed the square; then everything was quiet.

Exiled. From friendships, customs, human company—exiled. Not cloistered, but exiled, voluntarily exiled. All of us Argentines are. Exiled from the spirit, exiled from the civilization from which we came, from that ancestral knot in which, unlike ourselves, men produced art, thought, philosophy. If we can only understand that the good thing is not simply to want to escape from that exile, but to know what it is before escaping from it, for that voluntary residence in an aridness that wants to become fertile is what gives us the measure of our essential poverty and of our needs! All mystique stems from the loneliness of a heart, and that solitude, far from fundamentally isolating us, keeps us in deeper communication with everybody. Didn't our Unamuno say it well?: "Because the more I belong to myself and the more I am myself, the more I belong to others. From the fullness of myself I pour myself out to my brothers, and on pouring myself out to them, they come into me." There is nothing more powerfully universal than a fertile aloneness.

Thus, if I now felt a certain sadness, a bitter feeling of isolation and aloneness, all of this was destined to go away, to be changed to something not easy but immeasurably more fecund, immeasurably more efficient as regards its own relationship with the world, with men, with the spirit. Indeed, a man who exiles himself goes deeper within himself and "pours himself into others so that these others may pour themselves better into him." With each passing day, the world, the tangible world, became more and more my obligation, but the world through me and my people, the world bettered, enlarged, and extended along with myself and people. And the deeper my commitment to denude myself, to strip myself, to feel myself everything by dint of feeling myself nothing, but "nothing with much love," all the better will my awakening be in the company of this people who surrounded me at night—men, women, children, joys, sorrows.

I lifted my eyes to the height of those few countenances I found in my path. They were people, my people, my external country, my tangible country. The arms of that people were the spirit of liberty and the spirit of living; the body of those people was the severe exaltation of life. These arms and that body were turned outward like the image of the Creator, which is all human figure and road. That authentic people was the people who created; that invisible people was the great subterranean, submerged Creator. Wasn't its natural state a creative mystique? Severe exaltation of life! Wasn't this perhaps precisely the deep impulse, the motor, the *motus animi creandi*[13] of the great spiritual inventors, of human genius, of faith in the basic expression to true artists? Severe exaltation of life. John Milton, blind, the evangelical; Cervantes on his return from Lepanto;[14] John Donne;[15] Averroes[16] after his commentaries to the Stagirite; Rimbaud running through Charleville's sad streets—all of them at the height of their tragic inspiration, at the climax of their great fervor and anguish and suffering, at the dawn of their constant rebirth through the thing created, through the given son, through immortality finally conceived. The feeling that nourished them all was precisely this very one—the severe exaltation of life. Because this is the dramatic kernel of immortality. And you have it, you carry it inside, authentic people of Argentina, silent and dramatic people in your lack of speaking and in your doing from deep within.

"Yours is the feeling of the great creators. A lofty and severe state of exaltation of the spirit. A state of secret greatness thanks to which the sensitive soul pours forth from itself a rare prodigality. Be careful that they don't distort you! Stop and look that what you carry with you, you carry deep down in your being. Stop and look that what you carry only is visible on you for the eye that sees beyond your showy and empty jewels. I give thanks to the eye that looks into your inner essence. And to the one who sees how generously exalted your spirit is, how severe and stately is your living, enjoying, and suffering."

"Your silence is a deep pause, not death, not passing away; a deep pause. The fundamental pause, the pause of the dramatic reflection of the one who watches attentively before dawn. The pause of the one who ominously works in creative exile. Authentic people of Argentina, your true worth is your severe exaltation of life. It is deep, very deep; inexpugnable, very much inexpugnable; intimate, very intimate in the silence and solitude of your recondite life. What you are, in truth, is just that: severe exaltation of life. The opposite of your flowering, of your Boeotian vegetation, of your moss, of your golden verdigus."

"You work in the essence of your creative exile. I too am now in a similar exile. We are both genuine, we are both far away. We shall soon meet, we shall soon see each other and be happy to have our pores a little more open to the outside air of the universe."

I thought it, I felt it. This awakening to my transitory exile was my growth towards a higher possibility, towards the possibility of going forward within oneself, of not stopping in oneself, of going down to dwell in oneself in order to leave by the other door, by the narrow door and go beyond oneself. I started walking through other streets, then through still others, and saw very few people out so late at night.

I walked down to a street that had no lights, in darkness, and then to another street with more light. And I kept on walking—with the same hopeful despair—who knows until what time, until the timid trace of the first light began to appear at some spot in the sky with some strange, cold, imperceptible brightness.

I sobbed night's final cry in a new starless space. I felt a sort of shout within me, not broken but strangled. A sort of farewell, a "See you soon," a great effusion of the soul. I dragged myself like a ghost whose body was pain, a tragic form. Now there was no starlight, but almost dawn, the pale cry in which night ends. But wasn't I soon going to touch the land and men and the world, and for the better? Why was I crying? The night and I cried together. And a bit of light began to appear imminently. But I was just a few steps from home— imminently. I hurried. I could rest. I could rest a few hours. I wouldn't have to make my exile last a long time, but rather I would devour it, consume it, kill it by dint of frenzied, deeply felt work, by bleeding, by life itself.

I was almost rigid. I looked at that sky, the city, the life that begins again with its steel-colored early morning air. With how much love does one return from exile! One is new, one is the world. The authentic country has opened up and expanded. From exile I would return together with the incessant marching of that hidden army which is going to appear, which already does appear, the army of men carrying in its heart the feeling of the severe exaltation of life and in its hands the gesture of giving its free spirit and flesh. One comes back from exile full of love.

When I entered that solitary room and fell on the bed that had been undisturbed the whole night, oddly enough I did not act as if I were returning and settling down to rest, but rather as if I were rising up, strangely getting up, like the soldier's rising up in the dawn of battle. Like the rising of one who, after the whole night of vigil, suffering, cold, farewell, is perhaps going to unite the beginning of his day with death in a final gesture as a warrior and as a man, in the great forest of fear and desolation. Or like the rising of one who, if capable of another kind of glory, is going to go beyond, is not going to be thwarted by any force in that rapture, through which human fear despises itself and changes into intrepidness and joy.

Notes

1. Damascus. Capital of Syria, one of the oldest commercial cities in the Middle East. In A.D. 35, Paul accepted Christianity as he was traveling along the road to Damascus.

2. Tomás de Torquemada (1420–1498). Appointed Grand Inquisitor in 1487 by Pope Innocent VIII. His name has become synonymous with harshness and cruelty.

3. *La chair est triste, hélas! Et j'ai lu tous les livres.* Quotation from the French poet Stephane Mallarmé (1842–1898): "The flesh is sad, alas, and I've read all the books."

4. *De rerum natura.* The Latin phrase means "Concerning the Nature of Things." The words are the title of a long didactic poem by the Roman poet Titus Lucretius Carus (96–55 B.C.).

5. Paul Cézanne (1839–1906). French painter of the Post-Impressionist school. Works: "House of the Hanged Man," "Mont-Sainte-Victoire," "The Kitchen Table," "The Card Players."

6. Henri Matisse. (1869–1954). French painter, one of the leaders of the Fauve movement from about 1905–1910. Works: "Desserte," "The Red Studio," "Piano Lesson," "The Purple Robe."

7. Satrap. Title of the governor of a province in ancient Persia. The term here refers to a conniving or manipulative person.

8. *Ordo Amoris.* The Latin phrase means "The Order of Love." Mallea is referring to some Latin work, but I can find no reference to it.

9. *Paradise Regained.* John Milton's classic poem, written in 1671.

10. Etruscan hills. Reference to the extremely hilly area in central Italy controlled by the ancient Etruscans. This area is now Tuscany.

11. Strasbourg Needles. Spire of the Strasbourg Cathedral, completed in the 15th century. It is an excellent example of Gothic architecture.

12. Trafalgar. Trafalgar Square in London commemorates the British naval victory over the French and Spanish off Cape Trafalgar on October 21, 1805 in which Lord Nelson died in action. A column in the middle of Trafalgar Square bears a statue of Nelson.

13. *Motus animi creandi.* The Latin phrase means "Movement of the Creating Spirit."

14. Lepanto. Reference to the battle of Lepanto fought off Greece on October 7, 1571, in which the Moslem Turkish fleet was defeated by an allied force consisting of ships from Spain, Venice, and the Papal States, under the command of the Christian Don Juan of Austria. Miguel de Cervantes took part in the battle and permanently lost the use of his left arm.

15. John Donne (1572–1631). One of the English metaphysical poets. Donne's most famous poems include "Death, Be Not Proud" and "Go and Catch a Falling Star."

16. Averroes (1126–1198). Spanish-born Arabic scholar and philosopher whose commentaries on Aristotle the Catholic Church considered heretical. Mallea calls Aristotle the Stagirite, a reference to his birthplace in Stagira.

#62
L. H.